Children's World Atlas

Children's World Atlas

Malcolm Watson

Consultant: Clive Carpenter

Miles
Kelly

First published in 2007 by Miles Kelly Publishing Ltd
Harding's Barn, Bardfield End Green, Thaxted, Essex, CM6 3PX, UK

Copyright © Miles Kelly Publishing Ltd 2007

This edition updated 2018, printed 2019

2 4 6 8 10 9 7 5 3

Publishing Director Belinda Gallagher
Creative Director Jo Cowan
Editorial Director Rosie Neave
Editors Becky Miles, Amanda Askew
Editorial Assistant Carly Blake
Designers Simon Lee, Elaine Wilkinson
Cover Designer Simon Lee
Image Manager Liberty Newton
Production Elizabeth Collins, Jennifer Brunwin-Jones
Reprographics Stephan Davis, Callum Ratcliffe-Bingham
Assets Lorraine King

ISBN 978-1-78617-843-5 Hardback
ISBN 978-1-78617-844-2 Paperback

Printed in India

British Library Cataloguing-in-Publication Data
A catalogue record for this book is available from the British Library

All information correct at time of going to press

Made with paper from a sustainable forest

www.mileskelly.net

Contents

Using the atlas

Divided into continental areas, this atlas explores the world with amazing facts, statistics and photographs. Highly detailed maps show important cultural and geographical features, such as major towns, places of interest, mountain ranges and rivers.

1 Graticule
The coloured frame that runs around each map. It changes colour for each continental area and provides grid references that enable you to locate features on the map easily.

2 Main heading
Introduces the main countries on the page.

3 Locator globe
Highlights where in the world the countries are.

4 Introduction
Gives an insight into some of the countries that are mapped.

5 Scale
Shows the scale of the map in kilometres and miles.

6 Map
Shows towns, territories and islands, plus physical features such as mountain ranges.

7 Did You Know?
Amazing facts about people and places.

8 Image
Each photograph is accompanied by a detailed caption.

2 North Africa

4 The Sahara Desert dominates this region at 6000 km in width and 2000 km from north to south.
Only a narrow strip of land stands next to the Mediterranean Sea, but the fertile valleys of the Atlas Mountains and the banks of the Nile river have enough water to grow crops.

Algeria, Libya and Tunisia have bec wealthy by selling oil and natural g Europe. Egypt was the richest coun in the world when the pharaohs rul more than 3000 years ago. Egypt's well-preserved tombs and temples, especially the Great Pyramid of Giza, are a tourist attraction.

7 Did You Know?
The Sahara Desert region was wet and fertile 8000 years ago. As the climate has become drier, the desert has expanded.

8 In north Africa, many civilizations live in fortified cities, or ksars. *Ait Benhaddou* is situated near Marrakech [E2], Morocco. Few familes live here now as they have moved to modern villages nearby. Scenes from films including Alexander (2004) and The Mummy (1999) have been shot here.

9 In the next minute... ...the Sun will evaporate the equivalent of 110 million bottles of water from the Nile river.

62

6

KEY TO MAPS

Country border	State border	Disputed border	Country capital	State capital	Town
		Tarfaya WESTERN	**Madrid**	Lincoln■	• Rock Springs

Desert	Highest peak	River	Dependency/territory	Research station	Place of interest
	Tahat Peak 2918 m	Amazon	FALKLAND ISLANDS (UK)	Casey (Australia)	Mount Rushmore

NORTH AFRICA • AFRICA

Located on the Nile river, Cairo [F13] is the biggest city in Africa. Built in AD 988, **Al-Azhar University** is the second oldest university in the world, after the University of Al Karaouine Fez, Morocco. Al-Azhar Mosque stands alongside the university.

Facts and Stats

• Egypt's population of 95.2 million would fill 952 Olympic stadiums. Libya's population of 6.2 million would only fill 62 stadiums.

• Cairo [F13] is the biggest city with 20.3 million people. This would fill 203 Olympic stadiums, compared to Tripoli which would only fill 9.5 [E8].

• The average income per person in Libya is £6107, compared to a world average of £8196.

Search and Find

Algeria
• Algiers C6
Egypt
• Cairo, NAC (New Administrative Capital) F13

Libya
• Tripoli. E8
Morocco
• Rabat. D3
Tunisia
• Tunis D7

World Record
The Sahara sand sea in Algeria has the longest sand dunes in the world, with some more than 300 km.

Extreme Weather

The hottest temperature ever recorded was 58°C in Libya's Sahara Desert.

MEDITERRANEAN SEA

Tripoli
• Misurata
swiyah
Gulf of Sidra • Benghazi • Darnah
Surt • • Tubruq
• Ajdabiya
Alexandria • Tanta • Port Said
QATTARA DEPRESSION Cairo • Suez Canal
Giza • Suez
NAC* • Sinai Peninsula
GREAT SAND SEA
LIBYA
EZZAN LIBYAN DESERT
WESTERN DESERT
Nile
Sharm al Sheikh
• El Minya • Hurghada
Asyut • ISRAEL
Gulf of Aqaba
EGYPT RED SEA
• Qena
• Luxor
GILF KEBIR PLATEAU • Aswan
Lake Nasser
CHAD
SUDAN

*Egypt's New Administrative Capital (NAC) is currently being built 45 km east of Cairo.

THE DISTANCE separating Morocco from Spain, Europe, at the Strait of Gibraltar's [C3] narrowest point is only 13 km.

EGYPT has huge pyramids, built more than 3000 years ago. Each one held the body of a king.

Desert tribe people, such as the Berbers and Tuaregs, travel by camel from oasis to oasis across the Sahara Desert to trade cloth, salt and spices.

63

---

9 In the next minute...
Fascinating information about what is happening across the world in only one minute.

10 Search and Find
Each country or state is listed with its capital city and a grid reference.

11 The distance...
Measures the distance from one point to another and how long it would take to travel.

12 Place of interest
Provides extra information about a well-known sight or attraction.

13 World Record
Details a world record that a country holds.

14 Facts and Stats
Helps you to understand facts and figures. The highest peaks are compared to the Eiffel Tower in Paris, France, which is 320 m in height. Rivers are compared to the Nile river, Africa, which is 6670 km in length. Population is compared to an Olympic stadium, which would hold 100,000 people.

15 Extreme Weather
Details the highest and lowest temperatures, dramatic storms or high rainfall.

Planet Earth

Earth is a huge ball of rock with two thirds of its surface covered by seas and oceans. The third planet from the Sun in the Solar System, Earth is the only planet where life is known to exist, due to an atmosphere rich in oxygen and the water on its surface. Beneath the Earth's thin, solid crust is the liquid mantle, and at the centre is the core. The outer part of the core is liquid, but the inner core is solid metal.

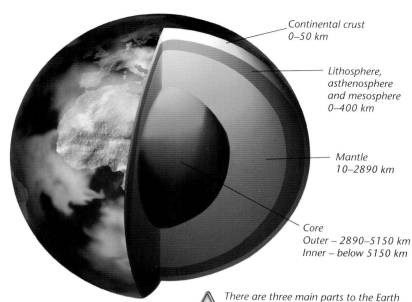

Continental crust
0–50 km

Lithosphere,
asthenosphere
and mesosphere
0–400 km

Mantle
10–2890 km

Core
Outer – 2890–5150 km
Inner – below 5150 km

There are three main parts to the Earth – the crust, mantle and core. Although the inner core reaches a temperature of 7000°C, it remains solid because the pressure is 6000 times greater than on the surface.

SPINNING EARTH

The Earth spins on its axis – an imaginary line through its centre – at a speed of more than 1600 km/h. It doesn't spin straight up, but leans to one side. As the Earth spins, the view of the Sun from different places on Earth constantly changes. This brings day and night, and the seasons.

In December, the South Pole leans towards the Sun. Places in the southern half of the world have summer. At the same time, places in the northern half have winter.

Seasons
There are four seasons – spring, summer, autumn and winter. Each season brings a change in temperature and weather. The changes in the seasons occur because the Earth tilts towards the Sun. When the Northern Hemisphere tilts towards the Sun, the northern part of the world has summer and the south has winter. Six months later, the opposite occurs – the Southern Hemisphere tilts towards the Sun. Then the north has winter and the south has summer. The tropics around the centre of the Earth are slightly different. They only have two seasons – wet and dry.

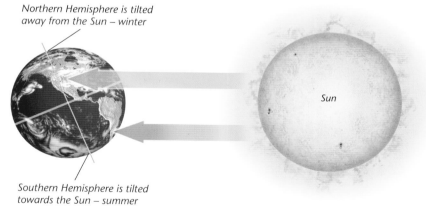

Northern Hemisphere is tilted away from the Sun – winter

Sun

Southern Hemisphere is tilted towards the Sun – summer

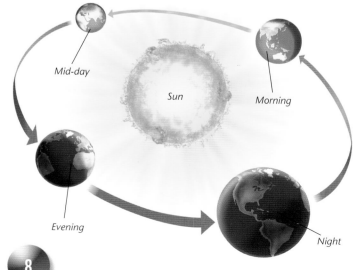

Mid-day

Sun

Morning

Evening

Night

When it is daylight on the half of the Earth facing towards the Sun, it is night on the half of the Earth facing away from it. As the Earth rotates, so the day and night halves shift gradually around the world.

Night and day
The Earth spins a complete turn on its axis every 24 hours. This gives us night and day. The Sun is the source of light for daytime. When it is night, it is dark because the Sun is shining on the opposite side of the Earth. When it is evening or early morning, the Sun is moving away or towards our part of the Earth.

Shaping the land

The Earth's crust is made up of pieces called tectonic plates, which are constantly moving, changing the shape of the land. This can create mountains and volcanoes, as well as cause natural disasters, such as earthquakes. Rocks can also be broken down or worn away by the weather, such as wind and rain, or by the movement of water, such as waves.

A volcano erupts, shooting molten magma into the air.

A sea arch, formed by waves wearing away the rock.

PLATE TECTONICS

The Earth's crust is split into several parts called tectonic plates. The plates float on the molten magma underneath, causing them to constantly move.

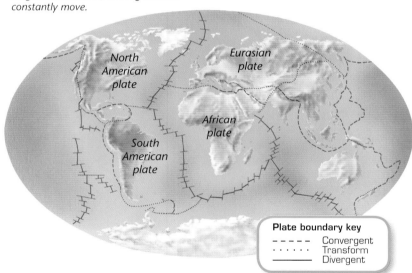

North American plate

Eurasian plate

African plate

South American plate

Plate boundary key
- - - - - Convergent
· · · · · · Transform
———— Divergent

Divergent plate boundaries
Where two plates move away from each other, molten rock, or magma, rises to fill the gap. This usually occurs beneath the oceans, forming a spreading ocean ridge, such as the mid-Atlantic ridge.

Mid-ocean ridge

Plates move apart

Ocean plate

Magma erupts through the gap

Mantle

Convergent plate boundaries
When two plates crash together, they crumple up and form major mountain chains, such as the Andes, as well as volcanoes. The Earth's crust is thin, so if cracks appear, the magma shoots up as the lava of a volcano. When an ocean plate is driven down into the Earth's magma, it is called subduction.

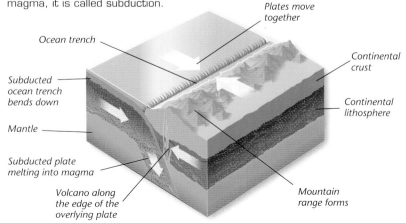

Ocean trench

Plates move together

Subducted ocean trench bends down

Continental crust

Mantle

Continental lithosphere

Subducted plate melting into magma

Volcano along the edge of the overlying plate

Mountain range forms

Transform plate boundaries
If two plates push past each other, pressure can build up, creating a break, or fault, which often causes an earthquake. Some earthquakes are so powerful that buildings collapse. Landslides can also occur, causing great damage. Undersea earthquakes can cause the massive waves of a tsunami, such as the tsunami that struck southeast Asia in 2004, killing 230,000 people.

Plates push past each other

Mantle

Climate

The Earth's climate is very simple. Near the Equator, the temperature is hot, and closer to the poles, the temperature is cold. All year round, daytime temperatures at the Equator are around 33°C and there are no seasons. At the poles, the temperature is usually below freezing, and in winter there are long hours of darkness and temperatures drop to −40°C. Rain and snowfall patterns are more complex. Countries at the Equator experience heavy rain, but the poles have very little rainfall.

Global warming

The increased level of carbon dioxide in the atmosphere causes global warming because the gas traps the Sun's heat. Carbon dioxide is emitted when carbon fuels are burnt – this happens in cars and factories. The effects of global warming are becoming evident. Large areas of ice around Antarctica have already disappeared. The Sahara Desert is expanding and droughts are more common in Australia, causing rivers, such as the Murray, to dry up (see below). Sea levels are slowly rising, threatening cities such as New York City and low-lying countries such as Bangladesh with flooding. Using alternative sources of energy, such as wind and solar power, is vital to slow down these changes.

TYPES OF CLIMATE

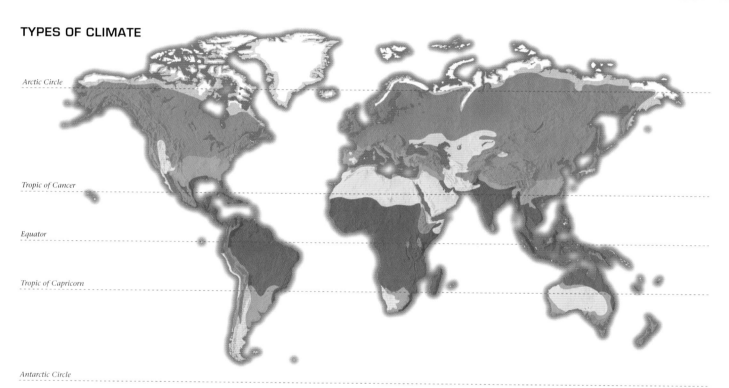

Arctic Circle

Tropic of Cancer

Equator

Tropic of Capricorn

Antarctic Circle

Polar and tundra
The lands around the Arctic Ocean and Antarctica are normally covered in snow. Northern Canada and Russia have a brief summer where the snow melts and the top layer of soil thaws to create a boggy ground called tundra.

Desert
Just north and south of the Equator lie desert areas. They have high daytime summer temperatures and are warm even in winter. Rain is very rare. Few plants grow and crops are only farmed where there are sources of water.

Cool temperate
Near the Arctic Circle, winters are cold and snowy, and summers are short. Closer to the Equator winters are milder, with little snow and warm summers. Forests are abundant and farming is common in the southern areas.

Warm temperate
In areas around the Mediterranean Sea and in some parts of North America, summers are hot and dry and winters are cool, but mild. Rainfall varies, so farming centres around growing citrus and olive trees.

Tropical
Close to the Equator, countries experience high temperatures and high rainfall for almost every month of the year. More animals and plants live in the tropical rainforests of the Amazon, central Africa and Indonesia than any other region.

Mountainous
Mountains have their own climate and snow can even be found at the Equator. At 5000 m in height, the temperature is 30°C colder than at sea level. Mountains also have more rainfall than the land surrounding them.

Population

The population of the world reached 7.6 billion in 2017. With around 250 babies being born each minute, and many people living longer due to a better quality of life, the population of the world is increasing rapidly. This rise puts pressure on the world's natural resources, and many cities are becoming overcrowded as people move in search of work. China is the most populated country with 1.39 billion people. Tokyo, the capital of Japan, is the largest city in the world with a population of 39.6 million.

WORLD POPULATION BY CONTINENT

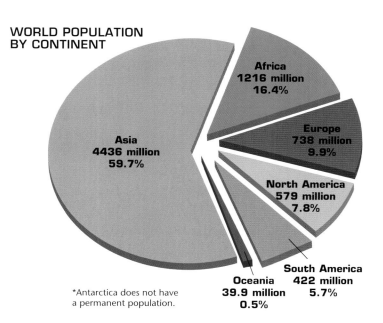

Asia 4436 million 59.7%
Africa 1216 million 16.4%
Europe 738 million 9.9%
North America 579 million 7.8%
South America 422 million 5.7%
Oceania 39.9 million 0.5%

*Antarctica does not have a permanent population.

TOP 10 COUNTRIES BY POPULATION DENSITY

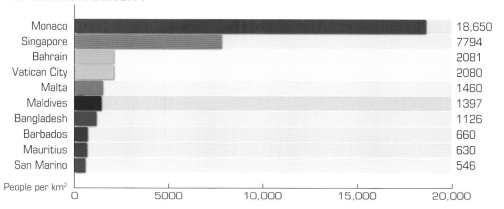

Country	People per km²
Monaco	18,650
Singapore	7794
Bahrain	2081
Vatican City	2080
Malta	1460
Maldives	1397
Bangladesh	1126
Barbados	660
Mauritius	630
San Marino	546

TOP 10 COUNTRIES BY POPULATION

1	China	1,391,700,000
2	India	1,339,200,000
3	USA	325,719,000
4	Indonesia	263,990,000
5	Pakistan	213,123,000
6	Brazil	207,661,000
7	Nigeria	193,393,000
8	Bangladesh	166,221,000
9	Russia	144,530,000
10	Mexico	129,200,000

TOP 20 CITIES BY POPULATION

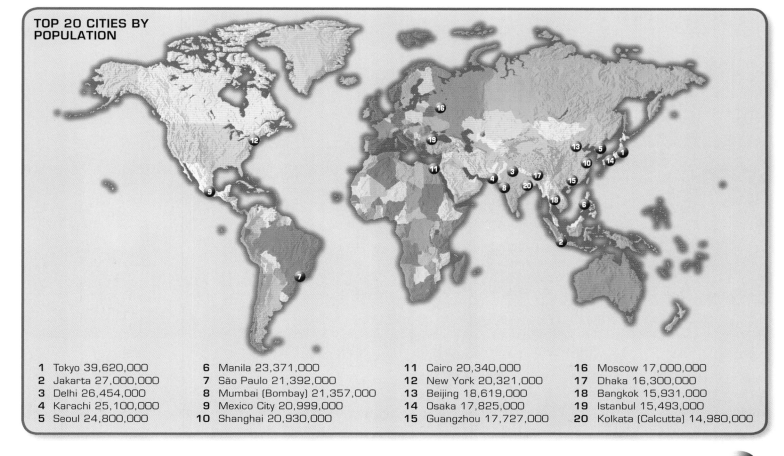

1	Tokyo	39,620,000
2	Jakarta	27,000,000
3	Delhi	26,454,000
4	Karachi	25,100,000
5	Seoul	24,800,000
6	Manila	23,371,000
7	São Paulo	21,392,000
8	Mumbai (Bombay)	21,357,000
9	Mexico City	20,999,000
10	Shanghai	20,930,000
11	Cairo	20,340,000
12	New York	20,321,000
13	Beijing	18,619,000
14	Osaka	17,825,000
15	Guangzhou	17,727,000
16	Moscow	17,000,000
17	Dhaka	16,300,000
18	Bangkok	15,931,000
19	Istanbul	15,493,000
20	Kolkata (Calcutta)	14,980,000

The Physical World

ARCT

QUEEN ELIZABETH ISLANDS

Ellesmere Island

BEAUFORT SEA

Baffin Bay

GREENLAND (DENMARK)

Victoria Island

Baffin Island

BROOKS RANGE

Great Bear Lake

Back

Davis Strait

Denmark Strait

NORWEG SEA

Yukon

Mackenzie

Little Bear Lake

HUDSON BAY

Gulf of Alaska

ROCKY MOUNTAINS

GREAT PLAINS

Lake Winnipeg

CANADIAN SHIELD

Newfoundland

ALEUTIAN ISLANDS

THE GREAT LAKES

Missouri

Mississippi

MID-ATLANTIC RIDGE

PACIFIC OCEAN

NORTH AMERICA

NORTH ATLANTIC OCEAN

CANARY ISLANDS (SPAIN)

Hawaii (US)

Rio Grande

SIERRA MADRE

GULF OF MEXICO

ATLAS MOUNT

SAH

WEST INDIES

MID-AMERICA TRENCH

CARIBBEAN SEA

Niger

Galápagos Islands (Ecuador)

LLANOS

Orinoco

GUIANA HIGHLANDS

MID-ATLANTIC RIDGE

GULF GUIN

Amazon

SOUTH AMERICA

ANDES

SELVAS

BRAZILIAN HIGHLANDS

SOUTH ATLANTI OCEAN

PERU-CHILE TRENCH

GRAN CHACO

PAMPAS

FALKLAND ISLANDS (UK)

WALVIS

Cape Horn

Antarctic

LONGEST RIVERS BY CONTINENT

River	Continent	Length km
Nile	Africa	6853
Chang Jiang (Yangze)	Asia	6300
Volga	Europe	3530
Mississippi-Missouri	North America	6020
Murray-Darling	Oceania	3750
Amazon	South America	6992

LOWEST POINTS BY CONTINENT

Area	Continent	Depth m
Lake Assal	Africa	−153
Dead Sea	Asia	−402
Caspian Sea shore	Europe	−28
Death Valley	North America	−86
Lake Eyre	Oceania	−16
Laguna del Carbón	South America	−105

HIGHEST POINTS BY CONTINENT

Mountain	Continent	Height m
Mount Kilimanjaro	Africa	5895
Mount Everest	Asia	8848
Mount Elbrus	Europe	5642
Denali	North America	6194
Puncak Jaya	Oceania	5030
Aconcagua	South America	6960

0 1000 2000 3000

0 1000 2000 3000 4000 500

OCEAN

SVALBARD
(NORWAY)

BARENTS
SEA

LAPLAND

Franz Josef Land

Novaya Zemlya

KARA
SEA

Severnaya Zemlya

LAPTEV SEA

NEW SIBERIAN
ISLANDS

EAST
SIBERIAN
SEA

BALTIC SEA

EUROPEAN PLAIN

EUROPE

Dvina

Volga

Dnieper

URAL MOUNTAINS

Ural

Yenisey

Ob

Ob

Yenisey

Irtysh

SIBERIAN
LOWLAND

CENTRAL
SIBERIAN
PLATEAU

Nizhnyaya Tunguska

ASIA

Angara

Lena

Lena

Aldan

BERING
SEA

CARPATHIAN
MOUNTAINS

Danube

BLACK SEA

CASPIAN SEA

Aral
Sea

Lake
Balkhash

SAYAN MOUNTAINS

Lake
Baikal

SEA OF
OKHOTSK

KURIL TRENCH

MEDITERRANEAN SEA

ZAGROS MOUNTAINS

Euphrates

Tigris

TIEN MOUNTAINS

HINDU KUSH

KUNLUN MOUNTAINS

GOBI
DESERT

SEA OF
JAPAN

PACIFIC
OCEAN

DESERT

Nile

NUBIAN
DESERT

Arabian
Peninsula

RED SEA

ARABIAN
SEA

Indus

TIBETAN
PLATEAU

HIMALAYAS

Ganges

Huang

Chang Jiang

EAST CHINA
SEA

MICRONESIA

AFRICA

GULF OF ADEN

ETHIOPIAN
HIGHLANDS

DECCAN

Irrawaddy

Mekong

SOUTH
CHINA
SEA

PHILIPPINE SEA

Uele

Congo

CONGO
BASIN

Kasai

GREAT RIFT VALLEY

Lake
Victoria

MID-INDIAN RIDGE

BAY OF
BENGAL

CELEBES
SEA

EAST INDIES

MELANESIA

KALAHARI
DESERT

Orange

Cape of
Good Hope

SOUTHWEST INDIAN RIDGE

INDIAN
OCEAN

JAVA TRENCH

SOUTHEAST INDIAN RIDGE

SOUTHERN
OCEAN

GREAT SANDY
DESERT

GREAT
VICTORIAN
DESERT

Great
Australian
Bight

GREAT DIVIDING RANGE

CORAL
SEA

OCEANIA

TASMAN
SEA

WORLD'S OCEANS	
Ocean	**Area km²**
Pacific	165,240,000
Atlantic	82,440,000
Indian	73,440,000
Southern	23,325,000
Arctic	14,090,000

LARGEST DESERTS		
Desert	**Continent**	**Area km²**
Sahara	Africa	8,600,000
Arabian	Asia	2,300,000
Australian	Australia	1,550,000
Gobi	Asia	1,300,000
Kalahari	Africa	930,000

LARGEST INLAND WATER BODIES		
Lake	**Continent**	**Area km²**
Caspian Sea	Asia–Europe	371,800
Superior	North America	82,350
Victoria	Africa	69,500
Huron	North America	59,600
Michigan	North America	57,800

The Political World

ARCTIC OCEAN

GREENLAND
(DENMARK)

Arctic Circle

Alaska
(US)

ICELAND

CANADA

UN
KIN

PACIFIC
OCEAN

REPUBLIC OF
IRELAND

FRA

UNITED STATES
OF AMERICA

ST. PIERRE AND
MIQUELON
(FRANCE)

ATLANTIC
OCEAN

PORTUGAL

BERMUDA (UK)

MOROCC

Tropic of Cancer

BAHAMAS

WESTERN
SAHARA

Hawaii
(US)

MEXICO

CUBA

HAITI

TURKS AND CAICOS ISLANDS (UK)

1 2   3 6 7
             8
              9
               12
      4 5 10
            13
           11
            14

MAURITANIA

CAPE VERDE
(CABO VERDE)

SENEGAL

BELIZE JAMAICA

GUATEMALA   HONDURAS
EL SALVADOR   NICARAGUA

22 21
      20
          15
        16   18
               17
              19

GAMBIA

GUINEA-BISSAU   GUINEA

KEY TO CARIBBEAN

1	DOMINICAN REPUBLIC
2	*PUERTO RICO* (US)
3	*VIRGIN ISLANDS* (US)
4	*SABA* (NETHERLANDS)
5	*ST. EUSTATIUS* (NETHERLANDS)
6	*ANGUILLA* (UK)
7	*ST. MARTIN* (FRANCE)/*SINT MAARTEN* (NETHERLANDS)
8	*ST. BARTHELÉMY* (FRANCE)
9	ANTIGUA AND BARBUDA
10	ST. KITTS AND NEVIS
11	*MONTSERRAT* (UK)
12	*GUADALOUPE* (FRANCE)
13	DOMINICA
14	*MARTINIQUE* (FRANCE)
15	ST. LUCIA
16	ST. VINCENT AND THE GRENADINES
17	BARBADOS
18	GRENADA
19	TRINIDAD AND TOBAGO
20	*BONAIRE* (NETHERLANDS)
21	*CURAÇAO* (NETHERLANDS)
22	*ARUBA* (NETHERLANDS)

COSTA RICA

PANAMA

VENEZUELA

GUYANA
SURINAME

FRENCH GUIANA
(FRANCE)

SIERRA LEONE

LIBERIA

CO
D'IVO

GHAN
TO
BEN

Equator

COLOMBIA

ECUADOR

KEY TO EUROPE

23	RUSSIA
24	LITHUANIA
25	NETHERLANDS
26	BELGIUM
27	LUXEMBOURG
28	GERMANY
29	CZECH REPUBLIC
30	SLOVAKIA
31	MOLDOVA
32	ROMANIA
33	HUNGARY
34	AUSTRIA
35	LIECHTENSTEIN
36	SWITZERLAND
37	SLOVENIA
38	CROATIA
39	BOSNIA AND HERZEGOVINA
40	SERBIA
41	MONTENEGRO
42	KOSOVO
43	MACEDONIA
44	ALBANIA
45	SAN MARINO
46	VATICAN CITY
47	MONACO
48	ANDORRA
49	MALTA

Galápagos
Islands
(Ecuador)

BRAZIL

PERU

BOLIVIA

PARAGUAY

CHILE

Tropic of Capricorn

URUGUAY

ARGENTINA

FALKLAND
ISLANDS
(UK)

SOUTH GEORGIA (UK)

COLOUR KEY

ANTARCTICA
NORTH AMERICA
SOUTH AND CENTRAL AMERICA
EUROPE
AFRICA
ASIA
OCEANIA

Antarctic Circle

ARCTIC OCEAN

FINLAND
SWEDEN
NORWAY
ESTONIA
DENMARK
LATVIA
23 24
BELARUS
POLAND
29
34 30
37 33 31
45 38 39 40 32
46 41 42
ITALY 44 43
49
BULGARIA
GREECE
TURKEY
CYPRUS
LEBANON
ISRAEL
LIBYA
EGYPT

RUSSIA

KAZAKHSTAN

MONGOLIA

UZBEKISTAN
KYRGYZSTAN
GEORGIA
AZERBAIJAN
TURKMENISTAN
TAJIKISTAN
ARMENIA
SYRIA
IRAQ
IRAN
AFGHANISTAN
JORDAN
KUWAIT
BAHRAIN
QATAR
SAUDI
ARABIA
PAKISTAN
UNITED
ARAB
EMIRATES
OMAN

CHINA

NORTH
KOREA
SOUTH
KOREA
JAPAN

PACIFIC
OCEAN

NEPAL
BHUTAN
BANGLADESH
INDIA
BURMA
(MYANMAR)
LAOS
THAILAND
VIETNAM
CAMBODIA
TAIWAN

CHAD
SUDAN
ERITREA
YEMEN
DJIBOUTI
CENTRAL
AFRICAN
REPUBLIC
SOUTH
SUDAN
ETHIOPIA
CAMEROON
SOMALIA
DEMOCRATIC
REPUBLIC
OF THE CONGO
KENYA
UGANDA
GABON
52
RWANDA
BURUNDI
TANZANIA
SRI
LANKA
MALDIVES
PHILIPPINES
BRUNEI
MALAYSIA
SINGAPORE
PALAU
MICRONESIA

MARSHALL
ISLANDS

INDONESIA

PAPUA
NEW
GUINEA
EAST TIMOR
(TIMOR-LESTE)

SOLOMON
ISLANDS

NAURU
KIRIBATI
TUVALU

SAMOA

SEYCHELLES

INDIAN
OCEAN

ANGOLA
ZAMBIA
MALAWI
COMOROS
MAYOTTE
(FRANCE)
MOZAMBIQUE
ZIMBABWE
MADAGASCAR
MAURITIUS
RÉUNION
(FRANCE)
NAMIBIA
BOTSWANA
ESWATINI
SOUTH
AFRICA
LESOTHO

VANUATU

CORAL SEA
ISLANDS TERRITORY
(AUSTRALIA)
NEW CALEDONIA
(FRANCE)

FIJI
NIUE
TONGA
COOK
ISLANDS

AUSTRALIA

0   1000   2000   3000 mi
0   1000 2000 3000 4000 5000 km

NEW
ZEALAND

KEY TO AFRICA

50 EQUATORIAL GUINEA
51 SÃO TOMÉ AND PRÍNCIPE
52 REPUBLIC OF THE CONGO
53 ANGOLA

SOUTHERN OCEAN

MOST WIDELY SPOKEN LANGUAGES

Language	Number of native speakers
Chinese Mandarin	955 million
Spanish	477 million
Hindi	425 million
English	371 million
Arabic	290 million
Bengali	220 million
Portuguese	218 million
Bahasa Indonesian	170 million
Russian	145 million
Japanese	128 million

ANTARCTICA

Antarctica

Just under 98 percent of Antarctica is covered by ice that is about 1.6 km thick. Although it is the coldest place on Earth, the region is heavily affected by global warming. The climate is becoming warmer due to an increased level of carbon dioxide, which traps the Sun's heat. Large areas of ice that cover the sea around Antarctica have already broken away and melted. Deep under the ice lie vast amounts of oil, coal and gold, but mining is prohibited.

| 0 | 200 | 400 | 600 | 800 mi |
| 0 | 400 | 800 | 1200 km |

Signy (UK)
Orcadas (Argentina)
South Orkney Islands

Sanae IV (South Africa)
Maitri (India)
Novolazervskaya (Russia)
Neumayer III (Germany)
Troll (Norway)
QUEEN MAUD LAND
Princess Elisabeth (Belgium)
Showa (Japan)

Chang Cheng (China)
Esperanza (Argentina)
Marambio (Argentina)
Presidente Eduardo Frei (Chile)
Palmer (US)
Rothera (UK)

WEDDELL SEA
COATS LAND
Halley (UK)
Belgrano II (Argentina)
Berkner Island
Ronne Ice Shelf
ELLSWORTH MOUNTAINS

Antarctic Peninsula
PALMER LAND
ELLSWORTH LAND
WEST ANTARCTICA

Mawson (Australia)
LAMBERT GLACIER
Zhongshan (China)
Davis (Australia)
PRINCESS ELIZABETH LAND
Mirny (Russia)

AMUNDSEN SEA

MARIE BYRD LAND

South Pole ★ Amundsen-Scott (US)

Vostok (Russia)

EAST ANTARCTICA

Roosevelt Island
Ross Ice Shelf
WILKES LAND
GEORGE V LAND
Casey (Australia)

Scott Base (New Zealand)
McMurdo (US)
ROSS SEA
Jang Bogo (South Korea)
Dumont d'Urville (France)

SOUTHERN OCEAN

Antarctic Circle

In the next ...at least five icebergs will fall into the oceans – enough fresh water to supply London for a day. **minute...**

Facts and Stats

• Antarctica does not have a permanent population.

• The area of the Arctic Ocean is 14 million km² – 136 times the area of Iceland.

• Antarctica now has nine permanently flowing meltwater streams, the longest of which, the Onyx, is 35 km long.

▷ *Emperor penguins* only live in Antarctica. Their bodies are adapted for the incredibly cold weather, and they have feathers on their legs down to their feet. The chicks do not grow their waterproof feathers until they are about ten months old.

Arctic Ocean

The Arctic is actually an ocean, not an area of land. Explorers have walked to the North Pole in spring when the ice is thickest, and a submarine once surfaced through the ice in late summer. The ice covering the Arctic Ocean is getting thinner and less extensive each year due to the effect of global warming – an increase in the temperature of the Earth's atmosphere. As a result, many animals, including polar bears, could eventually die out.

CHUKCHI SEA

Point Barrow

EAST SIBERIAN SEA

BEAUFORT SEA

Amundsen Gulf

Novosibirskiye Ostrova

Banks Island

LAPTEV SEA

Victoria Island

Melville Island

ARCTIC OCEAN

Severnaya Zemlya

Queen Elizabeth Islands

North Pole ✸

Ellesmere Island

Nares Strait

LINCOLN SEA

Franz Josef Land

Novaya Zemlya

Baffin Island

Kap Morris Jesup

WANDEL SEA

BARENTS SEA

KARA SEA

Baffin Bay

GREENLAND SEA

SVALBARD (NORWAY)

GREENLAND (DENMARK)

0	200	400	600	800 mi
0	400	800	1200 km	

Did You Know?

In Antarctica, the lowest temperature ever recorded was −94.7°C. The average summer temperature is −30°C – just 10°C warmer than a deep freezer.

NORWEGIAN SEA

Arctic Circle

THE DISTANCE from the North Pole [F11] to the South Pole [F4] is 19,996 km and would take 28 hours to travel by plane.

North America

ARCTIC OCEAN

Alaska
(US)

CANADA

PACIFIC
OCEAN

UNITED STATES
OF AMERICA

ATLANTIC
OCEAN

MEXICO

Hawaii
(US)

COUNTRY FACTFILE

Country	Life expectancy	Population to nearest thousand	Population growth %	Population as urban %	Area km²	Population density per km²	Capital city	Currency	Languages
Canada	82	36,286,000	0.7	82	9,970,610	3.6	Ottawa	Canadian Dollar	English, French
Mexico	76	129,200,000	1.1	80	1,958,201	66	Mexico City	Mexican Peso	Spanish
United States of America	80	325,719,000	0.8	82	9,629,091	33.8	Washington D.C.	US Dollar	English, Spanish

NB: Central America can be found as part of the South and Central America section.

Northeast USA

The northeast is the centre of the United States' industry and commerce with many large manufacturing companies. Ford and General Motor vehicles, as well as coal mines, steel works, the New York Stock Exchange, Washington White House and the Senate buildings are all situated here. Modern black music started in Cleveland and Detroit, whilst away from the cities there are many beaches, rivers, forests and lakes.

NORTH DAKOTA

Lake of the Woods

Red Lake

Isle Royale

Lake Superior

CANADA

Marquette

Upper Peninsula

MINNESOTA

Moorhead

Duluth

Green Bay

MICHIGA

Lower Peninsula

WISCONSIN

Minneapolis
Bloomington
Burnsville

St. Paul

Eau Claire

Green Bay
Appleton
Oshkosh

Lake Winnebago

Lake Michigan

Saginaw

Fli

SOUTH DAKOTA

Minnesota

Mississippi

Mankato

Rochester

La Crosse

Grand Rapids

Lansing

Wisconsin

Waukesha

Madison

Milwaukee

Ann Arb
Kalamazo

Mason City

Cedar

Janesville

Waterloo

Rockford

Elgin

IOWA

Sioux City

Cedar Rapids
Davenport

Aurora

Chicago

South Bend

Joliet

Gary

Fort Wayne

Des Moines

NEBRASKA

Des Moines

ILLINOIS

Wabash

Council Bluffs

Peoria

INDIANA

Munc

Champaign

Anderson

MISSOURI

Illinois

Decatur

Terre Haute

Indianap

Springfield

Bloomington

Mississippi

Jeffersonville

East St. Louis

Evansville

There are 30 major league baseball teams in two leagues, the American League (founded 1901) and the National League (founded 1876). 1903 was the first time that the World Series, between the winners of the two leagues, was played.

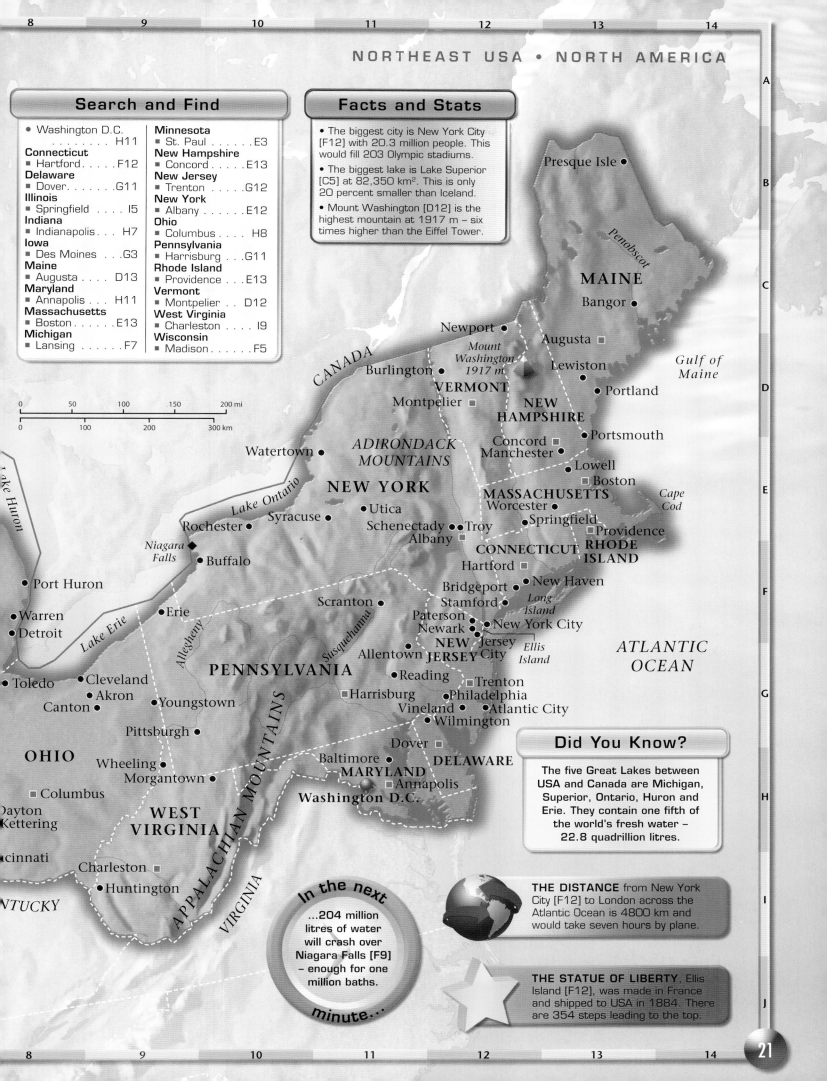

Search and Find

- Washington D.C. H11

Connecticut
- Hartford F12

Delaware
- Dover G11

Illinois
- Springfield I5

Indiana
- Indianapolis ... H7

Iowa
- Des Moines ... G3

Maine
- Augusta D13

Maryland
- Annapolis ... H11

Massachusetts
- Boston E13

Michigan
- Lansing F7

Minnesota
- St. Paul E3

New Hampshire
- Concord E13

New Jersey
- Trenton G12

New York
- Albany E12

Ohio
- Columbus H8

Pennsylvania
- Harrisburg ... G11

Rhode Island
- Providence ... E13

Vermont
- Montpelier .. D12

West Virginia
- Charleston I9

Wisconsin
- Madison F5

Facts and Stats

- The biggest city is New York City [F12] with 20.3 million people. This would fill 203 Olympic stadiums.
- The biggest lake is Lake Superior [C5] at 82,350 km². This is only 20 percent smaller than Iceland.
- Mount Washington [D12] is the highest mountain at 1917 m – six times higher than the Eiffel Tower.

Did You Know?

The five Great Lakes between USA and Canada are Michigan, Superior, Ontario, Huron and Erie. They contain one fifth of the world's fresh water – 22.8 quadrillion litres.

In the next ...204 million litres of water will crash over Niagara Falls [F9] – enough for one million baths. **minute...**

THE DISTANCE from New York City [F12] to London across the Atlantic Ocean is 4800 km and would take seven hours by plane.

THE STATUE OF LIBERTY, Ellis Island [F12], was made in France and shipped to USA in 1884. There are 354 steps leading to the top.

Southeast USA

The warm climate of Florida and the Gulf of Mexico coastal areas makes southeast USA popular with tourists. There is Disney World in Florida for fun, Cape Canaveral for space rocket launches, Miami for beaches, New Orleans for jazz, Nashville for country music and the Mississippi river for boat trips. Farming is the main occupation – mainly of tobacco, oranges, rice, peanuts, vegetables and cotton. There are many oil and gas rigs in the Gulf of Mexico to generate energy resources.

GRACELAND, Nashville [C8], is the home of Elvis Presley (1935–1977) and is visited by around 600,000 fans a year.

THE DISTANCE from the source to the mouth of the Mississippi–Missouri river is 6020 km and would take 20 days floating on a raft.

Extreme Weather

Hurricane Katrina, the largest hurricane ever recorded in the USA, caused 80 percent of New Orleans [H6] to flood. More than one million people were evacuated and 1833 died.

The **Kentucky Derby** takes place in Louisville [B8] on the first Saturday of May. The race is 2 km in length and more than 150,000 spectators attend the two-week-long festival every year.

World Record

The largest space rocket launch site in the world is at Cape Canaveral [H11].

IOWA

ILLINOIS

St. Joseph

Independence
Kansas City
Columbia
Jefferson City
St. Louis

Owensboro

KANSAS

MISSOURI
Cape Girardeau
Paducah

Springfield
Clarksville

OZARK PLATEAU

OKLAHOMA

ARKANSAS

Fort Smith
Memphis

Little Rock

Hot Springs
Pine Bluff

Mississippi

Yazoo

Ouachita

Greenville
Tuscaloo

Texarkana
El Dorado

MISSISSIPPI

TEXAS

Monroe
Meridian

Shreveport
Jackson

Pearl

LOUISIANA

Natchez
Hattiesburg

Red

Alexandria
Prichard
Mobil

Biloxi

Baton Rouge
Lafayette
Lake Charles
New Orleans

Marsh Island

Mississippi Delta

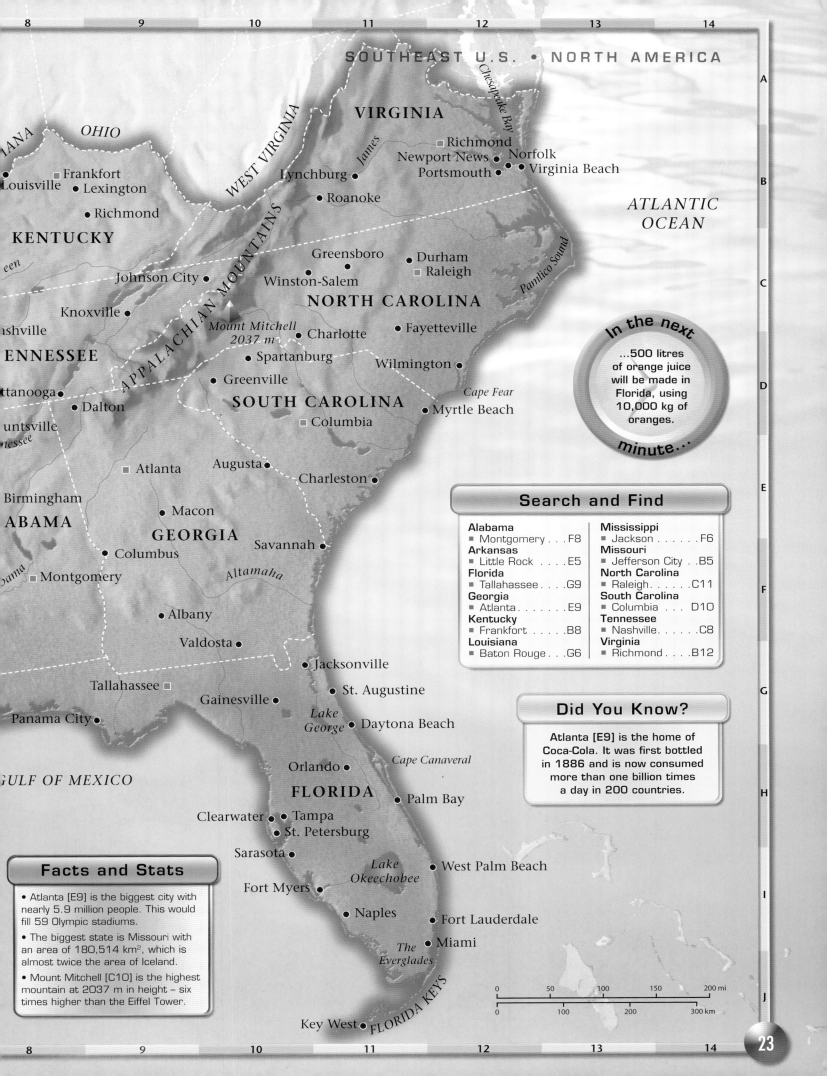

Southend SOUTHEAST U.S. • NORTH AMERICA

VIRGINIA

Chesapeake Bay

OHIO

Louisville
Frankfort
Lexington
Richmond

KENTUCKY

WEST VIRGINIA

Lynchburg
Roanoke

Richmond
Newport News Norfolk
Portsmouth Virginia Beach

James

ATLANTIC
OCEAN

Greensboro Durham
Johnson City Winston-Salem Raleigh

Knoxville

NORTH CAROLINA

Pamlico Sound

ashville

Mount Mitchell Charlotte Fayetteville
2037 m

ENNESSEE

ttanooga Dalton
Spartanburg
Greenville

Wilmington

Cape Fear

SOUTH CAROLINA Myrtle Beach

untsville Columbia

nessee

Augusta
Atlanta Charleston

Birmingham

LABAMA Macon

GEORGIA

Altamaha

Columbus Savannah

Montgomery

Albany

Valdosta

Jacksonville
St. Augustine
Gainesville Daytona Beach

*Lake
George*

GULF OF MEXICO

Tallahassee

Panama City

Orlando

Cape Canaveral

FLORIDA Palm Bay

Clearwater Tampa
St. Petersburg

Sarasota

*Lake
Okeechobee* West Palm Beach

Fort Myers

Naples Fort Lauderdale

*The
Everglades* Miami

Key West FLORIDA KEYS

In the next ...500 litres of orange juice will be made in Florida, using 10,000 kg of oranges. **minute...**

Search and Find

Alabama
■ Montgomery . . . F8
Arkansas
■ Little Rock E5
Florida
■ Tallahassee G9
Georgia
■ Atlanta E9
Kentucky
■ Frankfort B8
Louisiana
■ Baton Rouge . . . G6

Mississippi
■ Jackson F6
Missouri
■ Jefferson City . . B5
North Carolina
■ Raleigh C11
South Carolina
■ Columbia . . . D10
Tennessee
■ Nashville C8
Virginia
■ Richmond B12

Did You Know?

Atlanta [E9] is the home of
Coca-Cola. It was first bottled
in 1886 and is now consumed
more than one billion times
a day in 200 countries.

Facts and Stats

• Atlanta [E9] is the biggest city with
nearly 5.9 million people. This would
fill 59 Olympic stadiums.

• The biggest state is Missouri with
an area of 180,514 km², which is
almost twice the area of Iceland.

• Mount Mitchell [C10] is the highest
mountain at 2037 m in height – six
times higher than the Eiffel Tower.

| 0 | 50 | 100 | 150 | 200 mi |

| 0 | 100 | 200 | 300 km |

Northwest USA and Alaska

Inland areas in northwest USA are either stunning mountain scenery or vast ranches. Washington's Seattle is the only large urban area, with the Boeing aircraft factory, and the headquarters of Microsoft, UPS, Starbucks and Amazon. The USA's biggest apple-growing region stretches from the Pacific Ocean to the Great Plains of the Dakotas. Alaska is the USA's largest state. However, vast areas are uninhabited due to long, severe winters. Alaska is one of the leading oil-producing regions in the world.

In the next minute...
...Wyoming will produce 300 tonnes of coal – enough to produce electricity to power ten million TVs.

Bellingham

CANADA

OLYMPIC MOUNTAINS

Everett

Seattle

Columbia

WASHINGTON

Tacoma

Spokane

Coeur d'Alene

Flathead Lake

Olympia

Mount Rainier 4392 m

COLUMBIA BASIN

Pullman

ROCKY MOUNTAINS

Mount St. Helens 2549 m

Yakima

Pasco

Lewiston

Missoula
Helena

Vancouver

Portland

Pendleton

Butte

Salem
Corvallis

La Grande

COAST RANGES

Eugene

BLUE MOUNTAINS

Hells Canyon

IDAHO

PACIFIC OCEAN

OREGON

Burns

Boise

Medford

Malheur Lake

Snake

Idaho Falls

Klamath Falls

CALIFORNIA

Twin Falls

Pocatell

NEVADA

UTAH

*Cowboys take part in **rodeo competitions** to show off their ranching skills, including cattle roping. A lasso is used by the rider to catch the steer.*

Search and Find

Alaska		Oregon	
■ Juneau	C11	■ Salem	F3
Idaho		**South Dakota**	
■ Boise	G5	■ Pierre	G12
Montana		**Washington**	
■ Helena	E7	■ Olympia	D3
Nebraska		**Wyoming**	
■ Lincoln	I14	■ Cheyenne	I10
North Dakota			
■ Bismarck	F12		

ALASKA

CHUKCHI SEA

BERING SEA

Wainwright
Point Hope • Barrow
St. Lawrence Island
St. Matthew Island
Noatak
Colville
Nome
St. Paul Island
Nunivak Island
Hooper Bay • Alakanuk
Kobuk
Koyukuk
Yukon
Bethel • Kwethluk
Near Islands
St. George Island
Rat Islands
Aleutian Islands
Dillingham
Denali 6194 m
Tanana
Fort Yukon
Fairbanks
Andreanof Islands
Fox Islands
Unimak Island
Kenai
Seward
Anchorage
Cordova
Kodiak
Kodiak Island
Gulf of Alaska
Yakutat
PACIFIC OCEAN
Juneau
Sitka
Ketchikan
CANADA

0 100 200 300 400 500 mi
0 200 400 600 800 km

Facts and Stats

- Montana is 380,847 km² in area – 3.5 times the area of Iceland.
- Seattle [D4] is the biggest city with almost 3.9 million people. This would fill 39 Olympic stadiums.
- Alaska's Denali [B11] is the highest mountain at 6194 m – 19 times higher than the Eiffel Tower.

Did You Know?

In 1867, the USA bought Alaska from Russia for $7.2 million (£3.7 million) – cheaper than a modern New York apartment.

0 50 100 150 200 mi
0 100 200 300 km

Great Falls
Fort Peck Lake
Missouri
Williston
Minot
Grand Forks
Lake Sakakawea
MONTANA
NORTH DAKOTA
Miles City
Bismarck ■ Jamestown
Fargo
MINNESOTA
GREAT PLAINS
ozeman • Billings
Lake Oahe
Aberdeen
Watertown
wstone nal Park • Cody
BIGHORN MOUNTAINS
Gillette
Cheyenne
Pierre ■
SOUTH DAKOTA
ckson
Rapid City
White
Sioux Falls
Mount Rushmore
Lake Francis Case
WYOMING
Casper
Yanktown
Niobrara
SAND HILLS
Norfolk
Rock Springs
Loup
IOWA
Laramie
Cheyenne ■
NEBRASKA
COLORADO
North Platte • Grand Island
Omaha
Platte
Lincoln ■
Hastings

THE DISTANCE of the USA's Pacific coastline is 12,268 km and would take a migrating whale about 50 days to swim.

KANSAS

Southwest USA and Hawaii

PACIFIC
OCEAN

The nation's most dramatic landscape belongs to southwest USA, which is covered by the Rocky Mountains. Southern California, Nevada and Arizona are desert – the driest place being Death Valley. Texas is the home of the oil industry, and Nevada's Las Vegas attracts tourists visiting casinos and nearby scenery, such as the Grand Canyon. California has boomed due to the Hollywood film studios, Silicon Valley's large number of computer firms, and some of the most productive farmland in the country. Tropical Hawaii is a popular surfing and beach island 4800 km southwest of California.

OREGON

IDAHO

Mount Shasta
4322 m

Eureka

Redding

Winnemucca   Humboldt   Elko

Great
Salt

COAST RANGES

SIERRA NEVADA

Reno
Carson City

Sacramento

NEVADA

Santa Rosa

Oakland   Stockton
San Francisco   Yosemite
Palo Alto   Modesto   National
Sunnyvale   San Jose   Park

Tonopah

GREAT
BASIN

Salinas
Monterey   Fresno

Cedar City

Mount Whitney
4418 m

San Luis
Obispo   Bakersfield

DEATH VALLEY

Las
Vegas

CALIFORNIA

Hoover   Grand Can
Dam

Santa Barbara

ARIZONA

Oxnard
Pasadena
Los Angeles   San Bernardino
Long Beach   Riverside
Anaheim

Prescot

Oceanside

Phoenix
Gila   M

San Diego

Yuma

Search and Find

Arizona
- Phoenix F7

California
- Sacramento . . . C4

Colorado
- Denver C10

Hawaii
- Honolulu H3

Kansas
- Topeka D13

Nevada
- Carson City C5

New Mexico
- Santa Fe F10

Oklahoma
- Oklahoma City . F13

Texas
- Austin H13

Utah
- Salt Lake City . . C8

Mount
Kawaikini
1598 m   Kauai   Kapaa

KAUAI CHANNEL

Niihau

Oahu

Waialua   Kaneohe
Wahiawa
Honolulu   Kalaupapa

Molokai   Maui
Lanai City   Wailuku
Lanai

Kahoolawe

ALENUIHAHA CHANNEL

PACIFIC
OCEAN

Mauna Kea
4205 m   Hilo

Mauna Loa
4169 m

HAWAII

0   50   100   150 mi
0   100   200 km

Did You Know?

If California were its own country, it would have the fifth largest economy in the world.

Facts and Stats

- Texas is 691,027 km² in area – 6.5 times the area of Iceland.
- Los Angeles [F5] is the biggest city with 13.35 million people. This would fill 134 Olympic stadiums.
- Mount Whitney [D5] is the highest mountain at 4418 m in height – 14 times higher than the Eiffel Tower.

8 9 10 11 12 13 14

A

The Colorado river has carved a gorge over millions of years to form the **Grand Canyon** [E7]. It is up to 446 km in length and 1.6 km in depth.

B

0 50 100 150 200 mi

0 100 200 300 km

WYOMING

Brigham City
Ogden
Salt Lake City

C

Fort Collins • Sterling •
Greeley •
Boulder •
Lakewood • Denver
South Platte

• Provo

UTAH

Grand Junction •
Aspen •
COLORADO
Colorado Springs •

Mount Elbert 4399 m

Colorado

Pueblo •
Arkansas

NEBRASKA

St. Joseph •

Kansas City •

Hays • Salina • *Kansas* Topeka •

KANSAS

Lamar •
Dodge City • Hutchinson •
Wichita •

MISSOURI

D

E

Durango •
Farmington •

Humphreys Peak 3851 m

Gallup • Los Alamos •
Santa Fe •

Flagstaff
• Winslow Albuquerque •

NEW MEXICO

Clovis •

Rio Grande

Cimarron
Ponca City •
Enid •

North Canadian
Tulsa •
Muskogee •

OKLAHOMA

Oklahoma City •
Amarillo • Elk City • Norman •

ARKANSAS

F

Lawton •

Lubbock •
Wichita Falls •
Durant •

Plano •
Fort Worth • Dallas •
Arlington Longview •
Abilene • *Sabine*
Tyler •

LOUISIANA

Silver City •
Roswell •

Deming • Las Cruces •
Hobbs •
Carlsbad •

Tucson
• Douglas
El Paso •

MEXICO

Odessa • Midland •

TEXAS

Brazos
Leon Waco •

Trinity

G

Pecos •
Pecos
San Angelo •

S T O C K T O N   P L A T E A U

E D W A R D S   P L A T E A U

Colorado

Austin •

Beaumont •
Houston • Port Arthur •

H

In the next
...the Hoover Dam's [E6] power station will generate enough electricity to power 34.6 million light bulbs.
minute...

Del Rio •
San Antonio •
Galveston •

Eagle Pass •

San Antonio

I

THE DISTANCE across the Rocky Mountains [E9] is 1700 km and once took horse-drawn wagon trains more than six months to travel.

Laredo •
Corpus Christi •

MEXICO

GULF OF MEXICO

J

McAllen •
Brownsville •

8 9 10 11 12 13 14

Canada

Canada is the second largest country in the world. The Rocky Mountains of western Canada reach more than 3600 m above sea level and create stunning scenery. Tourists sail along the coast to see icebergs and to view migrating whales. The largest Canadian cities are Toronto and Montreal in the east, and Vancouver in the west. Quebec differs from the rest of Canada because of the large French-speaking population that lives there. Canada has a wealth of natural resources, including wood and petroleum, and is one of the top ten richest nations.

| 0 | 100 | 200 | 300 | 400 | 500 mi |
| 0 | 200 | 400 | 600 | 800 km |

Did You Know?

Canada has 10 percent of the world's forests. These are inhabited by a wide range of wildlife, including bears and moose.

Facts and Stats

- Canada is the second largest country in the world with an area of 9,970,610 km² – 97 times the area of Iceland.
- Toronto [J11] is the biggest city with a population of 5.9 million – this would fill 60 Olympic stadiums.

Deep in the Canadian Rockies is **Banff National Park** in Alberta, which was founded in 1885, and is Canada's oldest national park. Peyto Lake is a popular attraction as the water turns turquoise in colour as the surrounding glaciers melt.

ARCTIC OCEAN

BEAUFORT SEA

Ba
Isl

Inuvik

Mackenzie

ALASKA (US)

Kugluktuk

Dawson

Norman
Wells

MACKENZIE MOUNTAINS

YUKON
TERRITORY

NORTHWEST
TERRITORIE

*Mount Logan
5959 m*

Whitehorse

Yellowknife

*Gulf of
Alaska*

ROCKY

Fort Resolution

Fort Smith

PACIFIC
OCEAN

BRITISH
COLUMBIA

C A

Peace

Hazelton

Haida Gwaii

Prince Rupert

Peace Riv

COAST MOUNTAINS

Grande Prairie

Prince
George

ALBERTA

Edmo

MOUNTAINS

Fraser

Red D

*Vancouver
Island*

Kamloops

Calgary

Vancouver

Medicine Hat

Victoria

Lethbridge

UNITED STA

▷ **Aurora Borealis** *can be seen in the Northern Hemisphere. Also known as the Northern Lights, the bands of shimmering light are caused by atmospheric particles crashing into the Earth's atmosphere.*

Search and Find

Alberta
- Edmonton H7

British Columbia
- Victoria I5

Canada
- Ottawa I12

Manitoba
- Winnipeg I9

New Brunswick
- Fredericton . . . I13

Newfoundland and Labrador
- St. John's . . . H14

Northwest Territories
- Yellowknife F7

Nova Scotia
- Halifax I13

Nunavut
- Iqaluit. F11

Ontario
- Toronto J11

Prince Edward Island
- Charlottetown . I13

Quebec
- Quebec I12

Saskatchewan
- Regina I8

Yukon Territory
- Whitehorse. . . .F5

Axel Heiberg Island

Ellesmere Island

GREENLAND (DENMARK)

Bathurst Island

Devon Island

Baffin Bay

Prince of Wales Island

toria and

Baffin Island

• Iqalukyuuttiaq

NUNAVUT

Southampton Island

Iqaluit ☐

LABRADOR SEA

• Salliit

Hudson Strait

Kangiqtiniq (Rankin Inlet) •

Coats Island

Mansel Island

Ungava Peninsula

In the next

...Canadians will consume 25 litres of maple syrup – a natural sugar from the sugar maple tree.

minute...

HUDSON BAY

Feuilles

• Nain

LABRADOR

Churchill •

Churchill

Nelson

Goose Bay •

NEWFOUNDLAND AND LABRADOR

• Flin Flon

Prince Albert

MANITOBA

Severn

James Bay

La Grande Rivière

QUEBEC

Anticosti Island

• Gander

St. John's ☐

Newfoundland

askatoon

ONTARIO

Fort Albany •

Albany

Gaspé •

PRINCE EDWARD ISLAND

ST. PIERRE AND MIQUELON (FRANCE)

Chicoutimi •

NEW BRUNSWICK

☐ Charlottetown

• Regina

se

Winnipeg •

Fredericton ☐

☐ Halifax

v

• Brandon

Quebec ☐

St. John •

NOVA SCOTIA

MERICA

• Thunder Bay

Trois-Rivières •

Sherbrooke •

Bay of Fundy

Sudbury •

Montreal •

Ottawa ●

ATLANTIC OCEAN

Georgian Bay

Toronto •

• Oshawa

Kitchener •• Hamilton

• London

• Windsor

🌐 **THE DISTANCE** from St. John's [H14] to Vancouver [I6] is further than St. John's to Prague, Europe.

A
B
C
D
E
F
G
H
I
J

Mexico

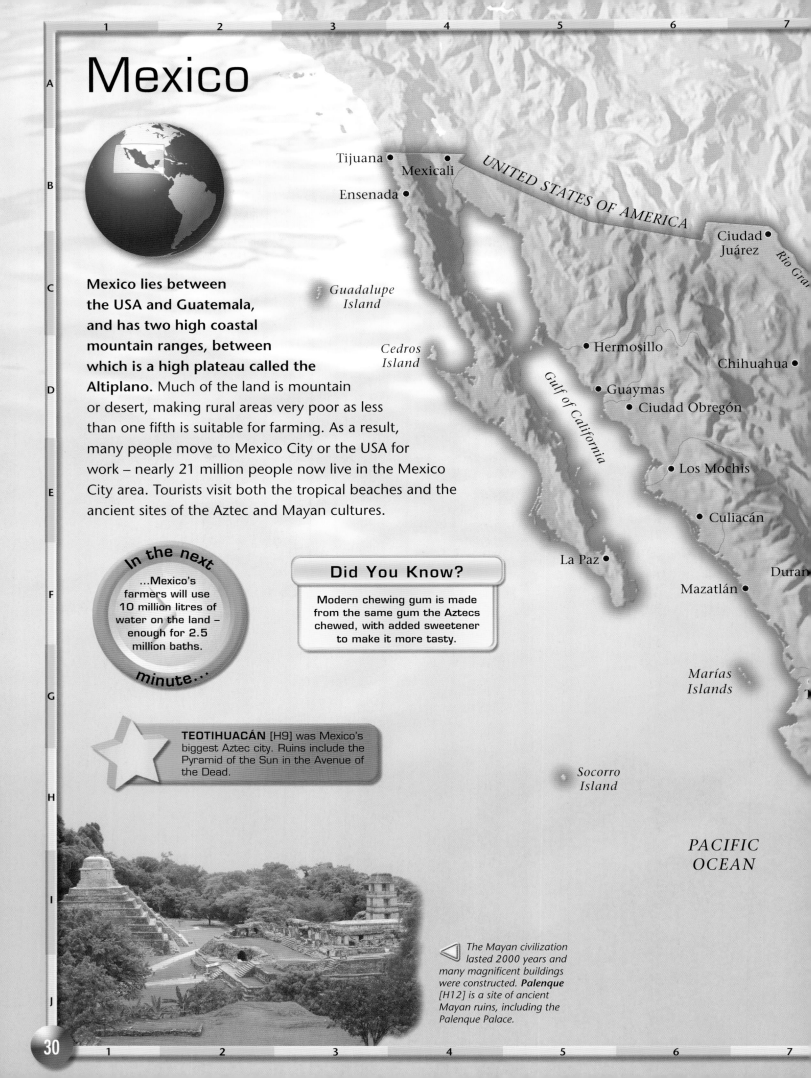

Mexico lies between the USA and Guatemala, and has two high coastal mountain ranges, between which is a high plateau called the Altiplano. Much of the land is mountain or desert, making rural areas very poor as less than one fifth is suitable for farming. As a result, many people move to Mexico City or the USA for work – nearly 21 million people now live in the Mexico City area. Tourists visit both the tropical beaches and the ancient sites of the Aztec and Mayan cultures.

In the next ...Mexico's farmers will use 10 million litres of water on the land – enough for 2.5 million baths. **minute...**

Did You Know?

Modern chewing gum is made from the same gum the Aztecs chewed, with added sweetener to make it more tasty.

TEOTIHUACÁN [H9] was Mexico's biggest Aztec city. Ruins include the Pyramid of the Sun in the Avenue of the Dead.

Tijuana
Mexicali
Ensenada

UNITED STATES OF AMERICA

Ciudad Juárez
Rio Gran

Guadalupe Island

Cedros Island

Hermosillo
Chihuahua

Gulf of California

Guaymas
Ciudad Obregón

Los Mochis

Culiacán

La Paz

Duran

Mazatlán

Marías Islands

Socorro Island

PACIFIC OCEAN

The Mayan civilization lasted 2000 years and many magnificent buildings were constructed. *Palenque* [H12] is a site of ancient Mayan ruins, including the Palenque Palace.

The stories of the ancient Mexican cultures are retold through ornately dressed **folk dancers**. The costumes and performances represent ancient Mayan dances for the gods.

Facts and Stats

• Mexico City [H9] has a population of nearly 21 million people – this would fill 210 Olympic stadiums.

• The Rio Grande [C7] is 3060 km in length – less than half the length of the Nile river.

• The highest mountain is Volcan Pico de Orizaba [H10] at 5700 m in height. It is 18 times higher than the Eiffel Tower.

THE DISTANCE from east to west across Mexico City [H9] is only 30 km, but it takes more than three hours by car at peak times.

The Xochimilco area of Mexico City [H9] has many **ancient canals**. During festivals, boats are covered with flowers to attract tourists.

UNITED STATES OF AMERICA

Nuevo Laredo •

ómez Palacio •   • Monclova
                              Reynosa •
Terreón •   Monterrey •   Matamoros •
        Saltillo •

MEXICO

                    • Ciudad Victoria

GULF OF MEXICO

                    • Ciudad Madero
San Luis Potosí • • Tampico
• Aguascalientes

                                              Cancún •
                              Mérida •   Cozumel Island
León •   Chichén Itzá
    Querétaro •
• Guadalajara   Bay of Campeche   Yucatán Peninsula
        • Pachuca
Teotihuacán ◆   Volcan Pico
        • Ecatepec de Orizaba   Chetumal •
Morelia •   5700 m
    Toluca •   • Veracruz
Colima   H
Mexico City   • Orizaba
    Cuernavaca • Puebla •   Villahermosa •
                  Coatzacoalcos •   BELIZE
Chilpancingo •   Palenque ◆
        Oaxaca •   GUATEMALA
    Acapulco •   Tuxtla Gutiérrez •

                Gulf of Tehuantepec

0   100   200   300 mi
0   200   400 km

South and Central America

BAHAMAS

CUBA

DOMINICAN
REPUBLIC

2

1

BELIZE

4

GUATEMALA

HONDURAS

3

HONDURAS

EL SALVADOR

NICARAGUA

6

5

9

7

COSTA RICA

8

10

GUYANA

PANAMA

VENEZUELA

SURINAME

COLOMBIA

ECUADOR

PERU

B R A Z I L

BOLIVIA

PACIFIC
OCEAN

CHILE

PARAGUAY

URUGUAY

ATLANTIC
OCEAN

ARGENTINA

KEY
1 HAITI
2 JAMAICA
3 ST. KITTS AND NEVIS
4 ANTIGUA AND BARBUDA
5 DOMINICA
6 ST. LUCIA
7 ST. VINCENT AND THE GRENADINES
8 GRENADA
9 BARBADOS
10 TRINIDAD AND TOBAGO

COUNTRY FACTFILE

Country	Life expectancy	Population to nearest thousand	Population growth %	Population as urban %	Area km²	Population density per km²	Capital city	Currency	Languages
Antigua and Barbuda	77	95,000	1.2	59	442	214.9	St. John's	East Caribbean Dollar	English, Creole
Argentina	77	44,045,000	0.9	92	2,766,890	15.9	Buenos Aires	Argentine Peso	Spanish
Bahamas	73	391,000	0.8	87	13,939	28.1	Nassau	Bahamian Dollar	English, Creole
Barbados	76	284,000	0.3	52	430	660.5	Bridgetown	Barbadian Dollar	English, Bajan (Creole)
Belize	69	398,000	1.8	52	22,965	17.3	Belmopan	Belizean Dollar	English, Creole, Spanish
Bolivia	70	11,146,000	1.5	69	1,098,581	10.1	La Paz, Sucre	Boliviano	Spanish, Quechua, Aymara
Brazil	74	207,661,000	0.7	87	8,502,728	24.4	Brasília	Real	Portuguese
Chile	80	17,574,000	0.8	88	756,626	23.2	Santiago, Valparaiso	Chilean Peso	Spanish
Colombia	74	48,292,000	1.0	81	1,141,748	43.1	Bogotá	Colombian Peso	Spanish
Costa Rica	79	4,948,000	1.2	79	51,100	96.8	San José	Costa Rican Colon	Spanish
Cuba	79	11,239,000	−0.3	77	110,861	101.4	Havana	Cuban Peso	Spanish
Dominica	77	74,000	0.2	71	739	100.1	Roseau	East Caribbean Dollar	English, French Creole
Dominican Republic	75	10,169,000	1.2	81	48,311	210.5	Santo Domingo	Domincan Peso	Spanish
Ecuador	77	16,777,000	1.3	79	269,178	62.3	Quito	US Dollar	Spanish, Quechua
El Salvador	75	6,582,000	0.3	72	21,041	312.8	San Salvador	US Dollar	Spanish
Grenada	75	108	0.4	40	344	314	St. George's	East Caribbean Dollar	English, French Creole
Guatemala	73	16,584	1.8	52	108,889	152	Guatemala City	Quetzal	Spanish
Guyana	69	778,000	0.3	36	215,083	3.6	Georgetown	Guyanese Dollar	English, Creole
Haiti	64	10,981,000	1.3	59	27,750	405.7	Port-au-Prince	Gourde	French, Creole
Honduras	71	8,866,000	1.8	57	112,088	78.8	Tegucigalpa	Lempira	Spanish
Jamaica	74	2,729,000	0.7	56	10,991	248.5	Kingston	Jamaican Dollar	English, Creole
Nicaragua	74	6,328,000	1.0	59	130,670	48.4	Managua	Gold Cordoba	Spanish
Panama	79	4,098,000	1.3	75	74,177	55.2	Panama City	Balboa, US Dollar	Spanish, English
Paraguay	77	6,954,000	1.2	62	406,752	17.1	Asunción	Guarani	Spanish, Guarani
Peru	74	29,328,000	1.0	79	1,285,216	22.9	Lima	New Sol	Spanish, Quechua
St. Kitts and Nevis	76	55,000	0.7	44	269	204.5	Basseterre	East Caribbean Dollar	English, Creole
St. Lucia	78	179,000	0.3	59	617	290.1	Castries	East Caribbean Dollar	English, French Creole
St. Vincent and the Grenadines	76	110,000	0	55	398	282.8	Kingstown	East Caribbean Dollar	English, Creole
Suriname	73	563,000	1.0	75	163,820	3.4	Paramaribo	Suriname Dollar	Dutch, Sranantonga, Hindi
Trinidad and Tobago	73	1,328,000	0	72	5128	259	Port-of-Spain	Trinidad and Tobago Dollar	English, Creole
Uruguay	77	3,493,000	0.3	95	175,016	20	Montevideo	Uruguayan Peso	Spanish
Venezuela *	76	28,930,000	1.5	88	916,445	34.3	Caracas	Sovereign Bolivar	Spanish

*Likely to change due to uncertain economic and political situation.

Central America and the Caribbean

Central America is a narrow area of land where the mountain chain continues from Antarctica up to Alaska. The only gap, which joins the Atlantic and Pacific Oceans, is the Panama Canal.

The manmade canal shortens the journey between the oceans by 13,000 km. The Caribbean islands are mainly agricultural, but their sandy beaches, warm seas and links to the USA and Europe make them popular tourist destinations.

MEXICO

BELIZE
● Belize City
Belmopan

MAYA MOUNTAINS

Quezaltenango ●

● San Antonio

GUATEMALA
Guatemala City San Pedro ● ● La Ceiba
Sula ● El Progreso
Escuintla ●

HONDURAS

San Salvador ● ● Tegucigalpa
EL SALVADOR

● Estelí
Chinandega ● **NICARAGUA**
León ●
Managua

COSTA RICA
Puntarenas ● ● Heredia
San José
Cerro Chirripó
Grande 3819 m

Havana
Pinar del Rio ● ● Cárdenas
Santa Clara ●
Nueva Gerona ● ● Cienfuegos **CU**
Isla de la Sancti Spíri
Juventud Camagüe

CAYMAN ISLANDS (UK)

Montego Bay

JAMAICA
Sp
T

Gulf of Barran
Darien
Cartage
Panama
Canal Colón ●
● San Miguelito
David ● Since le
PANAMA *CORDILLERA CENTRAL* **Panama City** Mont
Gulf of Panama

◁ *In many places in Central America,* **weaving** *is still done by hand rather than by machine. Colourful rugs and tapestries from the region are sold around the world.*

0	100	200	300	400 mi
0		200	400	600 km

Medellí
Quibdó ●
Manizale
Pereira ●
Armenia ●
Buenaventura ● Ibagu
Cali ●
Popayán ● *CORDILL*
Pasto ●
ECUADOR

Facts and Stats

● Colombia has a population of nearly 48.3 million people – this would fill 483 Olympic stadiums.

● The life expectancy of people in Haiti is only 64 years, compared to 79 years in Cuba and a world average of 69 years.

● The average income per person in Haiti is £586 and £23,682 in the Bahamas, compared to a world average of £8196.

There are two lakes in the craters of the **Poas volcano**, Costa Rica. Due to geothermal activity, it is believed that the lakes are turning into geysers. Since 1828, the volcano has erupted 46 times.

BAHAMAS

Nassau

TURKS AND CAICOS ISLANDS (UK)

Holguín
yamo
Guantánamo
ago
Cap-Haïtien
uba
Gonaïves

DOMINICAN REPUBLIC

Santiago
La Vega
San Francisco de Macorís

La Romana

Port-au-Prince
gston
Les Cayes   Jacmel
Santo Domingo

HAITI

VIRGIN ISLANDS (UK)

VIRGIN ISLANDS (US)
ANGUILLA (UK)

PUERTO RICO (US)

SABA (NETH.)

ST. MARTIN (FRANCE)/SINT MAARTEN (NETH.)
ST. BARTHELÉMY (FRANCE)
ST. EUSTATIUS (NETH.)

Basseterre
ST. KITTS AND NEVIS
MONTSERRAT (UK)

ANTIGUA AND BARBUDA
St. John's

GUADELOUPE (FRANCE)

DOMINICA
Roseau

MARTINIQUE (FRANCE)

Castries
ST. LUCIA

BARBADOS
Bridgetown

ST. VINCENT AND THE GRENADINES
Kingstown

GRENADA
St. George's

C A R I B B E A N   S E A

ARUBA (NETHERLANDS)
CURAÇAO (NETHERLANDS)
BONAIRE (NETHERLANDS)

Port-of-Spain
TRINIDAD AND TOBAGO

Pico Cristobal Colon 5800 m
Maracaibo
Caracas
Cumaná
Barquisimeto   Maracay   Barcelona
Valencia
Valera
Guanare
Barinas

cuta
San Cristóbal
Bucaramanga
rancabermeja

Ciudad Bolívar   Ciudad Guayana

VENEZUELA

Georgetown

Tunja
Río Meta
Angel Falls ◆
Puerto Ayacucho
GUIANA HIGHLANDS

Paramaribo

Bogotá
Villavicencio

GUYANA

FRENCH GUIANA (FRANCE)

SURINAME

BRAZIL

COLOMBIA

Río Vaupés
Río Apaporis
BRAZIL
Caquetá

BRAZIL

PERU

In the next
...Colombia, will pack 1313 kg of coffee into bags for export – that's nearly 200,000 cups.
minute...

World Record
At more than 979 m in height, Angel Falls [G11] is the highest waterfall in the world.

THE DISTANCE from one end of the Panama Canal [F6] to the other is only 77 km, but it saves 18 days sailing time.

Did You Know?
The Bermuda Triangle is an area in the Atlantic Ocean, northeast of the Caribbean. Many ships and aircraft have disappeared here without a trace.

South America

Stretching from the tropical forests of the Amazon to just a short distance from icy Antarctica, South America is a continent of contrasts. The Andes stretch the length of the continent, but the main feature is the Amazon rainforest. The rainforest is home to more plant and animal species than any other habitat in the world. However, around 25,000 km² of the rainforest is destroyed each year to make room for farmland. The forest not only provides a home to many animals, but it is also the source of many plant-derived medicines. By absorbing carbon dioxide, the forest helps to reduce global warming.

◁ At 6992 km in length, the **Amazon river** crosses the full width of Brazil. A wide range of wildlife live in the river, including the endangered boto, or Amazon river dolphin.

Search and Find

Argentina
- Buenos Aires . . G8

Bolivia
- La Paz D7
- Sucre. E7

Brazil
- Brasília. D10

Chile
- Santiago. G7
- Valparaíso. G6

Ecuador
- Quito B5

Paraguay
- Asunción E8

Peru
- Lima D5

Uruguay
- Montevideo G8

In the next ...9000 tonnes of the Amazon rainforest will be destroyed – about 100 trees and other plants. minute...

▷ The statue of Jesus, **Christ the Redeemer**, stands at the top of Mount Corcovado, Rio de Janeiro [E10]. At 38 m in height, it is one of the most famous landmarks in the world.

VENEZU
Negro
COLOMBIA
Esmeraldas
Ibarra
Manta
Quito
Portoviejo
Ambato
Guayaquil
Riobamba
ECUADOR
Iquitos
Amazon
AMAZON
BASIN
Piura
Chiclayo
Trujillo
Pucallpa
Porto Velho
Chimbote
Rio Branco
PERU
Huacho
Lima
Callao
Huancayo
BOLIV
Ayacucho
Cusco
Ica
Lake
Titicaca
Juliaca
Arequipa
Puno
Cochaba
La Paz
S
Oruro
Arica
Sucre
Nevado Sajama
6520 m
Potosí
Iquique
Tarija
Calama
San Salv
ATACAMA
de Ju
Antofagasta
DESERT
PACIFIC
OCEAN
CHILE
San Miguel
de Tucumán
A R
La Serena
Córd
Coquimbo
R
San Juan
Cu.
Godoy Cruz
Mendoz
Vina del Mar
Valparaíso
Cerro
Santiago
Aconcagu
Rancagua
6959 m
Talcahuano
Chillán
Concepción
Los Angeles
Temuco
Neuqu
Valdivia
Osorno
Comod
Puerto Montt
Rivada
PATAGONIA
Pue
Mac
Rio
Gall
Punta Arenas
Ush

GUYANA
SURINAME
FRENCH GUIANA (FRANCE)

Amapá
Macapá
Marajó Island
Belém
São Luis
Parnaíba
Amazon
Manaus
Santarém
Altamira
Fortaleza
Marabá
Imperatriz
Teresina
Mossoró
Natal
Campina Grande
João Pessoa
Araguaína
Juazeiro do Norte
Recife
Maceio
Tocantins
Juazeiro
Aracaju

BRAZIL

Feira de Santana
Salvador

Chiabá
Brasília
Itabuna
Anápolis
MATO GROSSO PLATEAU
Goiânia
Campo Grande
Uberlândia
Governador Valadares
Uberaba
Belo Horizonte
Rìo Préto
Vitoria
Nova Iguaçu
Niteroi
Pedro Juan Caballero
Campinas
Rio de Janeiro
São Paulo
PARAGUAY
Santos
Asunción
Ciudad del Este
Curitiba
ACO Resistencia
Corrientes
Florianópolio
TINA
Porto Alegre

ATLANTIC OCEAN

Salto
Rivera
Pelotas
nta Fe
Rio Grande
URUGUAY
osario
Buenos Aires
Montevideo
omas
Zamora
La Plata
Bahía Blanca
Mar del Plata
Punta Alta

0   200   400   600   800 mi
0   400   800   1200 km

One of the largest **street carnivals** in the world is held every February in Rio de Janeiro [E10]. People dress in elaborate costumes and parades take place in the city centre. More than 200,000 people take part.

FALKLAND ISLANDS
(UK)

SOUTH GEORGIA
(UK)

e Horn

37

Europe

ARCTIC OCEAN

ICELAND

FINLAND

NORWAY SWEDEN

ESTONIA

LATVIA

RUSSIA

DENMARK

1

2

UNITED
KINGDOM

REPUBLIC
OF IRELAND

3

POLAND

BELARUS

GERMANY

4

6

*ATLANTIC
OCEAN*

5

11

10

7

UKRAINE

FRANCE

12

9

8

15

16

ROMANIA

13

14

23

17

18

19

BULGARIA

GEORGIA

24

20

21

27

SPAIN

22

PORTUGAL

ITALY

GREECE

25

26

KEY

1 RUSSIA	15 SLOVENIA
2 LITHUANIA	16 CROATIA
3 NETHERLANDS	17 BOSNIA AND HERZEGOVINA
4 BELGIUM	18 SERBIA
5 LUXEMBOURG	19 MONTENEGRO
6 CZECH REPUBLIC	20 KOSOVO
7 SLOVAKIA	21 MACEDONIA
8 MOLDOVA	22 ALBANIA
9 HUNGARY	23 SAN MARINO
10 AUSTRIA	24 VATICAN CITY
11 LIECHTENSTEIN	25 MALTA
12 SWITZERLAND	26 CYPRUS
13 ANDORRA	27 ARMENIA
14 MONACO	

* Crimea is legally part of Ukraine but has been annexed by Russia. See page 58 for detailed map.

COUNTRY FACTFILE

Country	Life expectancy	Population to nearest thousand	Population growth %	Population as urban %	Area km²	Population density per km²	Capital city	Currency	Languages
Albania	79	2,870,000	0	60	28,748	99.9	Tiranë	Lek	Albanian
Andorra	83	75,000	0	95	468	161.1	Andorra la Vella	Euro	Catalan, Spanish
Armenia	75	2,973,000	−0.2	70	29,743	100	Yerevan	Dram	Armenian
Austria	82	8,823,000	0.5	68	83,879	105.2	Vienna	Euro	German
Belarus	73	9,492,000	−0.2	79	207,546	45.7	Minsk	Belarusian Rouble	Belarusian, Russian
Belgium	81	11,376,000	0.7	98	30,528	367.2	Brussels	Euro	Dutch, Flemish, French
Bosnia and Herzegovina	77	3,438,000	−0.2	49	51,129	67.1	Sarajevo	Marka	Croat, Serb
Bulgaria	75	7,050,000	−0.6	75	111,036	63.5	Sofia	Lev	Bulgarian, Turkish
Croatia	76	4,154,000	−0.5	77	56,542	73.4	Zagreb	Kuna	Croat
Cyprus *	79	1,141,000	1.3	70	9251	123.3	Nicosia	Euro	Greek, Turkish, English
Czech Republic	79	10,610,000	0.1	75	78,864	134.5	Prague	Czech Koruna	Czech
Denmark	80	5,781,000	0.2	88	43,094	134.1	Copenhagen	Danish Krone	Danish
Estonia	77	1,319,000	0	69	45,227	30.3	Tallinn	Euro	Estonian, Russian
Finland	81	5,513,000	0.4	85	338,145	16.4	Helsinki	Euro	Finnish, Swedish
France	82	66,448,000	0.4	85	639,176	102.4	Paris	Euro	French
Georgia	76	4,015,000	−0.02	68	69,492	57.8	Tbilisi	Lari	Georgian
Germany	81	82,522,000	0	88	357,021	230.9	Berlin	Euro	German
Greece	81	10,768,000	−0.1	79	131,957	81.6	Athens	Euro	Greek
Hungary	76	9,798,000	−0.3	71	93,022	105.3	Budapest	Forint	Hungarian
Iceland	83	348,000	1.1	94	102,819	3.4	Reykjavik	Icelandic Krona	Icelandic
Ireland, Republic of	81	4,758,000	1.2	63	70,285	67.7	Dublin	Euro	English, Irish (Gaelic)
Italy	82	60,484,000	0	71	301,277	201	Rome	Euro	Italian
Kosovo	77	1,799,000	0.3	51	10,828	166.1	Pristina	Euro	Albanian
Latvia	75	1,934,000	−1.1	69	64,610	30	Riga	Euro	Latvian, Russian
Liechtenstein	82	38,000	0.7	45	160	238.1	Vaduz	Swiss Franc	German
Lithuania	75	2,810,000	−1.1	68	65,301	43	Vilnius	Euro	Lithuanian, Russian
Luxembourg	82	602,000	2	91	2586	232.8	Luxembourg	Euro	Letzeburgish, German, French
Macedonia	70	2,074,000	0.2	67	25,713	80.7	Skopje	Macedonian Denar	Macedonian, Albanian
Malta	81	476,000	0.3	95	316	1511.1	Valletta	Euro	Maltese, English
Moldova	71	3,503,000	−1.1	48	33,873	103.5	Chisinau	Moldovan Leu	Romanian (Moldovan), Russian, Ukrainian
Monaco	89	37,000	0.3	100	2	18,650	Monaco	Euro	French, Monegasque, Italian
Montenegro	75	622,000	−0.3	67	13,894	44.8	Podgorica	Euro	Serb, Albanian, Montenegrin
Netherlands	81	17,184,000	0.4	92	41,546	413.6	Amsterdam, The Hague	Euro	Dutch, Frisian
Norway	82	5,214,000	1	82	323,878	16.1	Oslo	Norwegian Krone	Norwegian
Poland	78	38,434,000	−0.1	66	312,685	122.9	Warsaw	Zloty	Polish
Portugal	79	10,291,000	0	65	92,391	111.4	Lisbon	Euro	Portuguese
Romania	75	19,524,000	0	57	237,500	82.4	Bucharest	Leu	Romanian, Hungarian
Russia	71	144,530,000	0	78	17,075,400	8.5	Moscow	Rouble	Russian, Tatar, Ukrainian
San Marino	83	33,000	0.7	97	61	545.9	San Marino	Euro	Italian
Serbia	76	7,021,000	−0.5	56	77,468	90.5	Belgrade	Serbian Dinar	Serb, Hungarian
Slovakia	77	5,435,000	0	57	49,036	110.8	Bratislava	Euro	Slovak, Hungarian
Slovenia	78	2,067,000	0	55	20,273	101.9	Ljubljana	Euro	Slovenian
Spain	82	46,572,000	0.8	80	504,782	92.2	Madrid	Euro	Spanish (Castilian), Catalan, Basque, Gallego
Sweden	82	10,120,000	0.8	87	449,964	22.5	Stockholm	Swedish Krona	Swedish
Switzerland	83	8,484,000	0.7	74	41,285	205.5	Bern	Swiss Franc	German, French, Italian
Ukraine	72	44,737,000	−0.4	70	603,700	74.4	Kiev	Hryvnia	Ukrainian, Russian
United Kingdom	81	66,040,000	0.5	83	244,088	270.6	London	British Pound	English
Vatican City	N/A	1000	0	100	0.44	2080	Vatican City	Euro	Italian, Latin

*Cyprus is part of Europe, but the mapping can be found in the Asia section.

Britain and Ireland

The United Kingdom (England, Scotland, Wales and Northern Ireland) and the Republic of Ireland make up the British Isles. The UK has become one of the most influential and prosperous countries in the world.
By 1900, the British Empire ruled many countries, including Canada, South Africa, India and Australia, which is why so many nations speak English. Ireland declared independence in 1919, but it only came into effect in 1922. Scotland, Wales and Northern Ireland now have their own parliaments. Manufacturing was once the major industry, but most wealth is now generated by banking, insurance and high-tech equipment.

The **Giant's Causeway** [E7] in Northern Ireland is made up of 40,000 columns created by a volcanic eruption. The columns measure up to 12 m in height. According to legend, the giant Finn McCool began to build the causeway towards Scotland, but he fell asleep before he finished it.

Search and Find

England	Scotland
● London. H10	■ Edinburgh E8
Northern Ireland	**Wales**
■ Belfast F7	■ Cardiff H8
Republic of Ireland	
● Dublin G7	

THE DISTANCE from Land's End [I7] to John o'Groats [C9] once took a cyclist 41 hours and a runner 12 days to complete.

Outer Hebrides — *Lewis*

Sky

Giant's Causeway ◆

● Londonde

NORTHERN IRELAND

Sligo ● — B
● Arm

REPUBLIC OF IRELAND

Drogheda ●

IR
S

Galway ●

Liffey **Du**

Shannon

WICKLOW MOUNTAINS

ATLANTIC OCEAN

Limerick ●

Carrantuohill ▲ 1041 m — Waterford ●

Cork ●

ST. GEORGE'S CHAN

Edinburgh [E8], Scotland, is the second most visited city after London. More than 4 million people are attracted to the city each year to see historical sights, such as Edinburgh Castle, or to attend the Edinburgh Festival in August.

Isles of Scilly *Land's End*

8 9 10 11 12 13 14

A

Shetland Islands

Lerwick

▷ **Snowdonia National Park** [G8], Wales, was created in 1951 and covers 2142 km² of land. More than 26,000 people actually live within the area and it receives more than six million visitors a year. The area is a mixture of forest, open land, coast and mountains – making it popular with hikers.

B

Orkney Islands

John o'Groats

C

0   50   100   150 mi
0   100   200 km

Inverness

SCOTLAND

Ben Nevis 1343 m

Aberdeen

THE TOWER OF LONDON [H10] has been a castle, a royal palace, a prison, a zoo and the home of the crown jewels.

D

MPIAN MOUNTAINS

Perth   Dundee

Falkirk

Edinburgh

Motherwell

NORTH SEA

Ayr

Facts and Stats

E

Newcastle upon Tyne

Carlisle

Sunderland

Scafell Pike 977 m

PENNINES

Middlesbrough

In the next ...148 passengers will arrive or depart from London's Heathrow Airport, one of the busiest airports in the world. minute...

• London [H10] is the biggest city with nearly 10.5 million people. This would fill 1048 Olympic stadiums.

• The Shannon [G6] is the longest river at 386 km in length. However, it is more than 17 times shorter than the Nile river.

• Ben Nevis [D8] is the highest mountain at 1343 m in height – four times higher than the Eiffel Tower.

F

York

LE MAN K)

Blackpool

Leeds

Hull

owdon 085 m

Liverpool   Manchester

Chester   Sheffield

ENGLAND

Stoke-on-Trent

G

Wrexham

Nottingham

Derby

WALES

Leicester

Peterborough

Did You Know?

Avebury Stone Circle [I9] is 6000 years old, and is the largest ancient stone monument in the world.

Aberystwyth

Birmingham

Coventry

Norwich

AMBRIAN OUNTAINS

Northampton

Cambridge

H

Gloucester

Ipswich

ansea   Newport   Swindon   Oxford

Colchester

Cardiff

Bristol

Avebury Stone Circle ◆   Reading

London

◆ Stonehenge

Dover

Southampton   Portsmouth

I

Exeter   Bournemouth

Brighton

Plymouth

Isle of Wight

▷ The **Millennium Bridge**, London [H10], was opened in 2000, and is used as a pedestrian footbridge. It has been designed to hold 5000 people at any one time. St. Paul's Cathedral is situated at its north end and the Tate Modern art gallery is at the south end.

ENGLISH CHANNEL

J

Guernsey

CHANNEL Jersey

ISLANDS (UK)

8 9 10 11 12 13 14

Scandinavia

Norway, Sweden, Denmark, Finland and Iceland are Europe's most northerly and least populated countries. Mainland Scandinavia stretches from Norway's mountainous Atlantic coast in the west to Finland's low-lying forested countryside in the east. More than one third lies within the Arctic Circle where, during a 73-day winter period, the Sun never rises. Norway and Iceland are not members of the European Union. Living standards are high due to vast natural resources, such as oil, gas, timber and iron. Scandinavia has a reputation for stylish designs with brands such as Bang and Olufsen, Ikea and Volvo.

In the next ...minute...
...Sweden will make more than two million matches – enough to fill 40,000 boxes.

World Record
Finland has more of its territory covered by lakes than any other country – 187,888 lakes cover 10 percent of the country.

Facts and Stats

• Sweden's population of 10.1 million would fill 101 Olympic stadiums.

• The life expectancy of people in Sweden is 82 years, compared to 80 years in Denmark and a world average of 69 years.

• The average income per person in Norway is £57,452, compared to a world average of £8196.

Did You Know?

The first Legoland was opened in Billund [I6], Denmark, in 1968. On average, every person in the world owns 52 Lego bricks.

Sognefjord [F5], Norway, is the second largest fjord in the world. Towns are situated on the fjord and the stunning scenery attracts many tourists, which helps to support the economy.

Lofoten Islands · Bodø

ATLANTIC OCEAN

Kristiansund · · Trondheim · Östersund

Ålesund ·

NORWAY

Sognefjord · Galdhøpiggen 2469 m

Bergen · · Voss · Lillehammer
Hamar

Haugesund · · Oslo
Drammen ·
Stavanger · Skien · Fredrikstad · Karlstad
Öre...

Kristiansand · Linköpi...

Skagerrak · Göteborg · Borås

NORTH SEA · Jönköpi...

Ålborg · *Kattegat* · Halmstad · Vä...

DENMARK · Randers
Århus · Helsingborg · Karlsham...
Billund · Copenhagen · Karlskr...
Esbjerg · · Lund
Kolding · Odense · Roskilde · Malmö

BORNHOLM (DENMARK)

GERMANY

ARCTIC OCEAN

North Cape

Vadsø

omsø

Narvik

Kiruna

L A P L A N D

Gällivare

WEDEN

Rovaniemi

RUSSIA

Kemi

Luleå
Piteå

Oulu

Skellefteå

GULF OF BOTHNIA

Umeå

Kokkola

nsköldsvik

Kuopio

Vaasa

dsvall

Jyväskylä

FINLAND

Pori

Tampere

Søderhamn

Hämeenlinna
Lahti

Gävle

Vantaa
Kotka
Turku
Åland
Islands
Espoo
Helsinki

Mariehamn

Uppsala

ästerås

Stockholm

Södertälje

rrköping

Isafjördhur

Olafsfjördhur

Húsavik

Akureyri

Myvatn

stervik

Visby
Gotland

Seydisfjördhur

Eskifjördhur

Ólafsvik

orgholm
nd

BALTIC SEA

ICELAND

VATNAJÖKULL

Hvítá

Thórsá

Hvannadalshnúkur
2119 m

Höfn

Akranes

Reykjavik

Keflavik
Kopavogur

NORWEGIAN
SEA

ATLANTIC
OCEAN

Vestmannaeyar

0   50   100   150 mi
0   100   200   300 km

0   50   100   150 mi
0   100   200 km

Sweden's **Ice Hotel** near Kiruna [C8] is only open from December to April and is rebuilt each year. The hotel has more than 80 rooms and even has a church. Everything in the hotel, down to the glasses, is made of ice.

Search and Find

Denmark
● Copenhagen . . . I7
Finland
● Helsinki G10
Iceland
● Reykjavik. I11

Norway
● Oslo. G6
Sweden
● Stockholm. G8

THE DISTANCE from Norway's North Cape [A9] to the North Pole is shorter than the distance from Oslo [G6] to southern Italy.

LAPLAND [C9] is said to be where Santa Claus lives. In December, many tourists visit the region to see Santa with his elves and reindeer.

Spain and Portugal

The Iberian Peninsula is occupied by Spain and Portugal. Africa is less than 16 km from the Strait of Gibraltar, and to the north Spain is bordered by France and the mountain state of Andorra. Spain also includes the Balearic Islands in the Mediterranean Sea and the Canary Islands, including Tenerife and Gran Canaria, which lie 100 km west of Africa in the Atlantic Ocean. Well-known for olive, orange and lemon groves, as well as hot weather and sandy beaches, these countries attract millions of tourists each year.

The costas of Spain are popular coastal regions. **Costa Brava** [C13] in northeast Spain is in the vicinity of Barcelona. S'Agaró is an exclusive resort, and its hotels have even been used in films.

THE DISTANCE from the east to the west side of the border between Spain and Gibraltar [I7] is only 800 m.

BILBAO [B9] is home to many museums including the Fine Arts Museum and the world-famous Guggenheim Museum.

Facts and Stats

- Spain's population of nearly 46.6 million would fill 466 Olympic stadiums. However, the population of Andorra is only 67,000 and would only fill half a stadium.
- The life expectancy of people in Spain is 82 years, compared to a world average of 69 years.
- The average income per person in Andorra is £29,787, compared to a world average of £8196.

Did You Know?

Sardines are the most popular Portuguese seafood. The average consumption for a person is 6 kg a year.

El Ferrol
La Coruña
Gijón
Ovi
Lugo
Santiago de Compostela
León
CANTABRIAN
Sil
Orense
Vigo
E
Braga
Zamor
Guimaraes
Duero
Tormes
Porto
Salamanca
Aveiro
SIER
Coimbra
Tajo (T
Tajo (Tagus)
Santarém
Cáceres
PORTUGAL
Mérida
Estoril
Lisbon
Badajoz
Almada
Évora
Setúbal
Beja
Guadiana
Guadalq
Lagos
Huelva
Seville
ATLANTIC
OCEAN
Faro
Moron de la Frontera
Arcos
Ron
Jerez de la Frontera
Cádiz
GIBRAL
(UK
Algeciras
Strait of Gibr
CEU
(SPA
MOROC

8   9   10   11   12   13   14

Search and Find

Andorra
● Andorra la Vella C12
Portugal
● Lisbon G4

Spain
● Madrid E8

BAY OF BISCAY

Santander

San Sebastián

Bilbao

TAINS

FRANCE

Vitória-Gasteiz   Pamplona

*Pico de Aneto
3405 m*

ANDORRA

P Y R E N E E S

**Andorra
la Vella**

Logroño

Gállego

Burgos

Ebro

Girona

Palencia

Soria

Cinca

Manresa

Mataró

Terrasa

/alladolid

Duero

Zaragoza

Lleida

Barcelona

Reus   Tarragona

Costa Brava

Costa Dorada

ovia

GREDOS

Tortosa

vila

Morella

Madrid

Guadalajara

Alcalá de Henares

Teruel

Menorca

Mallorca

Mahón

oledo

Aranjuez

Cuenca

Castellón de la Plana

Costa del Azahar

Palma

Turia

Sagunto

SPAIN

Júcar

Valencia

*Gulf of
Valencia*

Ibiza

BALEARIC ISLANDS

Ciudad Real

Albacete

Ibiza

Alcoy

Benidorm

Formentera

Alicante
Elche

Segura

Costa Blanca

Linares

Córdoba

Murcia

Jaén

Lorca   Cartagena

0   50   100 mi
0   80   160 km

Genil

Granada

SIERRA NEVADA

Motril   Almería

Málaga

arbella   *Costa del Sol*

M E D I T E R R A N E A N   S E A

In the next

...the bark of Portugal's and Spain's cork trees will produce enough cork for 136,000 wine bottles.

minute...

▷ Bullfighting is popular in Spain. **Toreros** are performers who fight and kill bulls. There are various types, including matadors, depending on the skills used during the fight. Performances and costumes are elaborate, attracting tourists from all over the world.

*MELILLA
(SPAIN)*

8   9   10   11   12   13   14

France and Monaco

The third largest country in Europe, France has the third highest population. Despite having a rural landscape, more than 85 percent of the population lives in towns, with more than one sixth in Paris. France has an excellent health, education and social care system, and is the fifth wealthiest country in the world. Northern France is an industrialized, low-lying region, and the south has the snow-capped peaks of the Alps and Pyrenees as well as the sunny beaches of the Mediterranean Sea. Monaco is a tiny, independent, French-speaking country. One of the richest countries in the world, Monaco boasts more than 2000 millionaires and no taxes. Only three hours from the mainland by boat is the mountainous island of Corsica.

Search and Find

France	Monaco
• Paris C9	• Monaco H11

PARIS [C9] is one of the most visited places in the world, with attractions such as the Eiffel Tower and the Louvre.

THE DISTANCE from Calais [A9] to Dover, England, is 41 km and has been swum in less than eight hours.

*The Gothic cathedral **Notre Dame de Paris** [C9] was mainly constructed in the 13th and 14th centuries, but is constantly being restored. The famous Emmanuel bell weighs 13 tonnes.*

ENGLISH CHANNEL

Cherb

Île d'Ouessant

Brest •

St. Malo •

Quimper •

Laval •

Lorient •

Rennes •

Belle-Île

Angers •

St. Nazaire •

• Nantes

Île d'Yeu

Poitie

Île de Ré

• La Rochelle

BAY OF BISCAY

Cognac •

Angoulê

Périgue

Bordeaux •

Dordogne

Berg

Garonne

Mont-de-Marsan •

Agen •

Adour

Montaub

Bayonne •

• Pau

Tou

• Tarbes

• Lourdes

P Y R E N E E S

SPAIN

ANDORRA

In the next
...France will provide the UK with enough electricity to power one light bulb in every home.
minute...

8   9   10   11   12   13   14

FRANCE AND MONACO • EUROPE

Calais • • Dunkerque
Boulogne •
Roubaix
Lille •
Lens • Valenciennes
e Seine
Dieppe •
Le Havre •
Amiens •
St. Quentin •
en • Rouen

BELGIUM

LUXEM-
BOURG

Monaco has a population of only 37,000. **Monte Carlo** is well known for its casinos, harbour, glamour and racetrack.

Seine
Charleville Mézières •
St. Denis •
Versailles • Paris
Chartres •
Fontainebleau •
e Mans
Orléans •
Tours
Auxerre •
Cher

Reims •
Marne
Châlons-en-
Champagne
Troyes •

Verdun •
Metz •
Nancy •
Haguenau •
Strasbourg •
VOSGES
MOUNTAINS

GERMANY

Bourges •
Châteauroux •
FRANCE
Montluçon •
Limoges •
Clermont-Ferrand •
Puy de Sancy
1881 m
Lyon •
St. Étienne •
MASSIF
Tarn CENTRAL
Valence •
Montélimar •
Castres •
Nîmes •
Béziers •
Montpellier •
rcassonne
Sète •
ignan
Toulon •
Gulf of Lion

Dijon •
Saône
Besançon •
Chalon-sur-Saône •
Mâcon •
Bourg-en-Bresse •
Chamonix •
Chambéry •
Rhône
Grenoble •
Avignon •
Arles •
Aix-en-Provence •
Marseille •
St. Tropez •

Mulhouse •
JURA MOUNTAINS
SWITZERLAND
Mont Blanc
4810 m
ALPS
ITALY

MONACO
Antibes •
Cannes • Nice •
Monaco

Facts and Stats

• The longest river is the Loire [D7] at 1020 km in length – nearly seven times shorter than the Nile river.

• Mont Blanc [F11] is the highest mountain at 4810 m – 15 times higher than the Eiffel Tower.

• The average income per person in France is £29,277, compared to a world average of £8196.

Did You Know?

For three weeks every summer, more than 100 professional cyclists take part in a 4000-km race called the Tour de France.

Cape Corse
Bastia •
Corsica
Gulf of Sagone
Ajaccio •

MEDITERRANEAN SEA

0   50   100   150 mi
0   100   200 km

Strait of Bonifacio

World Record
Monaco has the highest population density in the world with 18,650 people per km².

8   9   10   11   12   13   14

A
B
C
D
E
F
G
H
I
J

47

Italy and the Balkans

Northern Italy is highly industrialized and produces many famous brands, such as Ferrari and Armani, while the south is mainly agricultural. Croatia, Bosnia and Herzegovina, Serbia, Montenegro, Kosovo and Macedonia were once part of Yugoslavia, but they have each become independent since 1991. Greece is one of Europe's oldest nations. The dry climate, steep slopes and thin soil limit farming to grapes, olives and citrus fruit. This area was home to the ancient Greek and Roman empires, which produced monuments such as Rome's Colosseum and the Parthenon in Athens, as well as Olympia – home to the first Olympic Games in 776 BC.

Facts and Stats

- Italy's population of 60.5 million would fill 605 Olympic stadiums. Montenegro's population of 622,000 would fill six stadiums.

- The life expectancy of people in San Marino is 83 years, compared to 76 years in Serbia and a world average of 69 years.

- The average income per person in Italy is £24,313, compared to £2963 in Kosovo and a world average of £8196.

In the next
...Italy will produce 5603 kg of pasta – that's about 70,000 adult portions!
minute...

Map labels

SWITZERLAND
AUST
SLOVEN
FRANCE
Bolzano
Aosta
Como
Lecco
Trento
Udine
Krar
Monza
Bergamo
Vicenza
Ljublj
Novara
Milan
Brescia
Verona
Treviso
Trieste
Turin
Lodi
Cremona
Padua
Venice
Ko
Alessandria
Piacenza
Mantua
Chioggia
Rije
Parma
Adria
Pu
Genoa
Reggio nell'
Ferrara
Gulf of Venice
Savona
Emilia
Bologna
Ravenna
La Spezia
Carrara
Forli
San Remo
Massa
Pistoia
Rimini
Viareggio
Prato
SAN MARI
Pisa
Florence
San Marino
Livorno
Empoli
Arezzo
Ancona
Siena
Perugia
Piombino
ITALY
Elba
Grosseto
Terni
Teram
Civitavecchia
Pe
VATICAN CITY (in Rome)
Rome
Latina
Campobass
Sassari
Gaeta
Beneve
Gulf of Gaeta
Na
Nuoro
Salerno
Sardinia
Gulf o Salern
Cagliari
TYRRHENIAN SEA
Palermo
Me
Trapani
Mount Etna 3326 m
Caltanissetta
Agrigento
Cata
Sicily
Ragusa
Si
Pantelleria
MALTA
Val

One of the most prominent sights in **Zagreb** [B8], the capital of Croatia, is the cathedral. The spires are 105 m in height and were built after an earthquake in 1880, which damaged much of the original structure.

Did You Know?

It costs the Italian government more money to keep the Tower of Pisa [D5] leaning than it would to straighten it.

8   9   10   11   12   13   14

A

▷ **The Grand Canal**, Venice [B6], is the main waterway through the city – public transportation is by water, rather than road. Venice is slowly sinking due to rising sea levels. The main squares flood about 60 times a year.

B

• Maribor

Celje   • Varazdin

o Mesto   • Bjelovar

Zagreb

• Sisak **CROATIA**

arlovac   • Osijek

Bihac   • Prijedor   Slavonski Brod

Banja Luka   • Brcko   • Bijeljina

BOSNIA AND   • Tuzla   • Sabac

HERZEGOVINA   • Zenica   • Valjevo

adar   **Sarajevo**   • Srebrenica

• Sibenik   • Uzice   • Cacak

• Split   **Mostar**   **SERBIA**

Foca

• Subotica

HUNGARY

• Zrenjanin

ROMANIA

• Novi Sad

• Pancevo

Belgrade

• Smederevo

• Kragujevac   • Negotin

Zajecar

• Krusevac

C

Search and Find

Albania		**Malta**	
• Tiranë	F10	• Valletta	I7
Bosnia and		**Montenegro**	
Herzegovina		• Podgorica	E9
• Sarajevo	D9	**San Marino**	
Croatia		• San Marino	D6
• Zagreb	B8	**Serbia**	
Greece		• Belgrade	C10
• Athens	H12	**Slovenia**	
Italy		• Ljubljana	B7
• Rome	E6	**Vatican City**	
Kosovo		• Vatican City	E6
• Pristina	E10		
Macedonia			
• Skopje	E11		

D

MONTENEGRO   Novi Pazar   • Nis

• Ivangrad   Kosovska

• Niksic   Mitrovica   • Leskovac

• Dubrovnik   • Podgorica   • Pejë   **Pristina**

Gjakove   • Vranje

• Cetinje   **KOSOVO**

• Bar   Prizren   • Kumanovo

• Shkodër   **Skopje**

E

ADRIATIC SEA

MACEDONIA   **BULGARIA**

TURKEY

Tiranë   Lake   • Prilep

ggia   Durrës •   Ohrid   • Kilkís   Sérrai • Drama

• Bari   Elbasan •   • Bitola   • Xánthi   • Komotiní

Lake   Florina • Edessa

ALBANIA   Prespa   Ptolemaïs   Kaválla   Alexandroúpolis

F

• Taranto   • Brindisi   Korçë   Kastoria   Veroia   Thessaloníki   Thásos   Samothrace

• Lecce   • Vlorë   Kozáni   • Kateríni   Mount Athos 2033 m

Mount Olympus   2917 m

• Metéora   Lemnos

G

• Cosenza   • Ioánnina

Corfu   • Trikala   • Larissa   **GREECE**   Lesbos

• Crotone   • Párga   • Vólos

Catanzaro   • Arta   • Kardhitsa

Préveza   • Lamía   Skíros   Chios

gio di Calabria   • Agriníon   • Thérmon   Euboea

H

Mesalóngion   Thebes   • Marathon   Sámos

Cephalonía   • Pátrai   Megara   • Káristos

Olympia   Piraeus   Andros   Ikaría

IONIAN SEA   Zákinthos   • Árgos   **Athens**   Tínos

• Pyrgos   Kéa   Mykonos

Peleponnese   Páros   Náxos

• Kalamata   Amorgos   Kos

Astipálaia   Rhódes •

I

0   50   100   150   200 mi

0   100   200   300 km

• Neápolis   **SEA OF CRETE**   Rhodes

Kíthira   Kárpathos

Khaniá •   • Iráklion

Crete

J

THE DISTANCE from the town of Marathon [H12] to Athens [H12] is 42 km, and was first run by a Greek soldier 2500 years ago.

8   9   10   11   12   13   14

Germany and the Low Countries

Luxembourg, Belgium and the Netherlands are the three nations that make up the low countries.

Much of the Netherlands is below sea level, and it relies on massive sea walls called dykes and thousands of pumps to drain the land. Brussels, the capital of Belgium, is home to the European Union's main centre of government, and Antwerp is the centre of the world's diamond-cutting industry. Luxembourg has the second-highest income per person in the world due to its banking industry. Germany has the fourth largest economy in the world after the United States, China and Japan, and produces machinery and cars such as BMW, Mercedes and Porsche. Parts of the former East Germany, which reunited with the West in 1990, are still not as prosperous.

NOR*
SE*

Terschelling Ameland
Vlieland
Waddenzee
Texel
Den Helder •
Leeuwarden
Groni*
NETHERLANDS • As*
Alkmaar •
Northeast
Polder
Emmer*
Haarlem •
Amsterdam
Flevoland • Zwolle
Leiden •
Polder Apeldoorn*
Hilversum •
Enschede•
The Hague
Utrecht •
Delft •
Gouda •
Arnhem •
Rotterdam •
Waal Nijmegen •
Mün*
Dordrecht •
Vlissingen •
Breda • Tilburg • 's-Hertogenbosch
Zeebrugge •
Maas (Meuse)
Ostend • • Bruges
Eindhoven •
Dortn*
Ghent •
• Antwerp
Duisburg •
Ess*
Roeselare •
Aalst • Mechelen
Krefeld •
Wupp*
Kortrijk •
Leuven Genk •
Düsseldorf •
Solingen •
Brussels Hasselt • Maastricht •
Colo*
Tournai •
Aachen •
Charleroi Namur • Liège
Bonn*
Mons •
Verviers •
Meuse (Maas)
• Dinant
BELGIUM
HUNSRÜCK
Bastogne •
Kobl*
Rhine
LUXEMBOURG
Luxembourg •
• Trier
Esch-sur-Alzette •
Kaiserslau*
Saarbrücken •
FRANCE
FRANCE
Karlsru*
Baden-B*
B*
F*
•
Freibu*
im Bre*
SW*

Search and Find

Belgium	Luxembourg
• Brussels E5	• Luxembourg . . . G6
Germany	**Netherlands**
• Berlin D11	• Amsterdam . . . D6
	• The Hague . . . D5

Amsterdam [D6] is well-known for its network of canals. The tall, leaning buildings were once used for storage. Hooks at the top of each house enabled goods to be pulled up to the top rooms.

0   50   100   150   200 mi
0   100   200   300 km

Facts and Stats

• Germany's population of 82.5 million would fill 825 Olympic stadiums. Luxembourg's population of 602,000 would only fill 60 stadiums.

• Mount Zugspitze [I9] is the highest mountain at 2964 m – nine times higher than the Eiffel Tower.

• The average income per person in Luxembourg is £79,314, compared to a world average of £8196.

COLOGNE [E7] holds one of the biggest carnivals in the world. Every November, more than one million people take part in the festival.

THE DISTANCE from the source of the Rhine river [F7] in the Swiss Alps to its mouth at the North Sea is 1320 km.

A

8 9 10 11 12 13 14

Sylt

DENMARK

Flensburg

Schleswig

Kiel Bay

Kiel

Fehmarn

Mecklenburg Bay

Rügen

B

an Islands

Cuxhaven

Lübeck

Rostock

Greifswald

elmshaven

Bremerhaven

Hamburg

Schwerin

enburg

Bremen

Lüneburg

Neubrandenburg

Elbe

C

abrück

Ems

Hannover

Wolfsburg

Brandenburg

Berlin

POLAND

D

Bielefeld

Braunschweig

mm

Hameln

Potsdam

Magdeburg

Frankfurt an der Oder

Paderborn

Dessau

Elbe

E

Göttingen

Cottbus

Kassel

Halle

GERMANY

gen

Leipzig

Görlitz

Eisenach

Weimar

Meissen

Erfurt

Dresden

F

Giessen

Jena

Chemnitz

Gera

Freital

Fulda

Zwickau

Frankfurt am Main

Plauen

CZECH REPUBLIC

inz

Offenbach

Main

G

Darmstadt

Bamberg

ms

Würzburg

Bayreuth

nheim

igshafen

delberg

Fürth

Nuremberg

BOHEMIAN FOREST

H

Heilbronn

forzheim

Stuttgart

Regensburg

Tübingen

Reutlingen

Ingolstadt

SWABIAN JURA

Ulm

Augsburg

Passau

I

Danube

Munich

Lake Constance

BAVARIAN ALPS

Mount Zugspitze 2964 m

Berchtesgaden

J

ND

AUSTRIA

8 9 10 11 12 13 14

Did You Know?

Each year, Belgium produces 600,000 tonnes of chocolate in more than 1900 chocolate shops and companies.

In the next ...the Netherlands will make 1648 kg of cheese – enough for 83,700 cheese slices. **minute...**

World Record The Netherlands has a greater percentage of its land below sea level – 26% – than any other country.

Cologne Cathedral [E7] is one of the tallest and most magnificent Gothic buildings in the world. Its construction began in the 13th century, but wasn't completed until the late 19th century. The cathedral has 12 bells, and 509 steps lead to the top of the south tower, nearly 100 m above the ground.

Switzerland and Austria

Landlocked Switzerland, Austria and Liechtenstein are dominated by the Alps, creating stunning mountain scenery. Millions of tourists are attracted to the natural beauty, spectacular mountain vistas and popular Alpine skiing. Switzerland guards its independence and was not involved in either of the two World Wars. As a neutral, independent state, Switzerland is part of the United Nations and many charitable and banking organizations. As a result, it is a very wealthy country. Many composers come from Austria, including Mozart, Haydn, Schubert and Strauss.

▷ *The Belvedere Palace, Vienna [E13], was built in the 17th and 18th centuries. Archduke Franz Ferdinand was the last person to live at the palace. It is now a museum and gallery, exhibiting many important collections, including the works of Renoir, Monet and Van Gogh.*

In the next **...14,509 kg of chocolate will be eaten worldwide. The Swiss are the world's biggest consumers.** *minute...*

FRANCE

GERMANY

Rhine
• Basel
• Schaffhausen
Aarau • • Baden • Winterthur
Olten • Lake Constance
• Solothurn • Zürich
• Biel St. Gallen • • Bregenz
Neuchâtel • • Zug • Feldkirch Innsbruck
Lake Neuchâtel
● **Bern** • Lucerne **Vaduz** •
Yverdon • Thun • **SWITZERLAND** **LIECHTENSTEIN** • St. Anton
Fribourg • • Interlaken
Lausanne • Chur • • Galtür
Lake Geneva • Saanen BERNESE ALPS • Andermatt LEPONTINE ALPS Davos •
• Montreux
• Geneva St. Moritz •
• Sion • Brig • Bellinzona
Mount Dufourspitze 4634 m
Zermatt • • Locarno •
Mount Matterhorn 4478 m
ITALY ITALY
• Lugano

Did You Know?

The Swiss invented the quartz watch, wristwatch and waterproof watch. Switzerland produces expensive watches, such as Rolex, and watch-making is its third largest industry.

▷ *Leukerbad, in the heart of the Bernese Alps [G3], is the largest thermal spa in Europe. Dating back to Roman times, the complex contains 3.9 million litres of water and is surrounded by picturesque mountain scenery.*

BERN [F3] is the city where Albert Einstein worked, the Toblerone chocolate bar is made, and Emmental cheese is manufactured.

THE DISTANCE of the St. Moritz [G5] bobsleigh run is 1585 m and it takes just 70 seconds to travel from one end to the other.

Search and Find

Austria
• Vienna E13
Liechtenstein
• Vaduz. F5

Switzerland
• Bern F3

Extreme Weather

In 1999, the biggest avalanche in Austria for 400 years smashed into the town of Galtür [G6], killing 31 people.

0   50   100 mi
0   80   160 km

CZECH REPUBLIC

SLOVAKIA

Zwettl Stadt

Inn
Braunau
Linz
Krems
Danube
Amstetten
Klosterneuburg
Wels
Steyr
Sankt Pölten
Vienna
Gmunden
Enns
Baden
Salzburg
Wiener Neustadt
Neusiedler See
Hallein
Bad Ischl
Kufstein
AUSTRIA
hwaz
Kitzbühel
Kapfenberg
Mount Grossglockner
3797 m
Leoben
NIEDERE TAUERN
Knittelfeld
HOHE TAUERN
Judenburg
Mur
HUNGARY
Graz
Gleisdorf
Spittal
Wolfsberg
Drau
ITALY
Villach
Klagenfurt

SLOVENIA

Facts and Stats

• The population of Liechtenstein is only 38,000 and wouldn't even fill half an Olympic stadium.

• Switzerland's Mount Dufourspitze [H3] is the highest mountain at 4634 m in height – 14 times higher than the Eiffel Tower.

• The average income per person in Switzerland is £61,156 compared to a world average of £8196.

▷ Switzerland is split into federal states, or cantons. Bern is the second largest Swiss canton, and is dominated by mountains, glaciers and waterfalls. The small village of **Gstaad** near Saanen [G2] is a popular ski resort with fantastic Alpine scenery.

Hungary, Romania and Bulgaria

Bulgaria and Romania became members of the European Union in 2007, with Hungary joining in 2004. These countries are now experiencing rapid economic growth after decades of communist rule. Romania is the largest of the three and Europe's longest river, the Danube, flows along its southern border to the Black Sea. Hungary's capital, Budapest, has a lively arts and music scene, and is host to a range of cultural and sporting festivals. The countryside is scenic with many lakes, historic towns and villages. Bulgaria also borders the Black Sea, but it is mainly mountainous and rural, and relatively undeveloped.

SLOVAKIA

Miskolc

AUSTRIA

Gyor

Esztergom

Budapest

Szombathely

Székesfehérvár   HUNGARY

Lake Balaton

Dunaujvaros

Kecskemét

SLOVENIA

Kaposvár

Tisza

Danube

Szeged

Ara

CROATIA

Pécs

Timisoa

SERBIA

Facts and Stats

• The Danube [D6/G10] is the longest river at 2860 km in length. The Nile river is twice as long.

• Mount Musala [I10] is the highest mountain at 2925 m, which is nine times higher than the Eiffel Tower.

• The average income per person in Hungary is £10,844, compared to a world average of £8,196.

On the bank of the Danube river in Budapest [C6] is **Hungary's Parliament building.** *Hungarian architect, Imre Steindl, designed the building, although he went blind before the project was completed. More than 40 kg of gold was used in its construction.*

Bran Castle in Romania is more commonly known as Dracula's Castle because Bram Stoker based his novel around the building. In 2007, the castle was put up for sale for £40 million.

Did You Know?

One of the few Bulgarian commercial crops is the rose. The petals are used in the perfume industry.

THE DISTANCE from the source to the mouth of the Danube river [D6/G10] is 2888 km – almost all of it is accessible to boats.

ESZTERGOM [C5] is a former capital of Hungary and home to the nation's largest church, the Esztergom Basilica.

Search and Find

Bulgaria
● Sofia I9

Hungary
● Budapest C6

Romania
● Bucharest. . . . F11

In the next ...61,000 litres of water will enter the Black Sea from the Danube river. **minute...**

UKRAINE

yíregyháza

● Satu Mare

ebrecen

● Baia Mare

● Oradea

● Suceava

CARPATHIAN MOUNTAINS

● Iasi

MOLDOVA

● Cluj-Napoca

● Bacău

● Târgu Mures

ROMANIA

Mures

● Alba Iulia

Olt

● Sibiu

● Brasov

● Focsani

UKRAINE

T R A N S Y L V A N I A N   A L P S

● Galati
● Braila

● Tulcea

esita

● Pitesti

● Ploiesti

● Drobeta-Turnu Severin

Bucharest ⬤

● Calarasi

● Constanta

● Craiova

Jiu

● Giurgiu
● Ruse

● Dobrich

● Vidin

Danube

SERBIA

● Montana

Iskur

● Pleven

● Shumen

● Varna

BULGARIA

BLACK SEA

● Vratsa

● Gabrovo

B A L K A N   M O U N T A I N S

● Sliven

● Burgas

● Pernik

⬤ **Sofia**

● Stara Zagora

● Yambol

▲ Mount Musala 2925 m

● Kyustendil

● Plovdiv

● Dimitrovgrad

● Blagoevgrad

R H O D O P E   M O U N T A I N S

● Khaskovo

Maritsa

TURKEY

MACEDONIA

Struma

GREECE

0	50	100 mi
0	80	160 km

Poland, Czech Republic and Slovakia

Poland, Slovakia and the Czech Republic are among the newest members of the European Union. Standards of living are much lower than western Europe and many workers have moved to the United Kingdom and Ireland for better-paid jobs. However, since joining the EU, Slovakia has become a major car producer, and has seen minimal emigration. The Baltic coast of Poland is industrial with steelworks and shipyards, but low-wage rates and money from the EU have attracted new industries. Prague, the capital of the Czech Republic, is situated on the Vltava river and receives more than 9 million tourists a year.

The **Prague Astronomical Clock** [G5] is mounted on the wall of the Old Town City Hall. The astronomical dial represents the Sun and Moon. The 12 figures of the Apostles appear every hour, and all 12 are seen at 12 p.m. Finally, the calendar dial represents the months.

In the next
...Poland will mine 249 tonnes of coal, generating enough electricity for 9.9 million light bulbs.
minute...

Zygmunt's Column sits in the centre of **Castle Square, Warsaw** [E10]. Built in 1644, the monument represents King Zygmunt III Waza. Markets, street entertainment and concerts take place here, making it a popular tourist site.

BALTIC SEA

Koszalin

Szczecin

Notéc

Warta

Gorzow Wielkopolski

Pozna

Zielona Gora

Ka

Oder

Legnica

Wrocla

Opole

Liberec

Walbrzych

Ústí nad Labem

Hradec Kralove

GERMANY

Karlovy Vary

Cheb

Elbe

Prague

Pardubice

Plzen

CZECH REPUBLIC

Olomouc

Vltava

Jihlava

Zli

BOHEMIAN FOREST

Brno

Morava

Ceské Budejovice

AUSTRIA

Trer

Trna

Bratislava

Komár

0   50   100 mi
0   80   160 km

Gulf of Danzig
KALININGRAD (RUSSIA)
LITHUANIA

• Gdynia
dansk
• Elblag
• Suwalki
• Olsztyn
BELARUS

Vistula

ydgoszcz
Narew
• Bialystok
• Torun
Bug
oclawek
• Plock
• Warsaw
POLAND
Lodz •
Pilica
• Radom
• Lublin
Chelm
• Czestochowa
Vistula
San
om
• Sosnowiece
ice • Katowice
uschwitz ◆
• Rzeszow
UKRAINE
rava • Bielsko-Biala
• Kraków • Tarnow
• Wieliczka
Gerlachovsky Stit
2655 m
• Zilina
artin •
• Poprad
• Presov
TATRA MOUNTAINS
• Kosice
nice
• Banská Bystrica
SLOVAKIA
HUNGARY
a
• Levice
e

Search and Find

Czech Republic
• Prague G5
Poland
• Warsaw E10

Slovakia
• Bratislava J7

AUSCHWITZ [G8] was the centre of the Holocaust mass killings. Now a World Heritage site, it has more than 2 million visitors a year.

THE DISTANCE across the Charles Bridge, Prague [G5] is 516 m. The bridge is lined with 30 statues dating from around 1700.

Facts and Stats

• The longest river is the Vistula river [G10] at 1047 km in length – six times shorter than the Nile river.

• The highest mountain is Gerlachovsky Stit [H9] at 2655 m – eight times higher than the Eiffel Tower.

• The average income per person in Poland is £10,530, compared to a world average of £8196.

Did You Know?

Under the town of Wieliczka [G9] is one of the oldest salt mines in the world. The mine is so large that it has passages, lakes, buildings and a church. It is now a popular tourist attraction.

▷ **Bojnice Castle [I8]** is the most visited Slovakian castle, attracting more than 200,000 visitors a year. Many films have been shot here and the International Festival of Ghosts and Monsters takes place every spring.

Eastern Europe

The former Soviet states of Estonia, Latvia and Lithuania are now democratic, independent countries. The area is mainly flat, low-lying land that is covered in snow during winter, but a fertile grain- and dairy-farming region in summer. Without industries to compete with western Europe, these countries remain poor. Russia controls much of Europe's natural gas supplies, but has struggled to improve its standard of living. In 2014, Russia annexed the Crimean peninsula from Ukraine. Armenia and Georgia are part of the Caucasus range with the Caucasus Mountains providing a border between Europe and Asia.

The town of Trakai, Lithuania, can be found west of Vilnius [G5]. Out of the area's 200 lakes, Lake Galve is the largest at 47 m in depth. Built in the 14th and 15th centuries on the lake, **Trakai Island Castle** can only be reached by a drawbridge.

Search and Find

Armenia
- Yerevan J8

Belarus
- Minsk. G6

Estonia
- Tallinn E5

Georgia
- Tbilisi I8

Latvia
- Riga. F5

Lithuania
- Vilnius G5

Moldova
- Chisinau H6

Russia
- Moscow F7

Ukraine
- Kiev G6

A kremlin is a Russian castle, the most famous is the **Moscow Kremlin [F7]** on the bank of the Moskva river. Surrounded by a wall, the Kremlin includes four palaces, four golden-domed cathedrals and 20 towers.

In the next ...Russia will export enough natural gas to supply 96.4 homes for a minute. *minute...*

BAREN

FINLAND

Murmansk

Onega

Lake Onega

Petrozav

Vyborg

Lake Ladoga

St. Petersburg

BALTIC SEA

Gulf of Finland

Tallinn

ESTONIA

Novgorod

Tartu

Lake Peipus

Rybinsk

Yarosla

Gulf of Riga

Tver

Liepaja

Riga

LATVIA

Vitsyebsk

Moscow

LITHUANIA

RUSSIA

Vilnius

Smolensk

Ryaza

Kaliningrad

Kaunas

BELARUS

Kirov

POLAND

Hrodna

Minsk

Bryansk

Pripyat Marshes

Homyel

Lipe

Voronez

Rivne

Kiev

Dnieper

Lviv

Kha

SLOVAKIA

UKRAINE

Dnipropetrov

Prut

Kryvyy Rih

Donets

MOLDOVA

Zaporizhzhya

Rosto

Chisinau

Dniester

Odessa

na-D

ROMANIA

Tiraspol

Sea of Azov

Crimea

Krasno

Sevastopol

BLACK SEA

ARCTIC OCEAN

Novaya Zemlya

KARA SEA

Kolguyev Island

Vorkuta •

Pechora

hangelísk

Severnaya Dvina

Ukhta •

• Syktyvkar

RUSSIA

URAL MOUNTAINS

• Perm

• Izhevsk

Nizhniy Novgorod •

• Kazan

• Simbirsk • Ufa

Tolyatti

• Penza Samara

Magnitogorsk •

Ural

Saratov •

Orenburg •
Orsk •

Volga

KAZAKHSTAN

• Volgograd

• Astrakhan

avropol

• Vladikavkaz
• Grozny

t Elbrus 5642 m

ORGIA

Tbilisi

MENIA

Yerevan

KEY

IRAN

CASPIAN SEA

Extreme Weather

For seven months, the far north of Russia has temperatures below freezing and only two months above 10°C. It is too cold even for trees to grow.

Facts and Stats

• The population of Russia is 144.5 million and would fill 1445 Olympic stadiums. It is more than 100 times larger than Estonia's population of 1.3 million.

• Russia's area is 17 million km² – 165 times the area of Iceland. It is the biggest country in the world.

• The average income per person in Moldova is £1747, compared to £15,029 in Estonia and a world average of £8196.

THE DISTANCE from Vilnius [G5] to Tallinn [E5] was once covered by two million citizens in a human chain stretching more than 300 km.

ST. PETERSBURG [E6] has many canals and hundreds of bridges. It is sometimes called the Venice of the North.

Did You Know?

The region contains three states which have declared independence: Trans-Dniester (eastern Moldova) and Abkhazia and South Ossetia (regions of Georgia). These states are independent in practice but go largely unrecognized.

0 100 200 300 400 500 mi

0 200 400 600 800 km

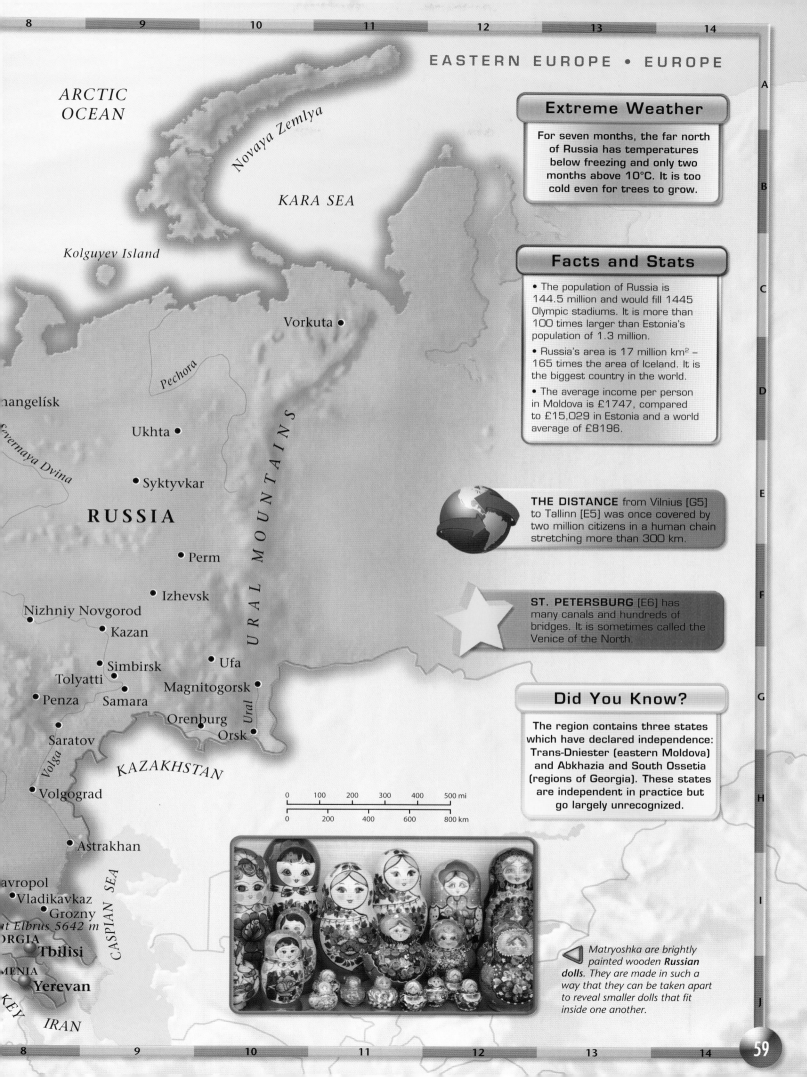

*Matryoshka are brightly painted wooden **Russian dolls**. They are made in such a way that they can be taken apart to reveal smaller dolls that fit inside one another.*

B C D E F G H I J

Africa

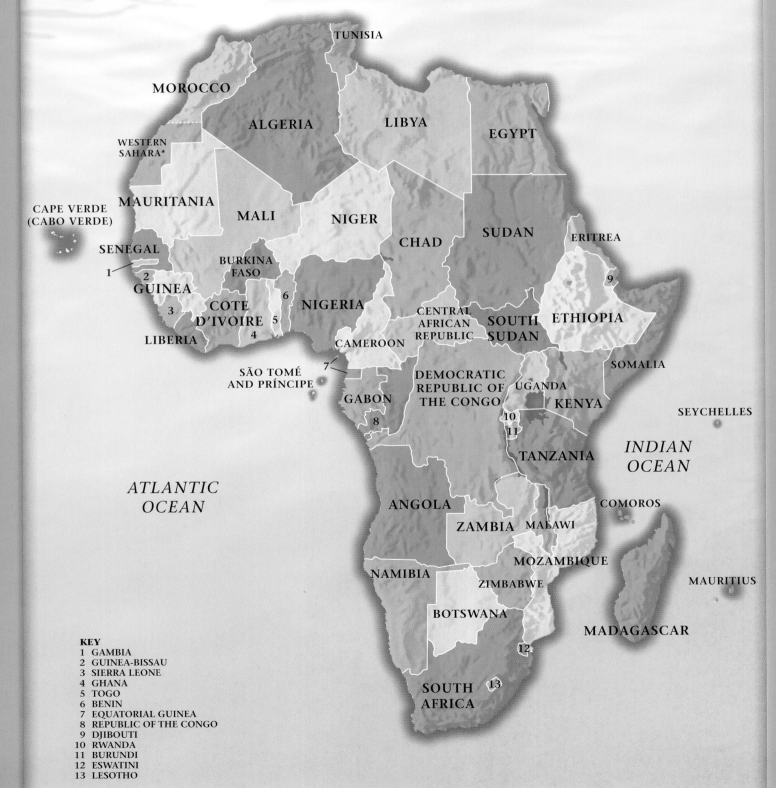

TUNISIA

MOROCCO

WESTERN
SAHARA*

ALGERIA

LIBYA

EGYPT

CAPE VERDE
(CABO VERDE)

MAURITANIA

MALI

NIGER

CHAD

SUDAN

ERITREA

SENEGAL

1
2

GUINEA

3

BURKINA
FASO

6

NIGERIA

9

CENTRAL
AFRICAN
REPUBLIC

SOUTH
SUDAN

ETHIOPIA

COTE
D'IVOIRE

5

4

LIBERIA

CAMEROON

SOMALIA

SÃO TOMÉ
AND PRÍNCIPE

7

DEMOCRATIC
REPUBLIC OF
THE CONGO

UGANDA

KENYA

SEYCHELLES

GABON

8

10
11

INDIAN
OCEAN

TANZANIA

ATLANTIC
OCEAN

ANGOLA

COMOROS

ZAMBIA

MALAWI

MOZAMBIQUE

NAMIBIA

ZIMBABWE

MAURITIUS

BOTSWANA

MADAGASCAR

12

KEY
1 GAMBIA
2 GUINEA-BISSAU
3 SIERRA LEONE
4 GHANA
5 TOGO
6 BENIN
7 EQUATORIAL GUINEA
8 REPUBLIC OF THE CONGO
9 DJIBOUTI
10 RWANDA
11 BURUNDI
12 ESWATINI
13 LESOTHO

SOUTH
AFRICA

13

*Western Sahara is a disputed territory in the Maghreb region of North Africa.

COUNTRY FACTFILE

Country	Life expectancy	Population to nearest thousand	Population growth %	Population as urban %	Area km²	Population density per km²	Capital city	Currency	Languages
Algeria	77	41,320,000	1.7	80	2,381,741	17.3	Algiers	Algerian Dinar	Arabic, Berber, French
Angola	60	29,250,000	3.5	66	1,252,145	23.4	Luanda	Kwanza	Portuguese, Umbundu
Benin	62	11,179,000	2.7	47	112,622	99.3	Porto-Novo, Cotonou	CFA Franc	French, Fon, Yoruba
Botswana	63	2,303,000	1.6	69	581,730	4	Gaborone	Pula	English, Tswana
Burkina Faso	56	19,632,000	3	30	270,764	74.8	Ouagadougou	CFA Franc	French, Mossi
Burundi	61	10,864,000	3.3	13	27,816	390.1	Bujumbura	Burundi Franc	Kirundi, French
Cameroon	59	22,189,000	2.6	58	466,715	47.5	Yaoundé	CFA Franc	French, English, Fang
Cape Verde (Cabo Verde)	75	538,000	1.3	66	4033	133.4	Praia	Cape Verdean Escudo	Portuguese, Crioulo
Central African Republic	53	4,660,000	2.1	41	622,436	7.5	Bangui	CFA Franc	French, Sangho
Chad	51	14,900,000	1.9	28	1,284,000	11.6	N'Djamena	CFA Franc	French, Arabic, Sara
Comoros	65	814,000	1.6	32	1862	437.2	Moroni	Comoran Franc	Comorian, French, Arabic
Congo, Democratic Republic of the	57	86,026,000	2.4	45	2,344,856	36.7	Kinshasa	Congolese Franc	French, Lingala, Swahili
Congo, Republic of the	60	5,260,000	2.1	67	342,000	15.4	Brazzaville	CFA Franc	French, Monokutuba, Kongo
Côte d'Ivoire (Ivory Coast)	59	24,295,000	1.8	54	320,783	75.7	Yamoussoukro, Abidjan	CFA Franc	French, Akan
Djibouti	64	1,049,000	2.2	85	23,200	45.2	Djibouti	Djiboutian Franc	Somali, French, Akan
Egypt	73	95,203,000	2.5	45	996,490	95.5	Cairo, NAC*	Egyptian Pound	Arabic
Equatorial Guinea	65	1,268,000	2.4	72	28,051	45.2	Ciudad de la Paz, Malabo	CFA Franc	Spanish, French, Fang
Eritrea	65	6,536,000	0.9	40	121,115	54	Asmara	Nakfa	Tigrinya, Arabic, Afar
Eswatini	52	1,093,000	1.1	34	17,363	62.9	Mbabane, Lobamba	Lilangeni	Swazi, English
Ethiopia	63	104,960,000	2.9	21	1,063,637	98.7	Addis Ababa	Birr	Amharic, Oromo, Tigrinya
Gabon	62	2,025,000	1.9	89	267,667	7.6	Libreville	CFA Franc	French, Fang
Gambia	65	2,100,000	2.1	61	10,689	195.6	Banjul	Dalasi	English, Malinke
Ghana	67	29,614,000	2.2	56	238,533	121.2	Accra	Cedi	Hausa, English, Akan
Guinea	61	12,720,000	2.6	37	245,857	51.7	Conakry	Guinean Franc	Fulani, French, Malinke
Guinea-Bissau	51	1,860,000	1.9	49	36,125	51.5	Bissau	CFA Franc	Crioulo, Portuguese, Balante
Kenya	64	49,700,000	1.7	30	582,646	85.3	Nairobi	Kenyan Shilling	Swahili, English, Kikuyu
Lesotho	53	2,230,000	0.3	27	30,355	73.5	Maseru	South African rand	Sesotho, English
Liberia	63	4,730,000	2.5	60	111,370	48.7	Monrovia	US Dollar, Liberian Dollar	Krio, English
Libya	77	6,375,000	1.6	88	1,777,060	3.6	Tripoli	Libyan Dinar	Arabic
Madagascar	66	25,570,000	2.5	37	587,041	43.6	Antananarivo	Madagascar Ariary	Malagasy, French
Malawi	62	17,373,000	3.3	20	118,484	146.6	Lilongwe	Malawian Kwacha	Chichewa, English
Mali	60	18,540,000	3	42	1,248,574	14.8	Bamako	CFA Franc	French, Bambara
Mauritania	63	3,984,000	2.2	59	1,030,700	3.9	Nouakchott	Ouguiya	Arabic
Mauritius	76	1,264,000	0.6	48	2040	629.8	Port Louis	Mauritius Rupee	French Creole, Bhojpuri, English
Morocco	77	34,665,000	1.0	63	446,550	77.6	Rabat	Moroccan Dirham	Arabic, Berber
Mozambique	54	28,862,000	2.5	38	801,590	36.1	Maputo	Metical	Emakhuwa, Portuguese
Namibia	64	2,414,000	2	50	824,269	2.9	Windhoek	Namibian Dollar	English, Ovambo, Nama
Niger	56	21,467,000	3.2	21	1,186,408	18.1	Niamey	CFA Franc	French, Hausa
Nigeria	54	193,393,000	2.4	50	923,103	209.5	Abuja	Naira	English, Hausa, Yoruba
Rwanda	64	12,210,000	2.7	28	25,314	482.3	Kigali	Rwandan Franc	Rwanda, French, English
São Tomé and Príncipe	66	202,000	1.7	73	1001	201.8	São Tomé	Dobra	Portuguese, Crioulo
Senegal	62	15,726,000	2.4	47	196,712	79.9	Dakar	CFA Franc	French, Wolof, Fulani
Seychelles	75	97,000	0.8	59	455	215.4	Victoria	Seychelles Rupee	Creole, English
Sierra Leone	59	7,092,000	2.4	42	71,740	98.9	Freetown	Leone	English, Krio, Mende
Somalia	53	14,700,000	2	45	637,657	23.1	Mogadishu	Somali Shilling	Somali, Arabic
South Africa	64	57,726,000	1	66	1,224,691	47.3	Pretoria, Cape Town	Rand	Xhosa, English, Zulu, Afrikaans
South Sudan	52	11,868,000	3.8	20	619,745	18.4	Juba	South Sudanese Pound	English, Dinka, Arabic
Sudan	64	37,960,000	1.6	40	1,840,687	22	Khartoum	Sudanese Dinar	Arabic, Nubian
Tanzania	63	50,144,000	2.8	34	945,037	56.6	Dar es Salaam, Dodoma	Tanzanian Shilling	Swahili, English
Togo	65	7,315,000	2.6	43	56,785	129.2	Lomé	CFA Franc	French, Ewe
Tunisia	76	11,304,000	1	69	163,610	69.1	Tunis	Tunisian Dinar	Arabic, French
Uganda	56	37,674,000	3.2	24	241,551	151.8	Kampala	Ugandan Shilling	Swahili, English, Ganda
Zambia	53	16,405,000	2.9	44	752,614	21.8	Lusaka	Zambian Kwacha	English, Bemba
Zimbabwe	58	13,573,000	1.6	38	390,757	34.7	Harare	US dollar	English, Shona

*New Administrative Capital.

North Africa

The Sahara Desert dominates this region at 6000 km in width and 2000 km from north to south.
Only a narrow strip of land stands next to the Mediterranean Sea, but the fertile valleys of the Atlas Mountains and the banks of the Nile river have enough water to grow crops.

Algeria, Libya and Tunisia have become wealthy by selling oil and natural gas to Europe. Egypt was the richest country in the world when the pharaohs ruled more than 3000 years ago. Egypt's well-preserved tombs and temples, especially the Great Pyramid of Giza, are a tourist attraction.

0   100   200   300 mi
0   200   400 km

Strait of Gibraltar
Tangier   *CEUTA* (SPAIN)
Tétouan   *MELILLA (SPAIN)*
Kénitra   Fes
Rabat   Oujda
Casablanca   Meknès
MOROCCO
Safi
Marrakech
Mount Toubkal 4176 m
Agadir
Sidi Ifni

ATLANTIC OCEAN

Tarfaya

WESTERN SAHARA

MAURITANIA

Tindouf

Ech-Cheliff   Blida
Oran   Sidi Bel Abbès
TELL ATLAS

Algiers
Bejaïa   Skikda   Bizerte
Constantine   Annaba   **Tunis**
Batna   Kairouan
Nab
Sou
S

TUNIS

SAHARAN ATLAS MOUNTAINS

Ghardaïa

Béchar

ATLAS MOUNTAINS

ALGERIA

Ghada

Adrar

In Salah

AHAGGAR
Tahat Peak 2918 m

S A H A R A   D E S

Tamanrasset

MALI

NIGER

Did You Know?

The Sahara Desert region was wet and fertile 8000 years ago. As the climate has become drier, the desert has expanded.

In north Africa, many civilizations live in fortified cities, or ksars. **Aït Benhaddou** is situated near Marrakech [E2], Morocco. Few families live here now as they have moved to modern villages nearby. Scenes from films including Alexander (2004) and The Mummy (1999) have been shot here.

In the next ...the Sun will evaporate the equivalent of 110 million bottles of water from the Nile river. *minute...*

Located on the Nile river, Cairo [F13] is the biggest city in Africa. Built in AD 988, **Al-Azhar University** is the second oldest university in the world, after the University of Al Karaouine Fez, Morocco. Al-Azhar Mosque stands alongside the university.

Facts and Stats

• Egypt's population of 95.2 million would fill 952 Olympic stadiums. Libya's population of 6.2 million would only fill 62 stadiums.

• Cairo [F13] is the biggest city with 20.3 million people. This would fill 203 Olympic stadiums, compared to Tripoli which would only fill 9.5 [E8].

• The average income per person in Libya is £6107, compared to a world average of £8196.

Search and Find

Algeria
• Algiers C6
Egypt
• Cairo, NAC (New Administrative Capital) F13

Libya
• Tripoli. E8
Morocco
• Rabat. D3
Tunisia
• Tunis D7

World Record
The Sahara sand sea in Algeria has the longest sand dunes in the world, with some more than 300 km.

Extreme Weather

The hottest temperature ever recorded was 58°C in Libya's Sahara Desert.

MEDITERRANEAN SEA

Tripoli
Misurata
Zawiyah
Surt
Gulf of Sidra
Benghazi
Darnah
Tubruq
Ajdabiya

Alexandria
Tanta
Port Said
Suez Canal
Cairo
Giza
Suez
NAC*
Sinai Peninsula
ISRAEL
Gulf of Aqaba

QATTARA DEPRESSION

GREAT SAND SEA

LIBYAN DESERT

LIBYA

FEZZAN

ha

WESTERN DESERT

EGYPT

Nile
Gulf of Suez
RED SEA

Sharm al Sheikh
El Minya
Hurghada
Asyut

Qena
Luxor

Aswan

GILF KEBIR PLATEAU

Lake Nasser

CHAD

SUDAN

*Egypt's New Administrative Capital (NAC) is currently being built 45 km east of Cairo.

THE DISTANCE separating Morocco from Spain, Europe, at the Strait of Gibraltar's [C3] narrowest point is only 13 km.

EGYPT has huge pyramids, built more than 3000 years ago. Each one held the body of a king.

Desert tribe people, such as the Berbers and Tuaregs, travel by camel from oasis to oasis across the Sahara Desert to trade cloth, salt and spices.

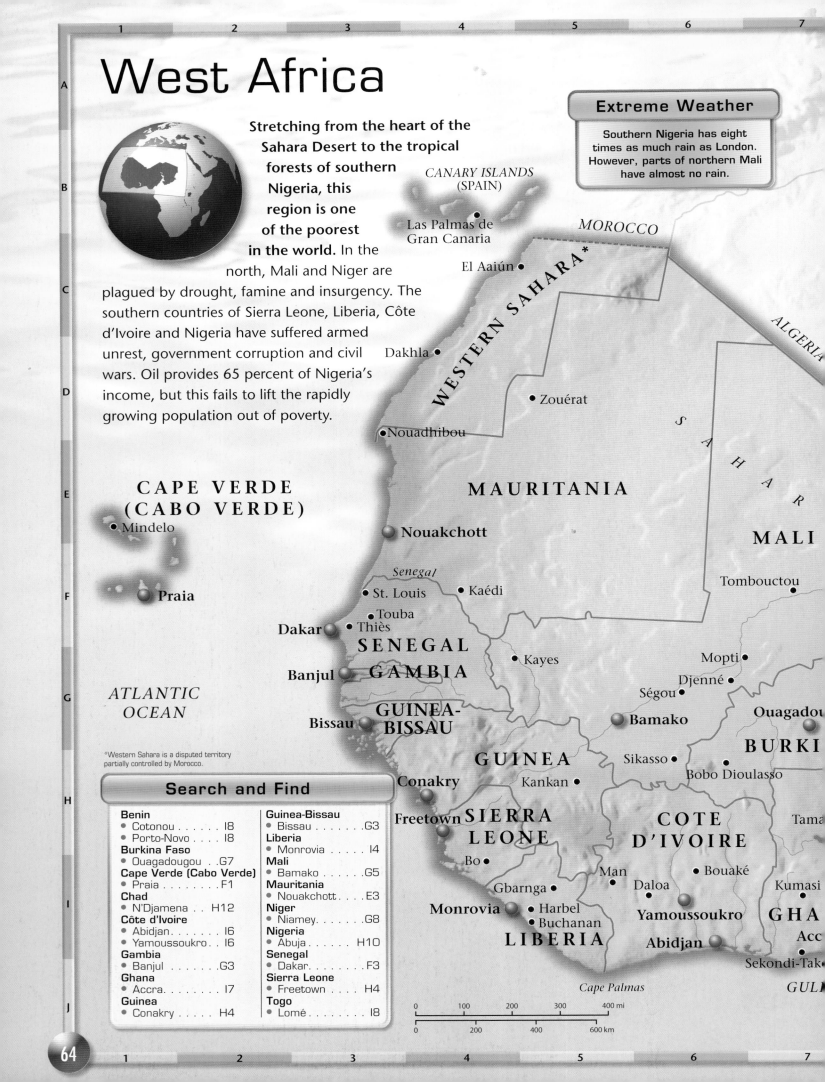

West Africa

Stretching from the heart of the Sahara Desert to the tropical forests of southern Nigeria, this region is one of the poorest in the world. In the north, Mali and Niger are plagued by drought, famine and insurgency. The southern countries of Sierra Leone, Liberia, Côte d'Ivoire and Nigeria have suffered armed unrest, government corruption and civil wars. Oil provides 65 percent of Nigeria's income, but this fails to lift the rapidly growing population out of poverty.

Extreme Weather

Southern Nigeria has eight times as much rain as London. However, parts of northern Mali have almost no rain.

*Western Sahara is a disputed territory partially controlled by Morocco.

CANARY ISLANDS (SPAIN)
Las Palmas de Gran Canaria

MOROCCO

El Aaiún

WESTERN SAHARA*

Dakhla

Zouérat

ALGERIA

Nouadhibou

MAURITANIA

SAHARA

CAPE VERDE (CABO VERDE)

Mindelo

Praia

Nouakchott

Senegal

St. Louis   Kaédi

Kayes

MALI

Tombouctou

Touba
Dakar   Thiès

SENEGAL

GAMBIA

Banjul

Mopti

Djenné

Ségou

ATLANTIC OCEAN

Bissau

GUINEA-BISSAU

Bamako

Ouagadou

BURKI

GUINEA

Sikasso

Bobo Dioulasso

Conakry

Kankan

Freetown   SIERRA
LEONE

COTE
D'IVOIRE

Tama

Bo

Man

Bouaké

Kumasi

Gbarnga

Daloa

Monrovia   Harbel
Buchanan

Yamoussoukro

GHA

LIBERIA

Abidjan

Acc

Sekondi-Tak

Cape Palmas

GUL

| 0 | 100 | 200 | 300 | 400 mi |
| 0 | 200 | 400 | 600 km |

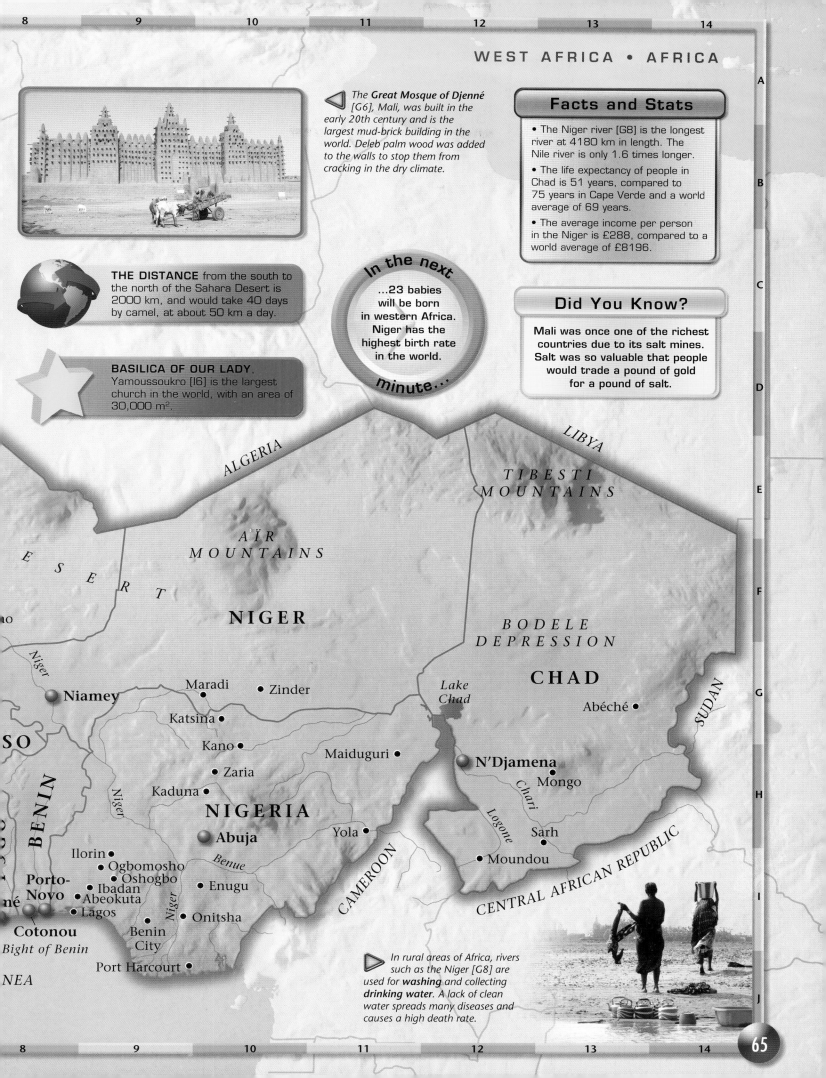

The **Great Mosque of Djenné** [G6], Mali, was built in the early 20th century and is the largest mud-brick building in the world. Deleb palm wood was added to the walls to stop them from cracking in the dry climate.

Facts and Stats

• The Niger river [G8] is the longest river at 4180 km in length. The Nile river is only 1.6 times longer.

• The life expectancy of people in Chad is 51 years, compared to 75 years in Cape Verde and a world average of 69 years.

• The average income per person in the Niger is £288, compared to a world average of £8196.

THE DISTANCE from the south to the north of the Sahara Desert is 2000 km, and would take 40 days by camel, at about 50 km a day.

In the next ...23 babies will be born in western Africa. Niger has the highest birth rate in the world. minute...

Did You Know?

Mali was once one of the richest countries due to its salt mines. Salt was so valuable that people would trade a pound of gold for a pound of salt.

BASILICA OF OUR LADY, Yamoussoukro [I6] is the largest church in the world, with an area of 30,000 m².

ALGERIA

LIBYA

TIBESTI MOUNTAINS

AÏR MOUNTAINS

D E S E R T

NIGER

BODELE DEPRESSION

CHAD

Niger

Niamey

Maradi   Zinder

Katsina

Kano

Zaria

Kaduna

Lake Chad

Abéché

Maiduguri

SUDAN

N'Djamena

Mongo

Chari

NIGERIA

SO

BENIN

Niger

Abuja

Yola

Sarh

Logone

Ilorin

Ogbomosho

Oshogbo

Porto-Novo

Ibadan

Abeokuta

Lagos

Enugu

CAMEROON

Moundou

CENTRAL AFRICAN REPUBLIC

Niger

Cotonou

Benin City

Onitsha

Bight of Benin

NEA

Port Harcourt

Benue

In rural areas of Africa, rivers such as the Niger [G8] are used for **washing** and collecting **drinking water**. A lack of clean water spreads many diseases and causes a high death rate.

A

B

C

D

E

F

G

H

I

J

East Africa

Due to the high altitude of Kenya, Tanzania and Uganda, the climate is suited to growing crops. These countries have strong economies based on exporting crops, such as tea and coffee, which are grown on large plantations run by European companies. The countries of Ethiopia, Somalia and Sudan are poorer as they have harsher climates and a history of unrest. The droughts that have repeatedly affected this southern fringe of the Sahara Desert have caused millions of deaths as well as the destruction of crops and animals.

EGYPT

LIBYA

*L I B Y A N
D E S E R T*   Wadi Ha

CHAD

*Japal Marrah
3089 m*   ● El Fasher

El Obeid

● Nyala

D A R F U R   **S U D A N**

CENTRAL AFRICAN REPUBLIC

BAHR AL-GHAZAL

● Wau

**S O U T
S U D A**

● Yambi

*DEMOCRATIC
REPUBLIC
OF THE CONGO*   A
La
Alb●

*Lake
Edward*

R W A N D
Kigali

Lake Kivu

B U R U N D
Bujumbura

Kigoma ●

*Lake
Tanganyi*

> *Lesser flamingos* are the smallest of the flamingo family. They are numerous throughout Africa and are always found in large groups called 'pats'. The colour of flamingos comes from their food – unhealthy birds are pale in colour.

Facts and Stats

- Mount Kilimanjaro [H9] is the highest mountain at 5895 m. It is 18 times higher than the Eiffel Tower.
- Sudan's area is 1.8 million km². This is 18 times the area of Iceland.
- Ethiopia has a population of 104.9 million. This would fill 1050 Olympic stadiums. Djibouti's population is 1 million and would fill 10 Olympic stadiums.

Extreme Weather

The Danakil Valley [D10], Ethiopia, has the hottest average daily temperature of 55°C.

Did You Know?

Somaliland declared itself independent from Somalia in 1991 but although it has been a separate country for 25 years, no other nation has recognized its independence.

0	100	200	300	400	500 mi

0	200	400	600	800 km

> The *Maasai people* of Kenya and Tanzania wear toga-like garments called shukkas, which can be bought at roadside shops. The official colour of the Maasai tribe is red, and is always worn as clothing or jewellery.

Map labels

NUBIAN DESERT

Port Sudan
rowe
bara
Khartoum
Omdurman
Kassala
Keren
Massawa
Asmara
ERITREA
DAHLAK ISLANDS
Wad Medani
Aksum
Ras Dashen 4533 m
Kosti
Gonder
Lake Tana
Asseb
Atbara
Blue Nile
Blue Nile
DJIBOUTI
Djibouti
Berbera
Debre Markos
Dire Dawa
SOMALILAND
DANAKIL VALLEY
lakal
Addis Ababa
Harer
Hargeisa
Gore
Nazret
Jima
OGADEN PLATEAU
nciel
ETHIOPIA
Eyl
Shebele
uba
Lake Turkana
SOMALIA
Jubba
ANDA
Mount Elgon 4322 m
KENYA
Baidoa
Mogadishu
Marka
Nanyuki
Baraawe
Kampala
Kisumu
Mount Kenya 5200 m
saka
Nakuru
GREAT RIFT VALLEY
Thika
Garissa
Kismaayo
ke
toria
Nairobi
Tana
Lake Natron
nza
Arusha
Galana
INDIAN OCEAN
Lake Eyasi
yanga
Malindi
Mount Kilimanjaro 5895 m
Mombasa
Tabora
Tanga
Pemba Island
ANZANIA
Dodoma
Zanzibar
Zanzibar Island
Rungwa
Bagamoyo
Kilosa
Dar es Salaam
Iringa
Mafia Island
Mbeya
Lake Malawi
Kilwa
Rufiji
Songea
Lindi
Mtwara
MALAWI
Ruvuma
MOZAMBIQUE

RED SEA

GULF OF ADEN

Cape Caseyr

Callouts

▷ *Seaweed is farmed in coastal areas throughout Africa and Asia. It can be used as food or fertilizer and also in medicines.*

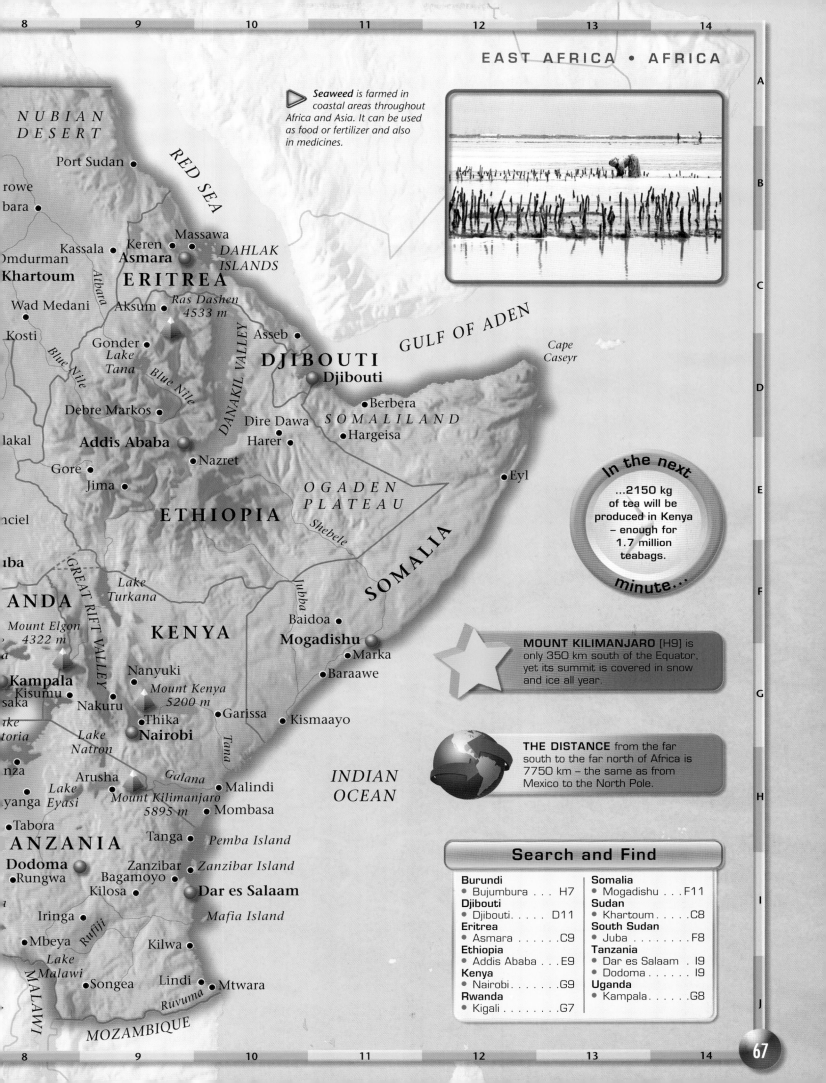

In the next ...2150 kg of tea will be produced in Kenya – enough for 1.7 million teabags. **minute...**

MOUNT KILIMANJARO [H9] is only 350 km south of the Equator, yet its summit is covered in snow and ice all year.

THE DISTANCE from the far south to the far north of Africa is 7750 km – the same as from Mexico to the North Pole.

Search and Find

Central and southern Africa

This region stretches from the tropical rainforests of Cameroon to the rich agricultural lands of South Africa. Only those countries with mineral wealth have prospered. Political unrest is widespread, bringing great poverty to the Central African Republic, DR Congo and Zimbabwe. Once an exporter of food and tobacco, Zimbabwe is now reliant on international aid. Farming, commerce, and gold and diamond mining have brought prosperity to many South Africans.

Victoria Falls [G8] on the Zambezi river tumbles more than 128 m into the gorge below, creating the largest sheet of falling water in the world. The local people called the waterfall 'the smoke that thunders'.

Facts and Stats

• The longest river is the Congo [C7]. At 4700 km in length, the Nile river is only 1.5 times longer.

• Mont Ngaliema (Mount Stanley) [C9] is the highest mountain at 5109 m in height – 16 times higher than the Eiffel Tower.

• The life expectancy of people in Eswatini is 52 years, compared to 76 years in Mauritius and a world average of 69 years.

Did You Know?

The Namib Desert [H6] is the oldest desert in the world. It covers 270,000 km² – more than twice the area of Iceland. Some parts have fewer than 2 cm of rain a year.

The **quiver tree** is a species of aloe found in southern Africa, especially throughout Namibia. Native people use the branches and bark of the tree to make containers, or quivers, for their arrows.

Map labels

NIGERIA
Garoua
Garba
CH
CEN
AFRICAN
Mount Cameroon 4071 m
Bamenda
CAMEROON
Bouar
Bambari
Malabo
Douala
Berbérati
Bioko Island
Yaoundé
Bangui
EQUATORIAL GUINEA
SÃO TOMÉ AND PRÍNCIPE
Príncipe
Ciudad de la Paz
REPUBLIC OF THE CONGO
São Tomé
São Tomé
Libreville
Mband
GABON
DEMOC OF T
Port-Gentil
Lake Mai-Ndombe
Bandundu
Brazzaville
Loubomo
Pointe-Noire
Kinshasa
Kikw
Matadi
Kwango
Kasai
Kwilu
Tsh
Luanda
Cuanza
Saurimo
Lue
ANGOLA
Luen
Lobito
Benguela
Huambo
Namibe
Lubango
Cubango
Cunene
Cuito
K
ETOSHA PAN
Cape Fria
Grootfontein
NAMIB DESERT
NAMIBIA
Windhoek
KALAH DESE
Swakopmund
Walvis Bay
Rehoboth
Lüderitz
Keetmanshoo
Alexander Bay
SO
Kenhardt
Carnarvo
Calvinia
Beaufort
Great Karoo
Cape Town
Word
Cape of Good Hope
Mosse
False Bay

8 9 10 11 12 13 14

THE DISTANCE to the bottom of South Africa's deepest gold mine is 3777 m – this would take four minutes in a high-speed lift.

In the next ...South Africa will mine 226 g of gold – enough for 75 18ct-gold wedding rings. minute...

0 100 200 300 400 500 mi
0 200 400 600 800 km

SOUTH SUDAN

akouma

Uele

Bondo

Watsa
Mount Ngaliema
5109 m

Basoko

Kisangani

UGANDA

Lake
Edward

C REPUBLIC
ONGO

Lake
Kivu

RWANDA

BURUNDI

Bukavu

Lomami

Congo

anie

Kalemie

TANZANIA

Lake Tanganyika

Mbuji-Mayi

Lake
Mweru

Kamina

Mbala

Kasama

wezi

Likasi

Lubumbashi

Lake
Bangweulu

MALAWI

Lake Malawi

Mufulira

Kitwe

Ndola

Kafue

Kabwe

Chipata

Lilongwe

AMBIA

Lake
Cahora
Bassa

Zomba

Lúrio

Nacala

Nampula

Moçambique

Lusaka

Blantyre

Tete

Zambezi

Livingstone

Lake
Kariba

Harare

Quelimane

rango

Victoria
Falls

Chitungwiza

Chimoio

MOZAMBIQUE

lta

Maun

ZIMBABWE

Beira

WANA

Bulawayo

Save

ancistown

Messina

Inhambane

ebi-Phikwe

Pietersburg

Limpopo

olepolole

Gaborone

Pretoria

atse

Mbabane

Maputo

Johannesburg

Soweto

Vaal

ESWATINI

Vereeniging

H AFRICA

Lobamba

Kimberley

Maseru

emfontein

Pietermaritzburg

LESOTHO

Durban

range

DRAKENSBERG MOUNTAINS

Port Shepstone

idelburg

Umtata

East London

Port Elizabeth

Cape
Delgado

COMOROS

Moroni

MAYOTTE
(FRANCE)

Antsiranana

Mahajanga

MADAGASCAR

Antananarivo

Fianarantsoa

SEYCHELLES

INDIAN
OCEAN

MAURITIUS

RÉUNION
(FRANCE)

Port
Louis

Victoria

MOZAMBIQUE CHANNEL

African elephants live in herds of females, led by a matriarch – normally the oldest female. They work together to keep the herd safe. When they walk in file, the youngsters stay close to the adults so they are protected from predators.

A

B

C

D

E

F

G

H

I

J

Asia

ARCTIC OCEAN

RUSSIA

KAZAKHSTAN

MONGOLIA

UZBEKISTAN

KYRGYZSTAN

1

NORTH
KOREA

TURKEY

TURKMENISTAN

TAJIKISTAN

JAPAN

SYRIA

AFGHANISTAN

CHINA

SOUTH
KOREA

2

IRAQ

3 4

IRAN

5

PAKISTAN

NEPAL

9

6

7

BANGLADESH

TAIWAN

8

SAUDI
ARABIA

INDIA

BURMA
(MYANMAR)

LAOS

*PACIFIC
OCEAN*

OMAN

YEMEN

THAILAND

VIETNAM

CAMBODIA

PHILIPPINES

SRI
LANKA

10

12

MALAYSIA

11

INDONESIA

*INDIAN
OCEAN*

EAST
TIMOR
(TIMOR-LESTE)

KEY
1 AZERBAIJAN
2 LEBANON
3 ISRAEL
4 JORDAN
5 KUWAIT
6 BAHRAIN
7 QATAR
8 UNITED ARAB EMIRATES
9 BHUTAN
10 BRUNEI
11 SINGAPORE
12 MALDIVES

COUNTRY FACTFILE

Country	Life expectancy	Population to nearest thousand	Population growth %	Population as urban %	Area km²	Population density per km²	Capital city	Currency	Languages
Afghanistan	52	28,224,000	2.4	27	645,807	43.2	Kabul	Afghani	Dari, Pashto
Azerbaijan *	73	9,828,000	0.9	57	86,600	110.8	Baku	Manat	Azeri
Bahrain	79	1,490,000	2.3	92	716	1836.6	Manama	Bahraini Dinar	Arabic, Urdu, English
Bangladesh	73	166,221,000	1	37	147,570	1126.4	Dhaka	Taka	Bangla, English
Bhutan	71	727,000	1.1	41	46,500	18.9	Thimphu	Ngultrum	Dzongkha, Nepali
Brunei	77	423,000	1.6	78	5765	73.4	Bandar Seri Begawan	Bruneian Dollar	Malay
Burma (Myanmar)	68	53,370,000	0.9	34	676,577	78.9	Naypyidaw	Kyat	Burmese, Shan
Cambodia	65	18,849,000	1.8	22	181,035	87.5	Phnom Penh	Riel	Khmer
China	76	1,391,700,000	0.4	59	9,559,686	148.5	Beijing	Yuan	Chinese (Guoyo), Wu, Yuëh
Cyprus†	79	1,141,000	1.3	70	9251	123.3	Nicosia	Euro	Greek, Turkish, English
East Timor (Timor-Leste)	68	1,184,000	2.1	33	14,874	79.6	Dili	US Dollar	Tetum, Portuguese
India	69	1,339,000,000	1.2	34	3,287,263	407.4	New Delhi	Indian Rupee	Hindi, English, Telegu, Bengali
Indonesia	73	263,990,000	0.9	55	1,904,413	138.6	Jakarta	Indonesian Rupiah	Bahasa Indonesian, Javanese, Sudanese
Iran	74	79,926,000	1.2	75	1,641,918	48.7	Tehran	Iranian Rial	Farsi (Persian), Azeri
Iraq	75	38,270,000	2.6	76	434,128	88	Baghdad	New Iraqi Dinar	Arabic, Kurdish
Israel	83	8,627,000	1.5	92	20,400	398.6	Jerusalem	Israeli Shekel	Hebrew, Arabic
Japan	85	127,095,000	-0.1	92	377,819	336.4	Tokyo	Yen	Japanese
Jordan	75	9,798,000	2.1	91	89,342	110.3	Amman	Jordanian Dinar	Arabic
Kazakhstan	71	18,157,000	1	64	2,717,300	6.7	Astana	Tenge	Kazakh, Russian
Korea, North	71	25,490,000	0.5	62	122,762	207.6	Pyongyang	North Korean Won	Korean
Korea, South	83	52,858,000	0.5	83	99,461	527.4	Seoul, Sejong	South Korean Won	Korean
Kuwait	78	4,438,000	1.5	98	17,818	261.5	Kuwait City	Kuwaiti Dinar	Arabic, Farsi, English
Kyrgyzstan	71	6,257,000	1.1	36	198,500	31.3	Bishkek	Som	Kyrgyz, Russian
Laos	65	6,850,000	1.5	39	236,800	28.6	Vientiane	Kip	Lao
Lebanon	78	6,106,000	3	90	10,201	486.8	Beirut	Lebanese Pound	Arabic
Malaysia	75	32,050,000	1.4	76	329,847	97	Kuala Lumpur, Putrajaya	Ringgit	Bahasa Melayu (Malay), Chinese, English
Maldives	76	435,000	1	46	298	1459.7	Male	Rufiyaa	Dhivehi (Maldivian)
Mongolia	70	3,132,000	1.2	72	1,564,100	2	Ulaanbaatar	Tugrik	Khalkha Mongol
Nepal	71	29,300,000	1.2	20	147,181	199	Kathmandu	Nepalese Rupee	Nepali, Maithili
Oman	76	4,414,000	2	85	309,500	14.3	Muscat	Omani Rial	Arabic, Baluchi
Pakistan	68	213,123,000	1.4	39	880,254	242.1	Islamabad	Pakistani Rupee	Urdu, Punjabi, Sindhi
Philippines	69	104,920,000	1.6	65	300,076	349.6	Manila	Philippine Peso	Filipino (Tagalog), Cebuano, English
Qatar	79	2,640,000	2.3	99	11,427	231	Doha	Qatari Rial	Arabic, Hindi, Malayalam
Russia	71	144,530,000	0	78	17,075,400	8.5	Moscow	Rouble	Russian, Tatar, Ukrainian
Saudi Arabia	76	32,950,000	1.5	86	2,149,803	15.3	Riyadh	Saudi Riyal	Arabic, Malayalam, Tagalog
Singapore	85	5,612,000	1.8	100	720	7794.4	Singapore	Singapore Dollar	Chinese, Malay, English
Sri Lanka	77	21,444,000	0.8	23	65,613	326.8	Colombo, Kotte	Sri Lankan Rupee	Sinhala, Tamil
Syria	75	18,270,000	0	58	185,180	98.7	Damascus	Syrian Pound	Arabic
Taiwan	80	23,540,000	0.2	78	36,179	650.7	Taipei	Taiwan dollar	Chinese (Mandarin), Min
Tajikistan	68	8,551,000	1.6	28	143,100	59.8	Dushanbe	Somoni	Tajik, Uzbek
Thailand	75	67,653,000	0.3	50	514,000	137.8	Bangkok	Baht	Thai, Chinese
Turkey	75	80,811,000	0.5	75	780,580	108.6	Ankara	Turkish Lira	Turkish, Kurdish
Turkmenistan	70	5,750,000	1.1	52	488,100	11.8	Ashgabat	Turkmen Manat	Turkmen, Uzbek
United Arab Emirates	78	9,121,000	2.4	90	83,600	112.4	Abu Dhabi	Emirati Dirham	Arabic, Hindu, Urdu
Uzbekistan	74	32,121,000	0.9	51	444,103	72.3	Tashkent	Uzbek Soum	Uzbek, Russian
Vietnam	74	92,695,000	0.9	36	329,315	281.5	Hanoi	Dong	Vietnamese
Yemen	66	28,250,000	2.3	37	527,970	53.5	Sana'a	Yemeni Rial	Arabic

* Although Azerbaijan is a member of some European organizations, it is historically and culturally part of western Asia.
† Cyprus is part of Europe, but the mapping can be found in this section.

The Near East

Mostly a poor, mountainous region, Turkey has a beautiful coastline and thriving tourist industry. The country is being transformed by the Great Anatolian project – reservoirs will be built along the Tigris and Euphrates rivers, to irrigate 16,000 km² of land. Although geographically closer to Asia, Turkey is internationally recognized as part of Europe. Israel was created in 1948. Land was taken from the Palestinians resulting in conflict with Syria, Jordan and Lebanon. Syria has been in civil conflict since 2011 as political power has been contested. Sheep and goats are the main livestock. Where irrigation is possible, vegetables and fruit are grown, much of which is exported to Europe.

BULGARIA

GREECE

Edirne

Tekirdag

Bosporus Strait

Istanbul

Sea of Marmara

Izmit

Bursa

Sak

Balikesir

Eskisehir

Kütahy

A N A T

P L A

Manisa

Usak

Izmir

Ephesus

Nazilli

Aydin

Denizli

Isp

Bodrum

T A

Antalya

The **Temple Mount** in Jerusalem [I9] is an important religious site. The Dome of the Rock is a Muslim shrine. The Western Wall dates back to 500 BC and is used by Jews for prayer.

THE DISTANCE from Europe to Asia across the Bosporus Strait [B6] is only 700 m and takes one minute by car across a bridge.

Search and Find

Cyprus
● Nicosia F8

Israel
● Jerusalem I9

Jordan
● Amman H10

Lebanon
● Beirut G9

Syria
● Damascus . . H10

Turkey
● Ankara C8

Did You Know?

Cyprus is the third largest island in the Mediterranean. The northern area of the island is Turkish Cypriot and the southern area is Greek Cypriot. Although geographically closer to Asia, Cyprus joined the EU in 2004.

Facts and Stats

● Turkey's area of 769,604 km² is 7.5 times the area of Iceland.

● Mount Ararat [D14] is the highest mountain at 5137 m – 16 times higher than the Eiffel Tower.

● The life expectancy of people in Israel is 83 years, compared to 75 years in Jordan and a world average of 69 years.

Pamukkale, which means 'cotton castle' in Turkish, was formed from the water of a very hot spring. The water contains a lot of chalk, which results in the limestone cliffs that can be seen today.

Scale

0 50 100 150 200 mi

0 100 200 300 km

The **Dead Sea** [I9] is the second saltiest body of water in the world and is called 'dead' because fish and other organisms cannot survive in it. Salty deposits cover the beaches and cliffs, and it is almost impossible to sink in the water because of the high salt content.

BLACK SEA

GEORGIA

ARMENIA

Zonguldak
Karabük
Samsun
Ordu
Trabzon
Çorum
PONTIC MOUNTAINS
Kars
Kelkit
Ankara
Kirikkale
Erzurum
TURKEY
Sivas
Erzincan
Mount Ararat 5137 m
IAN
AU
Lake Tuz
Kizilirmak
Kayseri
Elazig
Murat
Lake Van
Van
Konya
Malatya
Adiyaman
Diyarbakir
Batman
IRAN
IS MOUNTAINS
Firat
Tarsus
Adana
Osmaniye
Gaziantep
Khabur
Al Qamishli
Mersin
Al Hasakah
Antakya
Al Bab
Aleppo
Ar Raqqah
Euphrates

CYPRUS
Nicosia
Latakia
Lake Assad
aphos
Baniyas
Hamah
SYRIA
Dayr az Zawr
Limassol
Tartus
Homs
Tripoli
Abu Kamal
LEBANON
MEDITERRANEAN SEA
Beirut
LEBANON MOUNTAINS
SYRIAN DESERT
Sidon
Tyre
Damascus
IRAQ
Acre
Al Kiswah
Al Qunaytirah
Haifa
GOLAN HEIGHTS
Nazareth
Sea of Galilee
Dar'a
Hadera
WEST BANK
Irbid
Netanya
Ramallah
Az-Zarqa
Tel Aviv
Jordan
Amman
Jerusalem
Dead Sea
Gaza
Bethlehem
Ma'daba
GAZA STRIP
Beersheba
Al-Karak
ISRAEL
EGYPT
NEGEV DESERT
Ma'an
Wadi al Hasa
JORDAN
Elat
Aqaba
SAUDI ARABIA
Gulf of Aqaba

In the next ...Turkey will produce enough Turkish delight confectionery to create a pillar 305 m in height. **minute...**

The ruins of Ephesus [D5] are a major tourist attraction. Built in AD 135, the restored **Library of Celsus** is a monumental tomb for Celsus Polemaeanus, the governor of Asia. His grave is across the entrance, under the ground floor.

The Middle East

Vast oil and gas reserves have made several countries in the Middle East some of the wealthiest in the world. However, before oil was discovered, this was a poor region of desert tribes and coastal fishing. The area between the Euphrates and Tigris rivers was once home to the great civilization of Mesopotamia. Conflict and sanctions have damaged the economies of Iraq and Iran, but other countries such as the UAE are investing in tourism and other forms of industry. The city of Dubai now has the largest indoor ski slope in the world.

*For thousands of years, Iran has been the centre of the hand-woven **Persian carpet** industry. Although machinery is widely used today, traditional methods are still used in some areas. A medium-sized rug can take a skilled worker up to a year to complete.*

Extreme Weather

Midday temperatures can reach 50°C in the desert areas, but snow is common in the mountains of Iran and Iraq.

Did You Know?

The United Arab Emirates obtains more than 80 percent of its water supply by desalinating sea water.

*Millions of Muslims have made a pilgrimage, or Hajj, to Mecca [G5]. The holiest place in Islam is the **Kaaba**. Non-Muslims cannot enter Mecca.*

ARMEN

TURKEY

T

Mosul ● ● Arbil

Kirkuk ●

IRAQ

SYRIA

Bakht

Baghdad

SYRIAN DESERT

Karbala ●

Najaf ●

Tigris

Euphrates

JORDAN

An Nasiriyah

EGYPT

Al Jawf ● ● Sakakah

NAFUD DESERT

HIJAZ

Buraydah ●

Shaqra ●

Riyad

● Medina

● Yanbu

SAU

Jeddah
● ● Mecca
● Taif

RED SEA

As-Sulayyil ●

ASIR

● Abha

● Jizan
● Harad

Sana'a
● Al-Hudaydah

● Ta'izz

● Aden

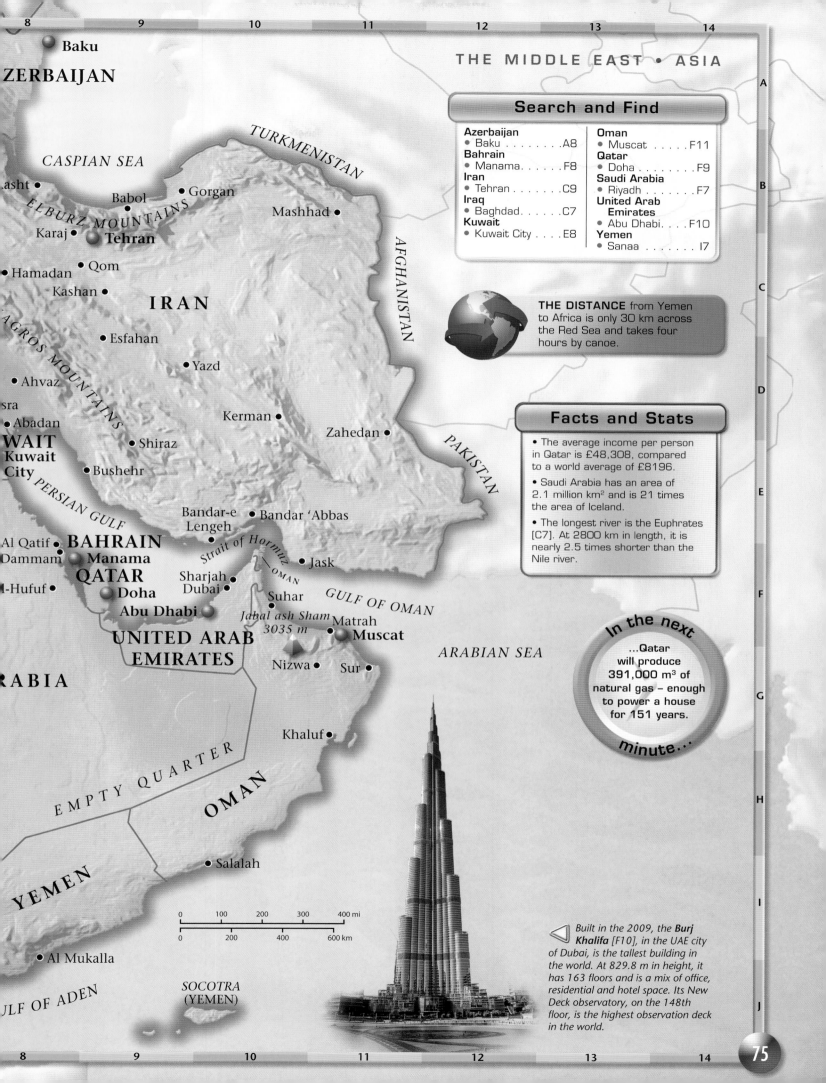

Baku

ZERBAIJAN

CASPIAN SEA

TURKMENISTAN

ELBURZ MOUNTAINS

Babol • Gorgan

Mashhad

asht

Karaj • **Tehran**

• Qom

• Hamadan

Kashan •

I R A N

AFGHANISTAN

• Esfahan

AGROS MOUNTAINS

• Ahvaz

• Yazd

sra

• Abadan

Kerman •

Zahedan •

PAKISTAN

WAIT

**Kuwait
City**

• Shiraz

• Bushehr

PERSIAN GULF

Bandar-e
Lengeh • Bandar 'Abbas

• Al Qatif

BAHRAIN

Strait of Hormuz

Dammam • **Manama**

• Jask

l-Hufuf •

QATAR

Sharjah

OMAN

• **Doha**

Dubai •

Abu Dhabi

Suhar •

GULF OF OMAN

*Jabal ash Sham
3035 m*

Matrah
• **Muscat**

**UNITED ARAB
EMIRATES**

Nizwa •

Sur •

ARABIAN SEA

RABIA

Khaluf •

EMPTY QUARTER

O M A N

YEMEN

• Salalah

• Al Mukalla

*SOCOTRA
(YEMEN)*

ULF OF ADEN

| 0 | 100 | 200 | 300 | 400 mi |
| 0 | 200 | 400 | 600 km |

Search and Find

Azerbaijan	Oman
● Baku A8	● Muscat F11
Bahrain	**Qatar**
● Manama. F8	● Doha F9
Iran	**Saudi Arabia**
● Tehran C9	● Riyadh F7
Iraq	**United Arab Emirates**
● Baghdad. C7	● Abu Dhabi. . . .F10
Kuwait	**Yemen**
● Kuwait City E8	● Sanaa I7

THE DISTANCE from Yemen to Africa is only 30 km across the Red Sea and takes four hours by canoe.

Facts and Stats

• The average income per person in Qatar is £48,308, compared to a world average of £8196.

• Saudi Arabia has an area of 2.1 million km² and is 21 times the area of Iceland.

• The longest river is the Euphrates [C7]. At 2800 km in length, it is nearly 2.5 times shorter than the Nile river.

In the next minute...

...Qatar will produce 391,000 m³ of natural gas – enough to power a house for 151 years.

Built in the 2009, the **Burj Khalifa** [F10], in the UAE city of Dubai, is the tallest building in the world. At 829.8 m in height, it has 163 floors and is a mix of office, residential and hotel space. Its New Deck observatory, on the 148th floor, is the highest observation deck in the world.

Indian subcontinent

With ice-covered mountains, tropical lowlands and hot deserts, this region is one of contrasts. Afghanistan is a war-torn, semi-desert nation that is in the process of rebuilding amidst ongoing conflicts. India has one of the most rapidly growing economies in the world. A highly educated, English-speaking workforce has resulted in many European and American companies establishing various support operations in India. The 'Bollywood' film studios are a worldwide success and cities are rapidly expanding. However, out of India's 1.34 billion population, two thirds remain poor, rural farmers. Pakistan, Bangladesh and the Himalayan states of Nepal and Bhutan remain relatively undeveloped.

The **Taj Mahal** in Agra [D9], India, was built for Mumtaz Mahal, the wife of Emperor Shah Jahan. When she died in 1629, the Emperor ordered the most beautiful tomb in the world to be built. It took 20,000 workers about 20 years to build. The Emperor and his wife are buried beneath the 60-m-high white dome.

Search and Find

Afghanistan
- Kabul B7

Bangladesh
- Dhaka E11

Bhutan
- Thimphu D11

India
- New Delhi D9

Nepal
- Kathmandu . . D10

Pakistan
- Islamabad B8

Sri Lanka
- Colombo J9
- Kotte J9

Did You Know?

Great Britain ruled India from 1858 until 1947. This is why English is widely spoken and cricket is the national sport.

THE DISTANCE from the Everest base camp to the summit is 10 km. In 2000, it was climbed in less than 17 hours.

World Record

In 1985, Mawsynram [E12] recorded the world's highest yearly rainfall – over 26,000 mm.

Many Hindus go to a mandir, or **temple**, to say prayers and to make offerings of food to the gods. The temples are beautifully decorated with carvings of gods and spirits.

TURKMENISTAN
Sheberghan •
Mazar-e Sh
• Herat
AFGHANISTA
Kab
• Farah

Helmand
RIGESTAN
DESERT
• Qandaha
Quetta •

PAKISTA
Larkana • • Suk
• Gwadar
Indus
Hyderabad •
Karachi • • Mirpur K

Gulf of
Kachchh
RANN O
KACHCH
Ahmada
Jamnagar •

ARABIAN
SEA
Bhavnaga
Su
Gulf of
Khambha

Mumb
(Bomba

INDIAN OCEAN

IRAN

8 9 10 11 12 13 14

TAJIKISTAN

K2
8611 m

Mardan

Islamabad

war

Srinagar

lpindi

alabad • Gujranwala

Lahore • Amritsar

tan • Sahiwel • Ludhiana

Sutlej

awalpur • Chandigarh

Meerut

Delhi

New Delhi

Jaipur • Agra

hpur • Ajmer

Ganges

Yamuna

NEPAL

H I M A L A Y A S

CHINA

Pokhara

Kathmandu

Mount Everest
8848 m

Lucknow

Kanpur

Allahabad • Varanasi

Patna • Biratnagar

Udaipur

Lalitpur

Rangpur

Thimphu

BHUTAN

Brahmaputra • Jorhat

Guwahati

NAGA HILLS

Mawsynram

Bhopal

Narmada

odara

Indore

I N D I A

Rajshahi

Dhanbad

Sylhet • Imphal

BANGLADESH

Dhaka

Agartala

Jamshedpur

Khulna

Chittagong

Nagpur • Raipur

Kolkata
(Calcutta)

BURMA (MYANMAR)

Cuttack

Godavari

ne

ona)

Solapur

Hyderabad

hapur

Krishna

Kurnool

EASTERN GHATS

Vijayawada

bli-Dhawar

Vishakhapatnam

BAY OF
BENGAL

Nellore

galore

Bengaluru
(Bangalore)

Mysore

Chennai
(Madras)

Puducherry

Kozhikode (Calicut)

Coimbatore

Tiruchirappalli

Kochi
Cochin)

Madurai

Palk Strait

Jaffna

iruvananthapuram
rivandrum)

Trincomalee

SRI LANKA

Kandy

Colombo

Kotte

Galle

ANDAMAN
ISLANDS
(INDIA)

NICOBAR
ISLANDS
(INDIA)

SIGIRIYA, or Lion's Mouth, was the fortress of Sri Lankan King Kashyapa (AD 477–495). Only the two giant paws of the lion remain.

Extreme Weather

The heaviest recorded hailstones, weighing up to one kilogram killed 92 people in Bangladesh on 14 April 1986.

Facts and Stats

- The longest river in the region is the Brahmaputra [D12]. At 2900 km in length, it is almost half the length of the Nile river.
- The highest mountain in the world is Mount Everest [D11] at 8848 m in height – 28 times higher than the Eiffel Tower.
- The life expectancy of people in Afghanistan is 52 years, compared to 76 years in Sri Lanka and a world average of 69 years.

▷ The **Ganges river** flows through the city of Varanasi [E10] and is believed to be sacred. Many Hindus make pilgrimages to pray and bathe in the holy water.

In the next
...more than 35 babies will be born in India – that's 50,400 every day.
minute...

0   100   200   300   400 mi
0   200   400   600 km

A B C D E F G H I J

8 9 10 11 12 13 14

Vietnam and the Philippines

Lush tropical rainforests lead to wonderful sandy beaches and warm seas. Rice fields and remote villages give way to sprawling cities. Despite the growth of tourism in Thailand and Vietnam, most of this area is poor. Many people live near the coast and they are still mainly dependent on fishing and farming. Rice is the main crop, grown in the river valleys in wet paddy fields. Vietnam has recovered from wars in the 20th century and is now a major coffee producer.

| 0 | 100 | 200 | 300 | 400 mi |
| 0 | 200 | 400 | 600 km |

INDIA

CHINA

BANGLADESH

Mandalay

Thai Nguyen

Hanoi Haiphong

Nam Dinh

BURMA (MYANMAR)

Thanh Hoa *Gulf of Tonkin*

Luang Prabang

Sittwe

Vinh

Irrawaddy

ARAKAN RANGE

Naypyidaw

LAOS

Prome

PEGU RANGE

Vientiane

Chiang Mai

Udon Thani

Hué

Da Nang

THAILAND

Savannakhet

Henzada

Pegu

Khon Kaen

Pakxe

Champassak

Bassein

Yangon (Rangoon)

Moulmein

Ubon Ratchathani

Mekong

VIETNAM

Gulf of Martaban

Nakhon Sawan

Qui Nhon

Angkor Wat

Tavoy

Nakhon Ratchasima

Siem Reap

ANDAMAN SEA

Bangkok

Batdâmbang

Nha Trang

Chon Buri

CAMBODIA

Da Lat

Mergui

Kampong Cham

BILAUKTAUNG RANGE

Phnom Penh

Ho Chi Minh City

GULF OF THAILAND

Can Tho

Facts and Stats

- The life expectancy of people in Laos is 65 years, compared to 75 years in Thailand and a world average of 69 years.
- The largest city in the region is Bangkok, with 13.2 million inhabitants.
- The average income per person in Cambodia is £495, compared to a world average of £6880.

Nakhon Si Thammarat

Phuket

In the next ...the Mekong river [G5] will deposit enough silt to fill 50 bathtubs – 30 million tonnes a year. *minute...*

Spratly Islands

Hat Yai Songkhla

MALAYSIA

◁ Many young men in Thailand temporarily become **Buddhist monks** to learn more about their faith. They shave their heads and beards and wear robes to show commitment to the holy life.

Search and Find

Cambodia	Philippines
● Phnom Penh . . H5	● Manila F10
Laos	**Thailand**
● Vientiane F4	● Bangkok H4
Burma (Myanmar)	**Vietnam**
● Naypyidaw F2	● Hanoi E5

THE DISTANCE from Yangon [G2] to Bangkok [H4] is 640 km and would take an elephant three days of non-stop walking.

Luzon Strait

Babuyan Islands

Laoag ●

● Tuguegarao

Luzon

PHILIPPINES

PACIFIC OCEAN

Angeles ● ● Cabanatuan

Manila ● ● Quezon City

Batangas ●

Mindoro

▷ The canals in Bangkok [H4] are used for **floating markets** where fresh produce, such as fruit, vegetables and flowers, is sold from boats.

● Calbayog
Samar

● Ormoc
Leyte

SOUTH CHINA SEA

Mindoro Strait

Panay Bacolod
Iloilo ● ● Cebu

Negros

● Butuan

Cagayan de Oro ●

Palawan Passage

● Puerto Princesa
Palawan

Mindanao

Pagadian ● ● Davao
Moro Gulf General Santos

SULU SEA

Zamboanga ●

Balabac Strait

CELEBES SEA

Did You Know?

The ruins of the ancient city of Angkor Wat [G5], complete with Hindu temples and royal palaces, were discovered in the Cambodian rainforest 150 years ago.

Extreme Weather

In July, the monsoon rains bring the city of Yangon [G2] as much rain as London gets in a year.

SULU ARCHIPELAGO

▷ Many tropical countries suffer from rainy seasons called monsoons, which result in serious flooding. In some parts of Asia, **houses are built on stilts** over bodies of water to protect them against water damage.

Indonesia, Malaysia and Singapore

Situated on the Equator, this region has a hot, wet climate. Malaysia is part of the Asian mainland and the large island of Borneo. It is developing rapidly with car and shipbuilding industries. Singapore is the richest country in this region, based on its technology industry, banking and high educational standards. A safe, law-abiding nation, laws against all types of crime, even dropping litter, are strictly enforced. Indonesia consists of over 13,000 islands. Natural disasters, poor communications and corruption have restricted economic growth. Although East Timor became independent from Indonesia in 2002, it remains impoverished.

THAILAND

George Town
Kuala Terengganu
Ipoh • MALAY
Medan • PENINSULA
Natuna Island
Kota Kinabalu • Sandakan
Bandar Seri Begawan
BRUNEI • SABAH
CELEBES SEA
Kelang • **Kuala Lumpur**
Putrajaya M A L A Y S I A
Strait of Malacca
Johor Baharu
Manado
Pekanbaru •
Singapore
SINGAPORE
S A R A W A K
• Kuching
Sumatra
Pontianak • Kapuas
MOLU SE
Padang •
Bangka
K A L I M A N T A N
• Palu
Jambi •
Belitung
Balikpapan
Makassar Strait
Sulawesi
Palembang •
Borneo
Barito
Banjarmasin

I N D O N E S I A
Makasar

Tanjungkarang
Telukbetung
Jakarta
JAVA SEA
FLORES SEA
Bandung • Java • Semarang
Surakarta • Surabaya
Malang • Komodo Flores
Bali Mataram • Ende
Lombok Sumbawa
Sumba Kupang

More than 450 m in height, the **Petronas Towers** in Kuala Lumpur [E2] contain 88 floors of offices, a shopping mall, a concert hall and parking for 4500 cars.

Extreme Weather

At the Equator, the climate is the same throughout the year – hot and very wet. Singapore's temperature averages at 27°C.

...seven new cars will be made in this region – that's 3.7 million a year.

Tea has been grown throughout Indonesia for more than 200 years, especially in Java and Sumatra. These small islands now produce 7 percent of the world's tea exports. The shoots are picked by hand, packed and exported.

Did You Know?

The 2004 tsunami in southeast Asia was caused by an undersea earthquake. The waves travelled at speeds of up to 800 km/h – 230,000 people were killed and five million were made homeless.

Search and Find

Brunei
- Bandar Seri Begawan E5

East Timor
- Dili. H7

Indonesia
- Jakarta H3

Malaysia
- Kuala Lumpur . . E2
- Putrajaya E2

Singapore
- Singapore F2

THE DISTANCE from Singapore to Malaysia is only 1056 m and the Joho–Singapore Causeway can be crossed by car in one minute.

| 0 | 100 | 200 | 300 | 400 mi |
| 0 | 200 | 400 | 600 km |

Imahera

Sorong

SERAM SEA

Seram

Ambon

Jayapura

New Guinea

DA SEA

Aru Islands

Tanimbar Island

ARAFURA SEA

ST TIMOR

The **Batak people** live in Sumatra, Indonesia. Easily recognizable, their houses are built on stilts and have high, thatched roofs. Often ornaments and paintings are placed on the outside to ward away evil spirits.

Facts and Stats

- The average income per person in Singapore is £43,899 compared to £1734 in East Timor and a world average of £8196.

- The life expectancy of people in Singapore is 85 years, compared to 68 years in East Timor and a world average of 69 years.

- Indonesia's area of 1.9 million km² is 18 times the area of Iceland.

Japan

Japan consists of four main islands – Kyushu, Hokkaido, Honshu and Shikoku. More than 70 percent of the country is covered with forested volcanic mountains such as Mount Fuji. Most of Japan's population lives on the flatlands along the coast, resulting in a very high population density. People live in high-rise flats or small houses, but frequent earthquakes can cause immense damage. Agriculture, industry, and urban development are concentrated on the main island of Honshu in the area between Osaka and Tokyo. Japan is one of the richest nations in the world, with well-known brands such as Toyota, Honda, Nissan, Sony, Panasonic and JVC.

The Golden Pavilion, Kyoto [G8], was originally built in the 14th century for a samurai general. The temple has been destroyed many times, and was most recently rebuilt in the 1950s. The pavilion, except the basement floor, is covered in pure gold leaf.

0	50	100	150	200 mi
0	100	200	300 km	

SEA OF JAPAN

MOUNT FUJI [G9] is an active volcano, but last erupted in 1707. More than 200,000 people walk to its snow-capped summit each year.

Oki Island

Matsue • Yonago •

THE DISTANCE from Tokyo [G10] to Osaka [H8] is 515 km. It only takes 2.5 hours by high-speed train, travelling at 206 km/h.

Matsue • Yonago • • Tot

Korea Strait

Tsushima

Hiroshima • Okayama • • K

Shimonoseki • Kure • Takamatsu •

Kitakyushu • Hofu • Waka•

Fukuoka • Matsuyama • Tokushima

Sasebo • Oita • *Shikoku*

Kumamoto • Saiki • • Kochi

Nagasaki • *Bungo Channel*

Amakusa Island Nobeoka •

Koshiki Island *Kyushu*

Sumo wrestling is a popular sport in Japan. Competitors have a body weight of up to 270 kg and their aim is to push their opponent out of the ring. Sumo is more than 2000 years old, and has strict rules and ceremonies.

• Miyazaki
• Miyakonojo
Kagoshima •

Tanega Island

Yaku Island

JAPAN • ASIA

Soya Strait

Rebun Island
Wakkanai
Rishiri Island

Abashiri

Ishikari
Asahikawa
Hokkaido

Otaru
Ebetsu
Sapporo
Chitose
Obihiro
Kushiro
Tomakomai

Muroran
Uchiura Bay

Hakodate
Cape Erimo

Tsugaru Strait

Aomori
Hirosaki
Hachinohe

Akita
Miyako
Hanamaki
Kamaishi

Sakata
Kesennuma

Ishinomaki
Yamagata
Sendai

Sado Island
Niigata
Fukushima

Nagaoka
Aizu
Koriyama

Shinano
Honshu
Iwaki

Toyama
Utsunomiya
Hitachi

zawa
Nagano
Takasaki
Mito
Komatsu

Matsumoto
Saitama
PACIFIC OCEAN

JAPAN
Kofu
Tokyo

Mount Fuji
3776 m
Chiba

Gifu
Kawasaki
Fuji
Yokohama
to

Nagoya
Toyota
Shizuoka

Toyohashi
Hamamatsu
ka
i

Miyake Island

Hachijo Island

> *Geisha* are female Japanese entertainers who are skilled in many traditional arts, such as music, singing and dancing. Although the make-up and clothing of geisha change throughout their career, they generally wear a white base, red lipstick and black outlines to their eyes.

In the next
...Japan will manufacture 15 cars and 50 computer consoles.
minute...

Did You Know?

People in Japan often wear face masks to protect themselves from fumes, pollution and germs.

Extreme Weather

The mountains of the northern island of Hokkaido have some of the heaviest snowfall in the world. The 1972 Winter Olympics were held there.

> With so many people, cars and businesses crammed into a small area, **Tokyo** [G10] is one of the most congested cities in the world. Tokyo Tower is based on the Eiffel Tower, Paris, although it is actually more than 8 m taller.

Facts and Stats

• The highest mountain is Mount Fuji [G9] at 3776 m. It is 12 times higher than the Eiffel Tower.

• The life expectancy of people in Japan is 85 years, compared to a world average of 69 years.

• The average income per person in Japan is £29,232, compared to a world average of £8196.

China and Korea

One fifth of the world's population lives in China. Once a poor, rural nation, China has the fastest-growing economy in the world. Each year, millions of farm workers move to the cities to work in factories. A new power station has to be built every week, making China the biggest user of coal and oil in the world. In contrast, Mongolia has a small, mainly rural population. North Korea is a Communist state with a low standard of living, but South Korea is much richer due to its shipbuilding, electronic and car industries.

In 210–209 BC, thousands of **terracotta soldiers** were buried with the first emperor of China, Qin Shi Huangdi, as it was believed to make him powerful in heaven. The tomb was discovered in 1974 near Xi'an [F10].

Search and Find

LHASA [H7] in the Himalayas is the capital of Tibet and home to many Buddhist monasteries and ancient palaces.

THE DISTANCE from one end of The Great Wall of China to the other is 8850 km. With all its branches the wall is over 21,000 km long.

Facts and Stats

- China has a population of 1391 million, which would fill 13,917 Olympic stadiums. Mongolia's population of 3.1 million would only fill 31 stadiums.
- China's area of 9.6 million km² is 93 times the area of Iceland.
- The Chang Jiang (Yangtze) [G10] is the longest river at 6300 km in length. The Nile river is nearly twice as long.

One of China's largest cities, **Shanghai** [F12] has a population of 20.9 million. The skyline is dominated by high-rise office buildings and the city is rapidly becoming one of the most important financial centres in the world. The Oriental Pearl Tower is the fifth highest tower in the world at 468 m.

Ulaang

ALTAI MOUNTAI

Uliast

KAZAKHSTAN

Tacheng

Yining

Urumqi

Turpan

Bosten Hu

Korla

TARIM BASIN

Kashi

SINKIANG

TAJIKISTAN

Shache

TAKLIMAKAN DESERT

AFGHANISTAN

Hotan

ALTUN SHAN

Golmud

KUNLUN SHAN

PAKISTAN

TIBET

Gar

Amdo

INDIA

PLATEAU

HIMALAYAS

NEPAL

Lhasa

Gyangzê

Mount Everest 8848 m

IN

BHUTAN

8 9 10 11 12 13 14

A

In the next
...China will generate enough electricity to make a cup of coffee for every person in the world.
minute...

B

0   100   200   300   400 mi
0   200   400   600 km

• Gulian

• Heihe

RUSSIA

• Nenjiang

• Hailar

• Qiqihar

• Sühbaatar

• Harbin

Hatgal • Darhan

• Choybalsan

• Tamsagbulag

• Jilin

• Erdenet

• Jargalan

• Changchun

• Chongjin

Ulaanbaatar ●

Hyesan • **NORTH**

SEA OF
JAPAN

MONGOLIA • Saynshand

INNER MONGOLIA

Fushun • **KOREA**

Shenyang •

Hamhung •

G O B I   D E S E R T

Anshan •

Wonsan •

andzadgad •

Jinzhou • Sinuiju •

Nampo • **Pyongyang**

SOUTH

• Hohhot

Sariwon •

KOREA

Baotou • • Zhangjiakou

Beijing ●

Dalian •

Seoul

Inchon •

• Taegu

• Yumen

• Tianjin

• Yantai

Sejong Busan •

• Yinchuan

Taiyuan •

• Zibo

Kwangju •

IAN SHAN

Qinghai
Hu

CHINA

Zhengzhou •

• Jinan

• Qingdao

YELLOW SEA

Huang

Xuzhou •

• Lianyungang

• Xining

• Luoyang

PACIFIC
OCEAN

• Lanzhou

• Xi'an

Nanjing •

BET

Hefei •

• Shanghai

Hangzhou •

• Ningbo

Wuhan •

Poyang
Hu

EAST
CHINA
SEA

Chang Jiang (Yangtze)

• Qamdo

Chengdu • • Nanchong

Dongting
Hu

Wenzhou •

Nu Jiang

Chongqing •

Changsha •

• Nanchang

• Fuzhou

Taipei

Hengyang •

TAIWAN

Guiyang •

Xiamen •

Mekong

• Kunming

Liuzhou •

Guangzhou • • Shenzen

• Hong Kong

BURMA

• Nanning

Macau •

Did You Know?

VIETNAM

• Zhanjiang

SOUTH
CHINA
SEA

More than 600 years ago, the Chinese began to bake pottery at temperatures high enough to produce porcelain. When this pottery came to Europe, it was called 'china'.

LAOS

Gulf of
Tonkin

• Haikou

Hainan

8 9 10 11 12 13 14

Central Asia and east Russia

Russia is the largest country in the world. However, eastern Russia contains large areas that are unpopulated. Vast areas north of the Arctic Circle suffer freezing conditions that make farming impossible. To the south, much is covered by forest or grassland. Towns are found only where there are natural resources, such as coal, oil, gas, iron and uranium. Kazakhstan is rapidly becoming wealthy due to selling oil, gas and metals to Europe and China, but Turkmenistan, Uzbekistan, Tajikistan and Kyrgyzstan remain underdeveloped.

Extreme Weather

In January 1926, Oymyakon [F10] recorded the lowest temperature for any permanently inhabited location on Earth at −71.2°C.

In the next minute...

...11,000 Russians will be playing chess, making it the nation's most popular sport.

SEVERNAYA ZEMLYA

ARCTIC OCEAN

KARA SEA

SIBERIA

RUSSIA

• Noril'sk

• Vorkuta

URAL MOUNTAINS

Yenisey

Tunguska

• Serov

Surgut • • Nizhnevartovsk

Ob

Angara

Lena

Krasnoyarsk

• Ust'Ilimsk

• Yekaterinburg

Tomsk •

• Kansk

• Kurgan

• Kemerovo

• Bratsk

YAB MO

• Chelyabinsk

• Novosibirsk

Semey •

• Omsk

Novokuznetsk • • Abakan

Usol'ye-Sibirskoye

Lake Baikal

• Kokshetau

Barnaul •

• Angarsk

Chita

Orenburg •

Pavlodar •

Irkutsk •

• Ulan-U

Ural

Astana

Oskemen •

MONGOLIA

• Aqtobe

Qaraghandy •

Lake Balkhash

• Atyrau

Zhezkazgan •

CHINA

Ustyurt Plateau

KAZAKHSTAN

Aral Sea

Qyzylorda • Taldyqorgan •

CASPIAN SEA

• Aktau

UZBEKISTAN

Almaty •

Search and Find

Tashkent • • **Bishkek**

KYRGYZSTAN

TURKMENISTAN

Turkmenabat •

Namangen

Balkanabat •

Dushanbe

Ashgabat

TAJIKISTAN

IRAN

AFGHANISTAN PAKISTAN

Kazakhstan	Tajikistan
● Astana H3	● Dushanbe J3
Kyrgyzstan	**Turkmenistan**
● Bishkek I4	● Ashgabat J3
Russian Federation	**Uzbekistan**
● Moscow (see page 45)	● Tashkent. I3

Lake Baikal [H7] is the oldest and deepest lake in the world at 1637 m in depth. It holds more than 20 percent of the world's fresh water.

Facts and Stats

- Turkmenistan's population of 5.75 million would fill 58 Olympic stadiums.
- The life expectancy in Russia is 71 years, compared to a world average of 69 years.
- The average income per person in Russia is £8172, compared to £609 in Tajikistan and a world average of £8196.

THE DISTANCE from Moscow in European Russia to the far east of Russia takes six days and four hours to travel by train at 62 km/h.

Did You Know?

Russia has 11 time zones. When it is 12 p.m. in Moscow, it is 3 p.m. in Novosibirsk [H5] and 7 p.m. in Vladivostok [I9].

LAPTEV SEA

EAST SIBERIAN SEA

CHUKCHI SEA

Lena

VERKHOYANSK MOUNTAINS

CHERSKIY MOUNTAINS

Kolyma

Yakutsk

Oymyakon

BERING SEA

Magadan

SEA OF OKHOTSK

| 0 | 250 | 500 | 750 | 1000 mi |
| 0 | 400 | 800 | 1200 | 1600 km |

V Y Y I N S

Amur

Petropavlovsk-Kamchatskiy

VLADIVOSTOK [I9] is home to the Russian navy's Pacific fleet. Until 1991, foreigners were not allowed into the city in case they were spies.

CHINA

Blagoveshchensk

Komsomol'sk-na-Amure

Khabarovsk

PACIFIC OCEAN

Yuzhno-Sakhalinsk

SIKHOTE-ALIN MOUNTAINS

Vladivostok

NORTH KOREA

The Aral Sea [I3] has shrunk by 90 percent since 1960. The remaining water has become very salty, killing off so many fish that the commercial fishing industry stopped and many boats have been abandoned.

Oceania

PACIFIC
OCEAN

MARSHALL
ISLANDS

PALAU

MICRONESIA

NAURU

PAPUA
NEW GUINEA

SOLOMON
ISLANDS

TUVALU

KIRIBATI

SAMOA

COOK ISLANDS

VANUATU

FIJI

TONGA NIUE

INDIAN
OCEAN

PACIFIC
OCEAN

AUSTRALIA

NEW
ZEALAND

SOUTHERN OCEAN

COUNTRY FACTFILE

Country	Life expectancy	Population to nearest thousand	Population growth %	Population as urban %	Area km²	Population density per km²	Capital city	Currency	Languages
Australia	82	24,599,000	1	90	7,702,315	3.2	Canberra	Australian Dollar	English
Cook Islands*	76	13,700	−2.7	75	237	57.8	Avarua	New Zealand Dollar	Cook Island Maori, English
Fiji	73	885,000	0.6	56	18,272	48.4	Suva	Fijian Dollar	English, Fijian
Kiribati	67	116,000	1.1	54	811	143	Bairiki	Australian Dollar	I-Kiribati, English
Marshall Islands	73	53,000	0	77	181	292.8	Majuro	US Dollar	Marshallese, English
Micronesia	73	106,000	0	26	701	151.2	Palikir	US Dollar	English, Chuukese, Pohnpeain
Nauru	67	11,000	0.5	N/A	21	523.8	Yaren	Australian Dollar	Nauruan
New Zealand	81	4,693,000	0.8	87	265,910	17.6	Wellington	New Zealand Dollar	English, Maori
Niue*	75	1400	−0.03	45	259	5.4	Alofi	New Zealand Dollar	Niuean, English
Palau	73	18,000	0	87	458	38.6	Ngerulmud-Melekeok	US Dollar	Palauan, English
Papua New Guinea	67	8,250,000	1.7	17	462,840	17.8	Port Moresby	Kina	Tok Pisin (Pidgin English), English
Samoa	74	192,000	0.6	34	2831	67.8	Apia	Tala	Samoan
Solomon Islands	76	653,000	1.9	24	28,370	23	Honiara	Solmon Islands Dollar	Melanesian languages
Tonga	76	101,000	−0.1	43	748	133.7	Nuku'alofa	Pa'anga	Tongan
Tuvalu	67	11,000	0.9	62	24	458.3	Vaiaku (Funafuti)	Australian Dollar	Mela
Vanuatu	74	272,000	1.9	26	12,190	22.3	Port-Vila	Vatu	Bislama, English, French

* Both the Cook Islands and Niue are self-governing states, but in free association with New Zealand, which is responsible for the aspects of foreign relations and defence that these countries agree to.

Australia

Much of Australia's inland is desert, known as the outback. Most people live in the eastern fertile land between Adelaide and Brisbane, and the capital, Canberra, is in the mountains of the Great Dividing Range. Many lakes in Australia vary in extent and some dry out in drought. Aboriginal people have lived in Australia for more than 40,000 years. In 1787, British settlers began to arrive and immigration has continued ever since. Aboriginals now make up just 2 percent of the population. Rich in gold, iron ore and coal, Australia is one of the wealthiest nations in the world.

Extreme Weather

To fight the effects of long periods of drought, Toowoomba [F13] may use recycled sewage in the water supply.

Did You Know?

The Great Barrier Reef [D12] stretches for more than 2000 km off the coast of Queensland.

SYDNEY [H12] is the largest city and has two of the most famous sights in the world – the Opera House and Sydney Harbour Bridge.

THE DISTANCE from the east coast to the west coast is 3000 km – the same as from London to Boston, USA.

Facts and Stats

- Australia's area of 7.7 million km² is 75 times the area of Iceland.
- The Murray–Darling [H11] is the longest river. At 3750 km, it is more than half the length of the Nile river.
- Mount Kosciuszko [H11] is the highest mountain at 2229 m in height – seven times higher than the Eiffel Tower.

At almost 50 m in width **Sydney Harbour Bridge** [H12] is one of the widest bridges in the world. It is 503 m in length, and has two railway tracks, eight lanes for cars, a bicycle path and a pedestrian path. About 160,000 vehicles cross the bridge each day.

Map labels

INDIAN OCEAN

Mel Isl

Bathurst Island

Darwin

Joseph Bonaparte Gulf

Drysdale

Wyndham

KIMBERLEY PLATEAU

Broome

Derby

Fitzroy

Halls Creek

Port Hedland

GREAT SANDY DESERT

Dampier

De Grey

Onslow

Exmouth

Ashburton

WESTERN AUSTRALIA

Ulu (Aye Roc

Carnarvon

GIBSON DESERT

Denham

Murchison

Meekatharra

Laverton

Geraldton

GREAT VICTORIA DESERT

Kalgoorlie

Perth

Freemantle

Mandurah

Balladonia

Norseman

Great Austra

Bunbury

Wagin

Augusta

Esperance

Albany

SOUTHERN OCEAN

AUSTRALIA • OCEANIA

Kangaroos can reach speeds of up to 50 km/h. They can be a danger on the roads, causing damage to vehicles in accidents as they weigh up to 90 kg. Therefore 'kangaroo crossing' signs are found throughout Australia.

A
B
C

HEM LAND
Groote Eylandt
Gulf of Carpentaria
Roper
erine

Cape York Peninsula

Wellesley Islands

Mitchell

• Cooktown

• Port Doulgas
Cairns •
Atherton • Innisfail

• Normanton
Burketown •
Flinders

PACIFIC OCEAN

NAMI SERT

• Tennant Creek

• Mount Isa
Norman
Georgina

GREAT BARRIER REEF

• Townsville
Bowen •

• Mackay

ERN TERRITORY

QUEENSLAND

D

• Alice Springs

NNELL RANGES

AUSTRALIA

Diamantina
Thomson
Barcoo

• Rockhampton
• Gladstone

GREAT DIVIDING RANGE

• Charleville

Warrego

Bundaberg
Fraser Island

E

Marla •

oober Pedy •

OUTH AUSTRALIA   • Marree

Tarcoola •

Ceduna •

• Bourke

NEW SOUTH WALES

Toowoomba •
• Sunshine Coast
• Brisbane
• Gold Coast

• Grafton
• Coffs Harbour
• Port Macquarie

F

Tamworth •

Port Augusta •
Whyalla •   • Port Pirie

Darling

Dubbo •

• Newcastle
• Gosford
• Sydney
• Wollongong

G

ht

Port Lincoln •   • Adelaide •

Mildura •

Murray

Wagga Wagga •

GREAT DIVIDING RANGE

Kangaroo Island

VICTORIA

Mount Kosciuszko 2229 m

Canberra
AUSTRALIAN CAPITAL TERRITORY

H

Bendigo •

Mount Gambier •

Ballarat •
Geelong •
• Melbourne
Sale •

TASMAN SEA

King Island
Bass Strait
Flinders Island
Cape Barren Island

I

Burnie • Devonport •
• Launceston

Queenstown •

TASMANIA

South East Cape

• Hobart

In the next
...six kangaroos will be born in Australia. There are twice as many kangaroos than humans.
minute...

J

100   200   300   400   500 mi

200   400   600   800 km

New Zealand and the Pacific Islands

New Zealand consists of two main islands and has a population of 4.7 million. The country generates a wealthy economy, mainly by selling its farm produce worldwide. English is the national language due to the many immigrants who started commercial farms and industries. The area of the Pacific Ocean east of Australia contains thousands of tropical islands including the Solomon Islands, Fiji, Vanuatu, Samoa, Kiribati, Tonga, Micronesia, Palau, the Marshall Islands, Papua New Guinea, Nauru and Tuvalu. Many people are leaving the Pacific Islands for education and work in Australia, New Zealand and the USA.

Bora-Bora is a small island in French Polynesia [I14] with a population of only 8000 people. The biggest industry is tourism as people are attracted to the stunning clear waters and tranquil atmosphere. Resorts with bungalows on stilts are a common feature.

In the next minute...
...New Zealand's wine growers will make more than 230 bottles of wine for export.

THE DISTANCE from the top to the bottom of the Nevis Highwire, New Zealand's highest bungee jump, is 135 m.

OTAGO PENINSULA [I7] is home to albatrosses, penguins, seals, whales and dolphins.

Facts and Stats

• The life expectancy of people in New Zealand is 81 years, compared to a world average of 69 years.

• There are 31 doctors per 10,000 people compared to a world average of 15 doctors.

• Aoraki/Mount Cook [H7] is the highest mountain at 3724 m – nearly 12 times higher than the Eiffel Tower.

The Maori were the first settlers in New Zealand, as they sailed from Polynesia 1000 years ago. Maori tikis are large carvings that are believed to protect sacred sites against evil.

TASMAN SEA

Cape Foulwind
Westport

Greymouth

Sou

Aoraki/Mount Cook 3724 m

SOUTHERN ALPS

Timaru
Waitaki

Oam

Otago Peninsu

Clutha

Dunedin

Cape Providence

Foveaux Strait

Invercargill

Codfish Island

Ruapuke Island

Stewart Island

North Cape

Whangarei

Great Barrier Island

Hauraki Gulf

Auckland
Manukau

Waikato

Bay of Plenty

Hamilton
Tauranga

East Cape

Rotorua

North Island

Gisborne

Lake Taupo

Poverty Bay

Mount Ruapehu 2797 m

New Plymouth

Wanganui

Cape Egmont

Hawke Bay

Napier
Hastings

NEW ZEALAND

Wanganui

Cape Farewell

Palmerston North

Cook Strait

Lower Hutt
Wellington

Nelson
Blenheim

Cape Palliser

...and

Christchurch

...nterbury Bight

SOUTH PACIFIC OCEAN

> Rotorua [C10] is well-known for geothermal activity including geysers and mud pools. Each day, soap is put into the opening of **Lady Knox Geyser** to make it erupt. The jets of water can reach up to 20 m in height.

Search and Find

Cook Islands	I13	Palau	H10
Fiji	I12	Papua New Guinea	
Kiribati	H12		I11
Marshall Islands		Samoa	I13
	H12	Solomon Islands	
Micronesia	H12		I12
Nauru	H12	Tonga	I13
New Zealand		Tuvalu	I12
● Wellington	F9	Vanuatu	I12
Niue	I13		

Extreme Weather

The mountains of South Island have hurricane winds of more than 250 km/h.

0   50   100   150 mi
0   100   200 km

PACIFIC OCEAN

NORTHERN MARIANA ISLANDS (US)

MARSHALL ISLANDS

GUAM (US)

PALAU

MICRONESIA

NAURU

0   500   1000 mi
0   800   1600 km

PAPUA NEW GUINEA

SOLOMON ISLANDS

TUVALU

KIRIBATI

TOKELAU (NEW ZEALAND)

WALLIS AND FUTUNA (FRANCE)

AMERICAN SAMOA (US)

SAMOA

CORAL SEA ISLANDS TERRITORY (AUSTRALIA)

VANUATU

COOK ISLANDS

TONGA

NEW CALEDONIA (FRANCE)

FIJI

NIUE

FRENCH POLYNESIA (FRANCE)

Did You Know?

The sea level is rising due to global warming. Two South Pacific islands in Kiribati, Tebua Tarawa and Abanuea, have already disappeared.

Countries of the world

Gazetteer

The gazetteer helps you to find towns and features on the maps. For example, **New York City** *Town* New York, USA 21 F12 shows that New York City is a town in the state of New York, USA. The town is on page 21 and can be found in square F12 by using the grid, or graticule. The letters run on the left and right, and the numbers run along the top and bottom. Trace where F and 21 meet to find New York City.

KEY: DRC – Democratic Republic of the Congo, UAE – United Arab Emirates, CAR – Central African Republic, RS – Research station

Aachen *Town* Germany 50 F6
Aalst *Town* Belgium 50 E5
Abadan *Town* Iran 75 D8
Abakan *Town* Russia 86 H5
Abéché *Town* Chad 65 G13
Aberdeen *Town* Scotland, UK 41 D9
Aberdeen *Town* S Dakota, USA 25 F13
Aberystwyth *Town* Wales, UK 41 H8
Abha *Town* Saudi Arabia 74 H6
Abidjan *Capital* Côte d'Ivoire 64 I6
Abilene *Town* Texas, USA 27 G12
Abkhazia *State* Georgia 58 I7
Abu Dhabi *Capital* UAE 75 F10
Abuja *Capital* Nigeria 65 H10
Abu Kamal *Town* Syria 73 G12
Acapulco *Town* Mexico 31 I9
Accra *Capital* Ghana 64 I7
Aconcagua, Cerro *Mountain* Argentina 36 G7
Adana *Town* Turkey 73 E9
Ad-Dammam *Town* Saudi Arabia 75 E8
Addis Ababa *Capital* Ethiopia 67 E9
Adelaide *Town* Australia 91 H9
Aden, Gulf of 67 C12, 74 J7
Aden *Town* Yemen 74 J7
Adirondack Mountains USA 21 E11
Adiyaman *Town* Turkey 73 E11
Adrar *Town* Algeria 62 F4
Adriatic Sea 49 E8
Afghanistan *Country* 76
Agadir *Town* Morocco 62 E2
Agen *Town* France 46 G7
Agra *Town* India 77 D9
Agrigento *Town* Sicily, Italy 48 H6
Aguascalientes *Town* Mexico 31 G8
Ahaggar *Mountain range* Algeria 62 G6
Ahmadabad *Town* India 76 E7
Ahvaz *Town* Iran 75 D8
Aïr Mountains Niger 65 F10
Aix-en-Provence *Town* France 47 H10
Aizu *Town* Japan 83 F10
Ajaccio *Town* France 47 J12
Akita *Town* Japan 83 D10
Akron *Town* Ohio, USA 21 G8
Aktau *Town* Kazakhstan 86 I2
Alabama *River* Alabama, USA 23 F8
Alabama *State* USA 23
Åland Island Finland 43 G9
Alaska, Gulf of 25 C11, 28 F4

Alaska *State* USA 25
Albacete *Town* Spain 45 F10
Alba Iulia *Town* Romania 55 E9
Albania *Country* 49
Albany *River* Ontario, Canada 29 H10
Albany *State capital* New York, USA 21 E12
Albany *Town* Australia 90 H5
Albany *Town* Georgia, USA 23 F9
Albert, Lake DRC/Uganda 66 F7
Alberta *Province* Canada 28
Albuquerque *Town* New Mexico, USA 27 F9
Alcoy *Town* Spain 45 G11
Aleppo *Town* Syria 73 F10
Alessandria *Town* Italy 48 C5
Aleutian Islands Alaska, USA 25 C9
Alexandria *Town* Egypt 63 E12
Alexandria *Town* Louisiana, USA 22 G5
Alexandroúpolis *Town* Greece 49 F13
Algeciras *Town* Spain 44 I7
Algeria *Country* 62
Algiers *Capital* Algeria 62 C6
Al Hasakah *Town* Syria 73 F12
Al-Hudaydah *Town* Yemen 74 I6
Al-Hufuf *Town* Saudi Arabia 75 F8
Alicante *Town* Spain 45 G11
Alice Springs *Town* Australia 91 E8
Al Jawf *Town* Saudi Arabia 74 D5
Al-Karak *Town* Jordan 73 I9
Alkmaar *Town* Netherlands 50 C6
Allahabad *Town* India 77 E9
Allegheny *River* Pennsylvania, USA 21 G9
Allentown *Town* Pennsylvania, USA 21 G11
Almaty *Town* Kazakhstan 86 I4
Almería *Town* Spain 45 H9
Al Mukalla *Town* Yemen 75 I8
Alps *Mountain range* France/Italy/ Switzerland 47 G10
Al Qamishli *Town* Syria 73 E12
Al Qunaytirah *Town* Syria 73 H9
Altai Mountains Mongolia/Russia 84 D7
Altamaha *River* Georgia, USA 23 F10
Altamira *Town* Brazil 37 B9
Altun Shan *Mountain range* China 84 F6
Amarillo *Town* Texas, USA 27 F11

Amazon *River* Brazil 36 B7, 37 B9
Amazon Basin Brazil 36 B7
Ambato *Town* Ecuador 36 B5
Ambon *Town* Indonesia 81 G8
American Samoa *Dep. territory* USA 93 I13
Amiens *Town* France 47 B9
Amman *Capital* Jordan 73 H10
Amritsar *Town* India 77 C8
Amsterdam *Capital* Netherlands 50 D6
Amu Dar'ya *River* Uzbekistan 86 J3
Amundsen Gulf 17 D9
Amundsen-Scott (US) *RS* Antarctica 16 F4
Amundsen Sea 16 F1
Amur *River* China/Russia 87 H8
Anaheim *Town* California, USA 26 F5
Anápolis *Town* Brazil 37 D9
Anatolian Plateau Turkey 72 D7
Anchorage *Town* Alaska, USA 25 C11
Ancona *Town* Italy 48 D7
Andaman Islands India 77 H12
Andaman Sea 78 H2
Anderson *Town* Indiana, USA 20 H7
Andes *Mountain range* 36 F7
Andorra *Country* 45
Andorra la Vella *Capital* Andorra 45 C12
Andreanof Islands Alaska, USA 25 C9
Angarsk *Town* Russia 86 H6
Angeles *Town* Philippines 79 F10
Angers *Town* France 46 C7
Angola *Country* 68
Angoulême *Town* France 46 E7
Anguilla *Dep. territory* UK 35 D12
Ankara *Capital* Turkey 73 C8
Annaba *Town* Algeria 62 D7
Annapolis *State capital* Maryland, USA 21 H11
Ann Arbor *Town* Michigan, USA 20 F7
An Nasiriyah *Town* Iraq 74 D7
Anshan *Town* China 85 D12
Antakya *Town* Turkey 73 F10
Antalya *Town* Turkey 72 E7
Antananarivo *Capital* Madagascar 69 G12
Antarctica 16
Antarctic Peninsula Antarctica 16 E2

Antibes *Town* France 47 H11
Anticosti Island Quebec, Canada 29 H13
Antigua and Barbuda *Country* 35
Antofagasta *Town* Chile 36 E6
Antsiranana *Town* Madagascar 69 F13
Antwerp *Town* Belgium 50 E5
Aomori *Town* Japan 83 D10
Aoraki/Mount Cook New Zealand 92 G7
Aosta *Town* Italy 48 B4
Apeldoorn *Town* Netherlands 50 D7
Appalachian Mountains USA 21 H10, 23 C10
Appleton *Town* Wisconsin, USA 20 F5
Aqaba *Town* Jordan 73 J9
Aqtobe *Town* Russia 86 H2
Arabian Sea 75 F12, 76 E6
Aracaju *Town* Brazil 37 C11
Arad *Town* Romania 54 D7
Arafura Sea 81 H9
Araguaína *Town* Brazil 37 C10
Arakan Range *Mountain range* Burma (Myanmar) 78 F2
Aral Sea Kazakhstan/Uzbekistan 86 I3
Ararat, Mount Turkey 73 D14
Arbil *Town* Iraq 74 B7
Arctic Ocean 17, 28, 43, 59, 86
Arequipa *Town* Peru 36 D6
Arezzo *Town* Italy 48 D6
Argentina *Country* 36
Århus *Town* Denmark 42 I6
Arica *Town* Chile 36 D6
Arizona *State* USA 26
Arkansas *State* USA 22
Arkhangelísk *Town* Russia 59 D8
Arles *Town* France 47 H9
Arlington *Town* Texas, USA 27 G13
Armenia *Country* 59
Armenia *Town* Colombia 35 H8
Arnhem *Town* Netherlands 50 D6
Arnhem Land Australia 91 B8
Ar Raqqah *Town* Syria 73 F11
Arua *Town* Uganda 66 F7
Aruba *Dep. territory* Netherlands 35 E9
Aru Islands Indonesia 81 G9
Arusha *Town* Tanzania 67 H9
Asahikawa *Town* Japan 83 B10

Ashgabat *Capital* Turkmenistan 86 J3

Asmara *Capital* Eritrea 67 C9

Assad, Lake Syria 73 F11

Assen *Town* Netherlands 50 C7

As-Sulayyil *Town* Saudi Arabia 74 G7

Astana *Capital* Kazakhstan 86 H3

Astrakhan *Town* Russia 59 H8

Asunción *Capital* Paraguay 37 E8

Aswan *Town* Egypt 63 H13

Asyut *Town* Egypt 63 G13

Atacama Desert Chile 36 E7

Atbara *Town* Sudan 67 B8

Athens *Capital* Greece 49 H12

Atlanta *State capital* Georgia, USA 23 E9

Atlantic City *Town* New Jersey, USA 21 G12

Atlantic Ocean 21, 23, 29, 37, 40, 42, 43, 44, 62, 64

Atlas Mountains Morocco 62 E3

Atyrau *Town* Kazakhstan 86 I2

Auckland *Town* New Zealand 93 C9

Augsburg *Town* Germany 51 I9

Augusta *Town* Georgia, USA 23 E10

Augusta *State capital* Maine, USA 21 D13

Aurora *Town* Illinois, USA 20 G6

Austin *State capital* Texas, USA 27 H13

Australia *Country* 90

Australian Capital Territory *State* Australia 91

Austria *Country* 40

Auxerre *Town* France 47 D9

Aveiro *Town* Portugal 44 E5

Avignon *Town* France 47 G9

Ávila *Town* Spain 45 E8

Axel Heiberg Island Nunavut, Canada 29 C9

Ayacucho *Town* Peru 36 D6

Aydin *Town* Turkey 72 D6

Azerbaijan *Country* 75

Azov, Sea of 58 I7

Az-Zarqa *Town* Jordan 73 H10

Az-Zawiyah *Town* Libya 73 H10

Bacău *Town* Romania 55 D12

Bacolod *Town* Philippines 79 G11

Badajoz *Town* Spain 44 F6

Baden-Baden *Town* Germany 50 H7

Baffin Bay Canada 17 G9, 29 D10

Baffin Island Canada 17 G8, 29 E10

Baghdad *Capital* Iraq 74 C7

Bahamas *Country* 35

Bahawalpur *Town* Pakistan 77 C8

Bahía Blanca *Town* Argentina 37 G8

Bahrain *Country* 75

Baikal, Lake Russia 86 H7

Bakersfield *Town* California, USA 26 E5

Bakhtaran *Town* Iran 74 C7

Baku *Capital* Azerbaijan 75 A8

Balaton, Lake Hungary 54 D5

Balearic Islands Spain 45

Bali *Island* Indonesia 80 H5

Balikesir *Town* Turkey 72 C6

Balikpapan *Town* Indonesia 80 F5

Balkanabat *Town* Turkmenistan 86 J2

Balkan Mountains Bulgaria 55 H10

Balkhash, Lake Kazakhstan 86 I4

Ballarat *Town* Australia 91 I10

Baltic Sea 43 H9, 56 B6, 58 F5

Baltimore *Town* Maryland, USA 21 H11

Bamako *Capital* Mali 64 G5

Bambari *Town* CAR 68 B7

Bamberg *Town* Germany 51 G9

Bamenda *Town* Cameroon 68 B5

Bandar 'Abbas *Town* Iran 75 E10

Bandar Seri Begawan *Capital* Brunei 80 E5

Banda Sea 81 G8

Bandundu *Town* DRC 68 D7

Bandung *Town* Indonesia 80 H3

Bangalore *See Bengaluru*

Bangkok *Capital* Thailand 78 H4

Bangladesh *Country* 77

Bangor *Town* Maine, USA 21 C13

Bangui *Capital* CAR 68 B7

Baniyas *Town* Syria 73 F10

Banja Luka *Town* Bosnia and Herz. 49 C8

Banjarmasin *Town* Indonesia 80 G5

Banjul *Capital* Gambia 64 G3

Banská Bystrica *Town* Slovakia 57 I8

Baotou *Town* China 85 E10

Bar *Town* Montenegro 49 E9

Barbados *Country* 35

Barcelona *Town* Spain 45 D13

Barcelona *Town* Venezuela 35 F11

Barents Sea 17 G13, 58 B7

Bari *Town* Italy 49 F8

Barinas *Town* Venezuela 35 F9

Barnaul *Town* Russia 86 H5

Barquisimeto *Town* Venezuela 35 F9

Barrancabermeja *Town* Colombia 35 G8

Barranquilla *Town* Colombia 35 F8

Basel *Town* Switzerland 52 E3

Basra *Town* Iraq 75 D8

Bassein *Town* Burma (Myanmar) 78 G2

Basseterre *Capital* St. Kitts and Nevis 35 D12

Bass Strait Australia 91 I11

Batangas *Town* Philippines 79 F10

Batdâmbang *Town* Cambodia 78 G5

Batman *Town* Turkey 73 E12

Batna *Town* Algeria 62 D6

Baton Rouge *State capital* Louisiana, USA 22 G6

Bayamo *Town* Cuba 35 C8

Bayreuth *Town* Germany 51 G10

Beaufort Sea 17 C9, 28 D6

Beaumont *Town* Texas, USA 27 H14

Béchar *Town* Algeria 62 E4

Beersheba *Town* Israel 73 I9

Beijing *Capital* China 85 E11

Beira *Town* Mozambique 69 G10

Beirut *Capital* Lebanon 73 G9

Beja *Town* Portugal 44 G5

Belarus *Country* 58

Belém *Town* Brazil 37 B10

Belfast *Capital* Northern Ireland, UK 40 F7

Belgium *Country* 50

Belgrade *Capital* Serbia 49 C10

Belgrano II (Argentina) *RS* Antarctica 16 E3

Belize *Country* 34

Belize City *Town* Belize 34 C5

Bellingham *Town* Washington, USA 24 C4

Belmopan *Capital* Belize 34 C5

Belo Horizonte *Town* Brazil 37 E10

Bendigo *Town* Australia 91 H11

Benevento *Town* Italy 48 F7

Bengal, Bay of 77 F11

Bengaluru (Bangalore) *Town* India 77 H8

Benghazi *Town* Libya 63 E10

Benguela *Town* Angola 68 F6

Benidorm *Town* Spain 45 G11

Benin *Country* 65

Benin City *Town* Nigeria 65 I9

Ben Nevis *Mountain* Scotland, UK 41 D8

Benue *River* Nigeria 65 I10

Berbera *Town* Somalia 67 D11

Bergamo *Town* Italy 48 B5

Bergen *Town* Norway 42 F5

Bergerac *Town* France 46 F7

Bering Sea 25 B9, 87 G13

Berlin *Capital* Germany 51 D11

Bern *Capital* Switzerland 52 F3

Besançon *Town* France 47 E10

Bethlehem *Town* Israel 73 I9

Béziers *Town* France 47 H8

Bhavnagar *Town* India 76 E7

Bhopal *Town* India 77 E8

Bhutan *Country* 77

Bialystok *Town* Poland 57 D11

Biel *Town* Switzerland 52 F3

Bielefeld *Town* Germany 51 D8

Bielsko-Biala *Town* Poland 57 H8

Bighorn Mountains Wyoming, USA 25 G9

Bihac *Town* Bosnia and Herz. 49 C8

Bilauktaung Range Thailand 78 G3

Bilbao *Town* Spain 45 B9

Billings *Town* Montana, USA 25 F9

Biloxi *Town* Mississippi, USA 22 G7

Biratnagar *Town* Nepal 77 D11

Birmingham *Town* Alabama, USA 23 E8

Birmingham *Town* England, UK 41 H9

Biscay, Bay of 45 A9, 46 E5

Bishkek *Capital* Kyrgyzstan 86 I4

Bismarck *State capital* N Dakota, USA 25 F12

Bissau *Capital* Guinea-Bissau 64 G3

Bitola *Town* Macedonia 49 F11

Bizerte *Town* Tunisia 62 C7

Black Forest Germany 50 I7

Blackpool *Town* England, UK 41 F8

Black Sea 55 H14, 58 I6, 73 B11

Blagoevgrad *Town* Bulgaria 55 I9

Blagoveshchensk *Town* Russia 87 H8

Blantyre *Town* Malawi 69 G10

Blida *Town* Algeria 62 D6

Bloemfontein *Town* South Africa 69 I8

Bloomington *Town* Indiana, USA 20 I6

Bloomington *Town* Minnesota, USA 20 E3

Blue Nile *River* Ethiopia/Sudan 67 D8

Bo *Town* Sierra Leone 64 I4

Boa Vista *Town* Brazil 37 A8

Bobo Dioulasso *Town* Burkina Faso 64 H6

Bodrum *Town* Turkey 72 E5

Bogotá *Capital* Colombia 35 H8

Bohemian Forest Czech Republic/ Germany 51 H11, 56 H4

Boise *State capital* Idaho, USA 24 G5

Bolivia *Country* 36

Bologna *Town* Italy 48 C6

Bolzano *Town* Italy 48 B6

Bombay *See Mumbai*

Bonaire *Dep. territory* Netherlands 35 F10

Bonifacio, Strait of 47 J12

Bonn *Town* Germany 50 F7

Borås *Town* Sweden 42 H7

Bordeaux *Town* France 46 F6

Borgholm *Town* Sweden 43 I8

Borneo *Island* Indonesia 80 G4

Bornholm *Dep. territory* Denmark 42 J7

Bosnia and Herzegovina *Country* 49

Boston *State capital* Massachusetts, USA 21 E13
Botswana *Country* 69
Bouar *Town* CAR 68 B6
Boulder *Town* Colorado, USA 27 C10
Boulogne *Town* France 47 A9
Bourges *Town* France 47 D9
Bourke *Town* Australia 91 F11
Bournemouth *Town* England, UK 41 I9
Bozeman *Town* Montana, USA 25 F8
Brahmaputra *River* Asia 77 E12
Braila *Town* Romania 55 E12
Brandenburg *Town* Germany 51 D11
Brasília *Capital* Brazil 37 D10
Brasov *Town* Romania 55 E10
Bratislava *Capital* Slovakia 56 J7
Bratsk *Town* Russia 86 G6
Braunschweig *Town* Germany 51 D10
Brazil *Country* 37
Brazzaville *Capital* Republic of the Congo 68 D6
Breda *Town* Netherlands 50 D5
Bremen *Town* Germany 51 C9
Bremerhaven *Town* Germany 51 C8
Brescia *Town* Italy 48 B5
Brest *Town* France 46 B5
Bridgeport *Town* Connecticut, USA 21 F12
Bridgetown *Capital* Barbados 35 E12
Brig *Town* Switzerland 52 G3
Brighton *Town* England, UK 41 I10
Brindisi *Town* Italy 49 F9
Brisbane *Town* Australia 91 F13
Bristol *Town* England, UK 41 H9
British Columbia *Province* Canada 28
Brive *Town* France 47 F8
Brno *Town* Czech Republic 56 H6
Broome *Town* Australia 90 C5
Brownsville *Town* Texas, USA 27 J13
Bruges *Town* Belgium 50 E4
Brunei *Country* 80
Brussels *Capital* Belgium 50 E5
Bryansk *Town* Russia 58 G6
Bucaramanga *Town* Colombia 35 G8
Bucharest *Capital* Romania 55 F11
Budapest *Capital* Hungary 54 C6
Buenaventura *Town* Colombia 34 H7
Buenos Aires *Capital* Argentina 37 G8
Buffalo *Town* New York, USA 21 F9
Bug *River* Poland 57 D10
Bujumbura *Capital* Burundi 66 H7

Bukavu *Town* DRC 69 D9
Bulawayo *Town* Zimbabwe 69 G9
Bulgaria *Country* 55
Buraydah *Town* Saudi Arabia 74 E7
Burgas *Town* Bulgaria 55 H12
Burgos *Town* Spain 45 C8
Burketown *Town* Australia 91 C10
Burkina Faso *Country* 64
Burlington *Town* Vermont, USA 21 D12
Burma (Myanmar) *Country* 78
Burns *Town* Oregon, USA 24 G4
Burnsville *Town* Minnesota, USA 20 E3
Bursa *Town* Turkey 72 C6
Burundi *Country* 66
Butuan *Town* Philippines 79 G12
Bydgoszcz *Town* Poland 57 D8
Bytom *Town* Poland 57 G8

Cabanatuan *Town* Philippines 79 E10
Cáceres *Town* Spain 44 F6
Cádiz *Town* Spain 44 I7
Caen *Town* France 47 B8
Cagayan de Oro *Town* Philippines 79 G11
Cagliari *Town* Sardinia, Italy 48 G4
Cairns *Town* Australia 91 C11
Cairo *Capital* Egypt 63 F13
Calais *Town* France 47 A9
Calama *Town* Chile 36 E7
Calarasi *Town* Romania 55 F12
Calbayog *Town* Philippines 79 F11
Calcutta *See* Kolkata
Calgary *Town* Alberta, Canada 28 H7
Cali *Town* Colombia 34 H7
Calicut *See* Kozhikode
California, Gulf of 30 D5
California *State* USA 26
Callao *Town* Peru 36 D5
Caltanissetta *Town* Sicily, Italy 48 H7
Camagüey *Town* Cuba 35 C8
Cambodia *Country* 78
Cambrian Mountains Wales, UK 41 H8
Cambridge *Town* England, UK 41 H10
Cameroon *Country* 68
Campeche, Bay of Mexico 31 H11
Campina Grande *Town* Brazil 37 C12
Campinas *Town* Brazil 37 E10
Campobasso *Town* Italy 48 E7
Campo Grande *Town* Brazil 37 E9
Canada *Country* 28
Canary Islands Spain 64 B4
Canberra *Capital* Australia 91 H12
Cancún *Town* Mexico 31 G14
Cannes *Town* France 47 H11

Cantabrian Mountains Spain 44 B7
Can Tho *Town* Vietnam 78 H5
Canton *Town* Ohio, USA 21 G9
Cape Horn Chile 37 J8
Cape Town *Capital* South Africa 68 J7
Cape Verde (Cabo Verde) Country 64
Cap-Haïtien *Town* Haiti 35 C9
Caracas *Capital* Venezuela 35 F10
Cárdenas *Town* Cuba 34 B7
Cardiff *Capital* Wales, UK 41 H8
Caribbean Sea 35 E9
Carlisle *Town* England, UK 41 F9
Carlsbad *Town* New Mexico, USA 27 G10
Carnarvon *Town* Australia 90 E3
Carpathian Mountains Poland/ Romania/Slovakia 55 D11
Carrara *Town* Italy 48 C5
Carson City *State capital* Nevada, USA 26 C5
Cartagena *Town* Colombia 35 F8
Cartagena *Town* Spain 45 H11
Casablanca *Town* Morocco 62 D3
Casey (Australia) *RS* Antarctica 16 G7
Casper *Town* Wyoming, USA 25 H9
Caspian Sea 59 I9, 75 B8, 86 I2
Cassai (Kasai) *River* Angola/DRC 68 E7
Castellón de la Plana *Town* Spain 45 E11
Castries *Capital* St. Lucia 35 E12
Catania *Town* Sicily, Italy 48 H7
Catanzaro *Town* Italy 49 G8
Cayman Islands *Dep. territory* UK 34 C7
Cebu *Town* Philippines 79 G11
Cedar City *Town* Utah, USA 26 D7
Cedar Rapids *Town* Iowa, USA 20 G4
Celebes Sea 79 H11, 80 E6
Celje *Town* Slovenia 49 B8
Central African Republic (CAR) *Country* 68
Ceské Budejovice *Town* Czech Republic 56 H5
Ceuta *Town* Spain 44 J7, 62 D3
Chad, Lake Chad 65 G12
Chad *Country* 65
Châlons-en-Champagne *Town* France 47 C10
Chalon-sur-Saône *Town* France 47 E10
Chambéry *Town* France 47 F10
Champaign *Town* Illinois, USA 20 H6
Chandigarh *Town* India 77 C8

Chang Cheng (China) *RS* Antarctica 16 D1
Changchun *Town* China 85 C12
Chang Jiang (Yangtze) *River* China 85 G10
Changsha *Town* China 85 G11
Channel Islands *Dep. territory* UK 41 J9
Charleroi *Town* Belgium 50 F5
Charleston *State capital* West Virginia, USA 21 I9
Charleston *Town* S Carolina, USA 23 E11
Charleville Mézières *Town* France 47 B10
Charlotte *Town* N Carolina, USA 23 C10
Charlottetown *Province capital* Prince Edward Islands, Canada 29 I13
Châteauroux *Town* France 47 D8
Chattanooga *Town* Tennessee, USA 23 D8
Cheb *Town* Czech Republic 56 G3
Chelm *Town* Poland 57 F11
Chelyabinsk *Town* Russia 86 G3
Chemnitz *Town* Germany 51 F11
Chengdu *Town* China 85 G9
Chennai (Madras) *Town* India 77 H9
Chester *Town* England, UK 41 G9
Chetumal *Town* Mexico 31 H13
Cheyenne *State capital* Wyoming, USA 25 I10
Chiang Mai *Town* Thailand 78 F3
Chiba *Town* Japan 83 G10
Chicago *Town* Illinois, USA 20 G6
Chichén Itzá Mexico 31 G13
Chiclayo *Town* Peru 36 C5
Chicoutimi *Town* Quebec, Canada 29 I12
Chihuahua *Town* Mexico 30 D7
Chile *Country* 36
Chillan *Town* Chile 36 G6
Chilpancingo *Town* Mexico 31 I9
Chimbote *Town* Peru 36 C5
Chimoio *Town* Mozambique 69 G10
China *Country* 85
Chinandega *Town* Nicaragua 34 E5
Chioggia *Town* Italy 48 C6
Chipata *Town* Zambia 69 F9
Chirripó Grande, Cerro *Mountain* Costa Rica 34 F5
Chisinau *Capital* Moldova 58 H6
Chita *Town* Russia 86 H7
Chitose *Town* Japan 83 B10
Chittagong *Town* Bangladesh 77 F12
Chitungwiza *Town* Zimbabwe 69 G9
Chon Buri *Town* Thailand 78 H4
Chongjin *Town* North Korea 85 C13

Chongqing *Town* China 85 H10
Choybalsan *Town* Mongolia 85 C10
Christchurch *Town* New Zealand 93 G8
Chukchi Sea 17 C11, 25 A10, 87 E13
Churchill *Town* Manitoba, Canada 29 G9
Cienfuegos *Town* Cuba 34 B7
Cincinnati *Town* Ohio, USA 21 H7
Ciudad Bolívar *Town* Venezuela 35 G11
Ciudad de la Paz *Capital* Equatorial Guinea 68 C5
Ciudad del Este *Town* Paraguay 37 F9
Ciudad Guayana *Town* Venezuela 35 G11
Ciudad Juárez *Town* Mexico 30 C7
Ciudad Madero *Town* Mexico 31 F10
Ciudad Obregón *Town* Mexico 30 D6
Ciudad Real *Town* Spain 45 F8
Ciudid Victoria *Town* Mexico 31 F9
Civitavecchia *Town* Italy 48 E6
Clarksville *Town* Tennessee, USA 22 C7
Clearwater *Town* Florida, USA 23 H10
Clermont-Ferrand *Town* France 47 E9
Cleveland *Town* Ohio, USA 21 G8
Clovis *Town* New Mexico, USA 27 F11
Cluj-Napoca *Town* Romania 55 D9
Coast Ranges California/Oregon, USA 24 F2, 26 B4
Coatzacoalcos *Town* Mexico 31 H11
Cochin *See Kochi*
Cognac *Town* France 46 E7
Coimbatore *Town* India 77 I8
Coimbra *Town* Portugal 44 E5
Colchester *Town* England, UK 41 H10
Colima *Town* Mexico 31 H8
Cologne *Town* Germany 50 E7
Colombia *Country* 35
Colombo *Capital* Sri Lanka 77 J9
Colón *Town* Panama 34 F7
Colorado *River* Mexico/USA 27 D8
Colorado *State* USA 27
Colorado Springs *Town* Colorado, USA 27 D10
Columbia *State capital* S Carolina, USA 23 D10
Columbia *Town* Missouri, USA 22 B5
Columbus *State capital* Ohio, USA 21 H8
Columbus *Town* Georgia, USA 23 F9
Como *Town* Italy 48 B5

Comodoro Rivadavia *Town* Argentina 36 H7
Comoros *Country* 69
Conakry *Capital* Guinea 64 H4
Concepción *Town* Chile 36 G6
Concord *State capital* New Hampshire, USA 21 E13
Congo *River* Western Central Africa 68 C7, 69 D8
Congo, Democratic Republic of the (DRC) *Country* 68
Congo, Republic of the *Country* 68
Connecticut *State* USA 21
Constanta *Town* Romania 55 F13
Constantine *Town* Algeria 62 D6
Coober Pedy *Town* Australia 91 F8
Cook Islands *Dep. territory* New Zealand 93 I13
Cook Strait New Zealand 93 F9
Cooktown *Town* Australia 91 B11
Copenhagen *Capital* Denmark 42 I7
Coquimbo *Town* Chile 36 F6
Coral Sea Islands Territory *Dep. territory* Australia 93 I11
Cordillera Central *Mountain range* Colombia/Panama 34 F6, 35 H8
Córdoba *Town* Argentina 36 F7
Córdoba *Town* Spain 45 G8
Corfu *Island* Greece 49 G10
Cork *Town* Republic of Ireland 40 H6
Corpus Christi *Town* Texas, USA 27 I13
Corrientes *Town* Argentina 37 F8
Corsica *Island* France 47 I12
Çorum *Town* Turkey 73 C9
Corvallis *Town* Oregon, USA 24 F3
Cosenza *Town* Italy 49 G8
Costa Rica *Country* 34
Côte d'Ivoire *Country* 64
Cotonou *Capital* Benin 65 I8
Cottbus *Town* Germany 51 E12
Council Bluffs *Town* Iowa, USA 20 H2
Coventry *Town* England, UK 41 H9
Craiova *Town* Romania 55 G9
Cremona *Town* Italy 48 C5
Crete, Sea of Greece 49 I12
Crete *Island* Greece 49 J12
Crimea Ukraine 58 I7
Croatia *Country* 49
Crotone *Town* Italy 49 G8
Cuba *Country* 34
Cúcuta *Town* Colombia 35 G8
Cuernavaca *Town* Mexico 31 H9
Cuito *River* Angola 68 G7
Culiacán *Town* Mexico 30 E6
Cumaná *Town* Venezuela 35 F11
Curaçao *Dep. territory* Netherlands 35 E10

Curitiba *Town* Brazil 37 F9
Cusco *Town* Peru 36 D6
Cuttack *Town* India 77 F10
Cuxhaven *Town* Germany 51 B9
Cyprus *Country* 73
Czech Republic Country 56
Czestochowa *Town* Poland 57 F8

Dakar *Capital* Senegal 64 F3
Dalandzadgad *Town* Mongolia 85 D8
Da Lat *Town* Vietnam 78 H6
Dalian *Town* China 85 E12
Dallas *Town* Texas, USA 27 G13
Damascus *Capital* Syria 73 H10
Dampier *Town* Australia 90 D4
Da Nang *Town* Vietnam 78 F6
Danube *River* Europe 51 I8, 40 E12, 54 D5, 55 G10, 57 J8
Danzig, Gulf of 57 B8
Dar'a *Town* Syria 73 H10
Dar es Salaam *Capital* Tanzania 67 I9
Darfur Sudan 66 D6
Darhan *Town* Mongolia 85 C9
Darien, Gulf of 34 F7
Darling *River* Australia 91 G10
Darmstadt *Town* Germany 51 G8
Darnah *Town* Libya 63 E10
Darwin *Town* Australia 90 B7
Davao *Town* Philippines 79 H12
Davenport *Town* Iowa, USA 20 G5
David *Town* Panama 34 F6
Dayr az Zawr *Town* Syria 73 F12
Dayton *Town* Ohio, USA 21 H8
Daytona Beach *Town* Florida, USA 23 G11
Dead Sea Jordan 73 I9
Death Valley California, USA 26 E6
Debrecen *Town* Hungary 55 C8
Decatur *Town* Illinois, USA 20 H6
Delaware *State* USA 21
Delft *Town* Netherlands 50 D5
Delhi *Town* India 77 D9
Del Rio *Town* Texas, USA 27 I11
Democratic Republic of the Congo (DRC) *See* Congo, Republic of the
Denali Alaska, USA 25 B11
Den Helder *Town* Netherlands 50 C6
Denizli *Town* Turkey 72 D6
Denmark *Country* 42
Denver *State capital* Colorado, USA 27 C10
Derby *Town* England, UK 41 G9
Des Moines *State capital* Iowa, USA 20 G3
Dessau *Town* Germany 51 E11
Detroit *Town* Michigan, USA 20 F8

Devon Island Nunavut, Canada 29 D9
Dhaka *Capital* Bangladesh 77 E11
Dhanbad *Town* India 77 E10
Dieppe *Town* France 47 B8
Dijon *Town* France 47 D10
Dili *Capital* East Timor (Timor-Leste) 80 H7
Dimitrovgrad *Town* Bulgaria 55 I11
Dire Dawa *Town* Ethiopia 67 D10
Diyarbakir *Town* Turkey 73 E12
Djibouti *Capital* Djibouti 67 D11
Djibouti *Country* 67
Dnieper *River* Ukraine 58 H6
Dniester *River* Ukraine 58 H6
Dnipropetrovsik *Town* Ukraine 58 H7
Dobrich *Town* Bulgaria 55 G13
Dodge City *Town* Kansas, USA 27 E12
Dodoma *Capital* Tanzania 67 I9
Doha *Capital* Qatar 75 F9
Dominica *Country* 35
Dominican Republic *Country* 35
Don *River* Russia 59 H8
Donetsk *Town* Ukraine 58 H7
Dordogne *River* France 46 F7
Dordrecht *Town* Netherlands 50 D5
Dortmund *Town* Germany 50 E7
Douala *Town* Cameroon 68 B5
Douglas *Town* Arizona, USA 27 G8
Dover *State capital* Delaware, USA 21 G12
Dover *Town* England, UK 41 I11
Drakensberg Mountains South Africa 69 J8
Drama *Town* Greece 49 F12
Drammen *Town* Norway 42 G6
Dresden *Town* Germany 51 F12
Drobeta-Turnu Severin *Town* Romania 55 F8
Drogheda *Town* Republic of Ireland 40 F7
Dubai *Town* UAE 75 F10
Dublin *Capital* Republic of Ireland 40 G7
Dubrovnik *Town* Croatia 49 E9
Duisburg *Town* Germany 50 E7
Duluth *Town* Minnesota, USA 20 D3
Dumont d'Urville (France) *RS* Antarctica 16 H5
Dunaujvaros *Town* Hungary 54 D6
Dundee *Town* Scotland, UK 41 D9
Dunedin *Town* New Zealand 92 I7
Dunkerque *Town* France 47 A9
Durango *Town* Colorado, USA 27 E9
Durango *Town* Mexico 30 F7
Durban *Town* South Africa 69 I9
Durham *Town* N Carolina, USA 23 C11
Durrës *Town* Albania 49 F9

Dushanbe *Capital* Tajikistan 86 J3
Düsseldorf *Town* Germany 50 E7

East Cape New Zealand 93 C11
East China Sea Pacific Ocean
   85 G13
Eastern Ghats *Mountain range* India
   77 G9
East London *Town* South Africa
   69 J8
East Siberian Sea Arctic Ocean
   17 C13, 87 E11
East Timor (Timor-Leste) *Country*
   81
Eau Claire *Town* Wisconsin, USA
   20 E4
Ebetsu *Town* Japan 83 B10
Ebro *River* Spain 45 C10
Ecuador *Country* 36
Edinburgh *Capital* Scotland, UK
   41 E8
Edirne *Town* Turkey 72 B5
Edmonton *Province capital* Alberta,
   Canada 28 H7
Edward, Lake DRC/Uganda 66 G7,
   69 C9
Edwards Plateau Texas, USA 27 H12
Egypt *Country* 63
Eindhoven *Town* Netherlands 50 E6
El Aaiún *Capital* Western Sahara
   64 C5
Elat *Town* Israel 73 J9
Elazig *Town* Turkey 73 D11
Elbasan *Town* Albania 49 F10
Elbe *River* Czech Republic/Germany
   51 E11, 56 G6
Elblag *Town* Poland 57 B8
Elbrus, Mount Russia 59 I8
Elche *Town* Spain 45 G11
El Fasher *Town* Sudan 66 C6
Elgin *Town* Illinois, USA 20 G6
Ellesmere Island Canada 17 F10,
   29 C9
Ellsworth Land Antarctica 16 F2
El Minya *Town* Egypt 63 F13
El Obeid *Town* Sudan 66 D7
El Paso *Town* Texas, USA 27 G9
El Progreso *Town* Honduras 34 D5
El Salvador *Country* 34
Emmen *Town* Netherlands 50 C7
Empty Quarter *Desert* Saudi Arabia
   75 H9
Ende *Town* Indonesia 80 H6
England *Country* UK 41
English Channel France/UK 41 I9,
   46 A6
Enid *Town* Oklahoma, USA 27 E13
Enschede *Town* Netherlands 50 D7
Ensenada *Town* Mexico 30 B4
Enugu *Town* Nigeria 65 I10

Equatorial Guinea *Country* 68
Erdenet *Town* Mongolia 85 C9
Erfurt *Town* Germany 51 F10
Erie, Lake USA 21 F9
Erie *Town* Pennsylvania, USA 21 F9
Eritrea *Country* 67
Erzincan *Town* Turkey 73 D11
Erzurum *Town* Turkey 73 C13
Esbjerg *Town* Denmark 42 I5
Escuintla *Town* Guatemala 34 D4
Esfahan *Town* Iran 75 C9
Eskisehir *Town* Turkey 72 C7
Esmeraldas *Town* Ecuador 36 A5
Esperance *Town* Australia 90 H6
Esperanza (Argentina) *RS* Antarctica
   16 D1
Espoo *Town* Finland 43 G10
Essen *Town* Germany 50 E7
Estonia *Country* 58
Eswatini *Country* 69
Ethiopia *Country* 67
Etna, Mount Italy 48 H7
Eugene *Town* Oregon, USA 24 F3
Euphrates *River* Iraq/Syria/Turkey 73
   F12, 74 C8
Evansville *Town* Indiana, USA 20 J6
Everest, Mount China/Nepal
   77 D11, 84 H6
Everett *Town* Washington, USA
   24 D4
Everglades, The Florida, USA 23 J11
Évora *Town* Portugal 44 G5
Exeter *Town* England, UK 41 I8

Fairbanks *Town* Alaska, USA 25 B11
Faisalabad *Town* Pakistan 77 C8
Falkland Islands *Dep. territory* UK
   37 J8
Fargo *Town* N Dakota, USA 25 F13
Fayetteville *Town* N Carolina, USA
   23 C11
Feira de Santana *Town* Brazil
   37 D11
Ferrara *Town* Italy 48 C6
Fes *Town* Morocco 62 D3
Feuilles *River* Quebec, Canada
   29 G11
Fianarantsoa *Town* Madagascar
   69 H12
Fiji *Country* 93 I12
Finland, Gulf of 58 E5
Finland *Country* 43
Firat *River* Turkey 73 E11
Fitzroy *River* Australia 90 C6
Flagstaff *Town* Arizona, USA 27 F8
Flensburg *Town* Germany 51 A9
Flint *Town* Michigan, USA 20 F7
Florence *Town* Italy 48 D6
Flores Sea 80 H6
Florianópolio *Town* Brazil 37 F9

Florida *State* USA 23
Florida Keys *Island group* Florida,
   USA 23 J11
Focsani *Town* Romania 55 E12
Foggia *Town* Italy 49 E8
Fontainebleau *Town* France 47 C9
Forli *Town* Italy 48 C6
Fort Albany *Town* Ontario, Canada
   29 H10
Fortaleza *Town* Brazil 37 B11
Fort Collins *Town* Colorado, USA
   27 C10
Fort Lauderdale *Town* Florida, USA
   23 I12
Fort Myers *Town* Florida, USA 23 I11
Fort Smith *Town* Arkansas, USA
   22 D4
Fort Wayne *Town* Indiana, USA
   20 G7
Fort Worth *Town* Texas, USA 27 G13
Foveaux Strait New Zealand 92 J5
Fox Islands Alaska, USA 25 C9
France *Country* 46
Francistown *Town* Botswana 69 H8
Frankfurt am Main *Town* Germany
   51 G8
Frankfurt an der Oder *Town*
   Germany 51 D12
Fraser Island Australia 91 E13
Fredericton *Province capital* New
   Brunswick, Canada 29 I13
Fredrikstad *Town* Norway 42 G6
Freemantle *Town* Australia 90 G4
Freetown *Capital* Sierra Leone
   64 H4
Freiburg im Breisgau *Town*
   Germany 50 I7
French Guiana *Dep. territory* France
   35 H14
French Polynesia *Dep. territory*
   France 93 I14
Fresno *Town* California, USA 26 D5
Fuji, Mount Japan 83 G9
Fuji *Town* Japan 83 G9
Fukui *Town* Japan 83 G8
Fukuoka *Town* Japan 82 H5
Fukushima *Town* Japan 83 F10
Fulda *Town* Germany 51 F9
Fürth *Town* Germany 51 H9
Fushun *Town* China 85 D12
Fuzhou *Town* China 85 H12

Gabon *Country* 68
Gaborone *Capital* Botswana 69 H8
Gabrovo *Town* Bulgaria 55 H11
Gainesville *Town* Florida, USA
   23 G10
Gallup *Town* New Mexico, USA
   27 E9
Galveston *Town* Texas, USA 27 I14

Galway *Town* Republic of Ireland
   40 G6
Gambia *Country* 64
Gander *Town* Newfoundland and
   Labrador, Canada 29 H14
Ganges *River* India 77 D9
Gao *Town* Mali 65 F8
Gar *Town* China 84 G5
Garland *Town* Texas, USA 27 G13
Garonne *River* France 46 F7
Garoua *Town* Cameroon 68 A6
Gary *Town* Indiana, USA 20 G6
Gaspé *Town* Quebec, Canada
   29 H13
Gävle *Town* Sweden 43 G8
Gaza *Town* Israel 73 I9
Gaza Strip *Disputed region*
   Near East 73 I9
Gaziantep *Town* Turkey 73 E10
Gbarnga *Town* Liberia 64 I5
Gdansk *Town* Poland 57 B8
Gdynia *Town* Poland 57 B8
Geelong *Town* Australia 91 I11
General Santos *Town* Philippines
   79 H12
Geneva, Lake Switzerland 52 G1
Geneva *Town* Switzerland 52 G1
Genk *Town* Belgium 50 E6
Genoa *Town* Italy 48 C5
Georgetown *Capital* Guyana
   35 G13
George Town *Town* Malaysia 80 E2
Georgia *Country* 59
Georgia *State* USA 23
Gera *Town* Germany 51 F10
Germany *Country* 50
Ghana *Country* 64
Ghardaïa *Town* Algeria 62 E6
Ghent *Town* Belgium 50 E5
Gibraltar *Dep. territory* UK 44 I7
Gibraltar, Strait of Morocco/Spain
   44 I7, 62 C3
Gibson Desert Australia 90 E5
Giessen *Town* Germany 51 F8
Gifu *Town* Japan 83 G8
Gijón *Town* Spain 44 B7
Gillette *Town* Wyoming, USA 25 G10
Girona *Town* Spain 45 C13
Gisborne *Town* New Zealand
   93 D11
Giurgiu *Town* Romania 55 G11
Gjakove *Town* Kosovo 49 E10
Glasgow *Town* Scotland, UK
   41 E8
Gliwice *Town* Poland 57 G8
Gloucester *Town* England, UK 41 H9
Gobi Desert Mongolia 85 D9
Godavari *River* India 77 F9
Godoy Cruz *Town* Argentina 36 G7
Goiânia *Town* Brazil 37 D9

Golan Heights *Mountain range* Syria 73 H9

Golmud *Town* China 84 F7

Gómez Palacio *Town* Mexico 31 E8

Gonaïves *Town* Haiti 35 C9

Gonder *Town* Ethiopia 67 D9

Gore *Town* Ethiopia 67 E9

Gorgan *Town* Iran 75 B9

Görlitz *Town* Germany 51 F12

Gorzow Wielkopolski *Town* Poland 56 D6

Gosford *Town* Australia 91 G12

Göteborg *Town* Sweden 42 H6

Gotland *Island* Sweden 43 H8

Göttingen *Town* Germany 51 E9

Gouda *Town* Netherlands 50 D6

Governador Valadares *Town* Brazil 37 E10

Grafton *Town* Australia 91 F13

Grampian Mountains Scotland, UK 41 D8

Granada *Town* Spain 45 H9

Gran Chaco Argentina 36 F7

Grand Canyon Arizona, USA 26 E7

Grand Forks *Town* N Dakota, USA 25 E13

Grand Rapids *Town* Michigan, USA 20 F7

Graz *Town* Austria 40 G12

Great Australian Bight Australia 90 G7

Great Barrier Island New Zealand 93 B9

Great Barrier Reef Australia 91 C12

Great Basin Nevada, USA 26 D6

Great Dividing Range Australia 91 D12

Great Falls *Town* Montana, USA 25 E8

Great Karoo South Africa 68 J7

Great Rift Valley Kenya 67 F9

Great Sandy Desert Australia 90 D6

Great Victoria Desert Australia 90 G5

Greece *Country* 49

Greeley *Town* Colorado, USA 27 C10

Green Bay *Town* Wisconsin, USA 20 E5

Greenland Sea 17 H11, 43 G12

Greensboro *Town* N Carolina, USA 23 C11

Greenville *Town* Mississippi, USA 22 E6

Greenville *Town* S Carolina, USA 23 D10

Greifswald *Town* Germany 51 B12

Grenada *Country* 35

Grenoble *Town* France 47 F10

Greymouth *Town* New Zealand 92 G7

Groningen *Town* Netherlands 50 C7

Grootfontein *Town* Namibia 68 G7

Grosseto *Town* Italy 48 D6

Grozny *Town* Russia 59 I8

Guadalajara *Town* Mexico 31 G8

Guadalajara *Town* Spain 45 E9

Guadeloupe *Dep. territory* France 35 D12

Guam *Dep. territory* USA 93 H11

Guanabacoa *Town* Cuba 34 B7

Guanare *Town* Venezuela 35 F9

Guangzhou *Town* China 85 I11

Guantánamo *Town* Cuba 35 C8

Guatemala *Country* 34

Guatemala City *Capital* Guatemala 34 D4

Guayaquil *Town* Ecuador 36 B5

Guaymas *Town* Mexico 30 D5

Guernsey *Island* Channel Islands, UK 41 J9

Guiana Highlands *Mountain range* Guyana/Venezuela 35 G12

Guinea, Gulf of 64 J7

Guinea *Country* 64

Guinea-Bissau *Country* 64

Guiyang *Town* China 85 H10

Gujranwala *Town* Pakistan 77 C8

Guwahati *Town* India 77 E12

Guyana *Country* 35

Gwadar *Town* Pakistan 76 D5

Gyor *Town* Hungary 54 C5

Haarlem *Town* Netherlands 50 D6

Hachinohe *Town* Japan 83 D10

Hadera *Town* Israel 73 H9

Haifa *Town* Israel 73 H9

Haikou *Town* China 85 J11

Hailar *Town* China 85 B11

Haiphong *Town* Vietnam 78 E5

Haiti *Country* 35

Hakodate *Town* Japan 83 C10

Halifax *Province capital* Nova Scotia, Canada 29 I13

Halle *Town* Germany 51 E10

Halley (UK) *RS* Antarctica 16 D3

Halmstad *Town* Sweden 42 I7

Hamadan *Town* Iran 75 C8

Hamah *Town* Syria 73 F10

Hamamatsu *Town* Japan 83 G9

Hamar *Town* Norway 42 G6

Hamburg *Town* Germany 51 C9

Hamhung *Town* North Korea 85 D13

Hamilton *Town* New Zealand 93 C9

Hamilton *Town* Ontario, Canada 29 J11

Hamm *Town* Germany 51 E8

Hanamaki *Town* Japan 83 E10

Hangzhou *Town* China 85 G12

Hannover *Town* Germany 51 D9

Hanoi *Capital* Vietnam 78 E5

Harare *Capital* Zimbabwe 69 G9

Harbel *Town* Liberia 64 I5

Harbin *Town* China 85 C12

Harer *Town* Ethiopia 67 E10

Hargeisa *Town* Somalia 67 D11

Harrisburg *State capital* Pennsylvania, USA 21 G11

Hartford *State capital* Connecticut, USA 21 F12

Hasselt *Town* Belgium 50 E6

Hastings *Town* New Zealand 93 E10

Hat Yai *Town* Thailand 78 J4

Haugesund *Town* Norway 42 G5

Havana *Capital* Cuba 34 B7

Hawaii *State* USA 26

Hefei *Town* China 85 F12

Heidelberg *Town* Germany 51 G8

Heilbronn *Town* Germany 51 H8

Helena *State capital* Montana, USA 24 E7

Helsingborg *Town* Sweden 42 I7

Helsinki *Capital* Finland 43 G10

Hengyang *Town* China 85 H11

Henzada *Town* Burrma (Myanmar) 78 F2

Herat *Town* Afghanistan 76 A6

Heredia *Town* Costa Rica 34 F5

Hermosillo *Town* Mexico 30 D5

Hilversum *Town* Netherlands 50 D6

Himalayas Asia 77 D10, 84 H6

Hims *Town* Syria 73 G10

Hirosaki *Town* Japan 83 D10

Hiroshima *Town* Japan 82 H6

Hitachi *Town* Japan 83 F10

Hobart *Town* Australia 91 J11

Ho Chi Minh City *Town* Vietnam 78 H6

Hofu *Town* Japan 82 H6

Hohhot *Town* China 85 E10

Hokkaido *Island* Japan 83 B11

Holguín *Town* Cuba 35 C8

Homyel *Town* Belarus 58 G6

Honduras *Country* 34

Hong Kong *Town* China 85 I11

Honolulu *State capital* Hawaii, USA 26 H3

Honshu *Island* Japan 83 F9

Hormuz, Strait of Iran/Oman 75 E10

Houston *Town* Texas, USA 27 H14

Hradec Kralove *Town* Czech Republic 56 G6

Hrodna *Town* Belarus 58 G5

Huacho *Town* Peru 36 C5

Huambo *Town* Angola 68 F6

Huancayo *Town* Peru 36 D6

Huang *River* China 85 F11

Hudson Bay Canada 29 G10

Hué *Town* Vietnam 78 F6

Huelva *Town* Spain 44 H6

Hull *Town* England, UK 41 F10

Hungary *Country* 54

Huntington *Town* West Virginia, USA 21 I9

Huntsville *Town* Alabama, USA 23 D8

Huron, Lake USA 20 E8

Hyderabad *Town* India 77 G8

Hyderabad *Town* Pakistan 76 D7

Hyesan *Town* North Korea 85 D13

Iasi *Town* Romania 55 C12

Ibadan *Town* Nigeria 65 I9

Ibagué *Town* Colombia 35 H8

Ibarra *Town* Ecuador 36 A5

Ibiza Balearic Islands, Spain 45 F12

Ibiza *Town* Ibiza, Spain 45 F12

Ica *Town* Peru 36 D5

Iceland *Country* 43

Idaho *State* USA 24

Idaho Falls *Town* Idaho, USA 24 G7

Illinois *River* Illinois, USA 20 H5

Illinois *State* USA 20

Iloilo *Town* Philippines 79 G11

Ilorin *Town* Nigeria 65 I9

Imperatriz *Town* Brazil 37 B10

Imphal *Town* India 77 E12

Inchon *Town* South Korea 85 E13

Independence *Town* Missouri, USA 22 B4

India *Country* 77

Indiana *State* USA 20

Indianapolis *State capital* Indiana, USA 20 H7

Indian Ocean 67, 69, 76, 90

Indonesia *Country* 80

Indore *Town* India 77 E8

Indus *River* Pakistan 76 D7

Ingolstadt *Town* Germany 51 H10

Inhambane *Town* Mozambique 69 H10

Innsbruck *Town* Austria 52 F7

In Salah *Town* Algeria 62 F5

Invercargill *Town* New Zealand 92 J6

Inverness *Town* Scotland, UK 41 C8

Ioánnina *Town* Greece 49 G10

Ionian Sea 49 H9

Iowa *State* USA 20

Ipoh *Town* Malaysia 80 E2

Ipswich *Town* England, UK 41 H10

Iqaluit *Province capital* Nunavut, Canada 29 F11

Iquique *Town* Chile 36 E6

Iquitos *Town* Peru 36 B6

Iráklion *Town* Crete, Greece 49 I12

Iran *Country* 75

Iraq *Country* 74

Irbid *Town* Jordan 73 H9

Ireland, Republic of *Country* 40

Iringa *Town* Tanzania 67 I9
Irish Sea 40 F7
Irkutsk *Town* Russia 86 H6
Irrawaddy *River* Burma (Myanmar) 78 F2
Ishinomaki *Town* Japan 83 E10
Islamabad *Capital* Pakistan 77 B8
Isle of Man *Dep. territory* UK 41 F8
Isparta *Town* Turkey 72 E7
Israel *Country* 73
Istanbul *Town* Turkey 72 B6
Itabuna *Town* Brazil 37 D11
Italy *Country* 48
Iwaki *Town* Japan 83 F10
Izhevsk *Town* Russia 59 F9
Izmir *Town* Turkey 72 D5
Izmit *Town* Turkey 72 C7

Jackson *State capital* Mississippi, USA 22 F6
Jacksonville *Town* Florida, USA 23 G10
Jaén *Town* Spain 45 H8
Jaffna *Town* Sri Lanka 77 I9
Jaipur *Town* India 77 D8
Jakarta *Capital* Indonesia 80 H3
Jamaica *Country* 35
Jambi *Town* Indonesia 80 F2
Jamnagar *Town* India 76 E7
Jamshedpur *Town* India 77 E10
Janesville *Town* Wisconsin, USA 20 G5
Jangbono (South Korea) *RS* Antarctica 16 H5
Japan, Sea of 82 F7, 85 D13
Japan *Country* 82
Java *Island* Indonesia 80 H4
Java Sea 80 H4
Jayapura *Town* Indonesia 81 F11
Jefferson City *State capital* Missouri, USA 22 B5
Jena *Town* Germany 51 F10
Jersey *Island* Channel Islands, UK 41 J9
Jerusalem *Capital* Israel 73 I9
Jiddah *Town* Saudi Arabia 74 G5
Jihlava *Town* Czech Republic 56 H6
Jilin *Town* China 85 C12
Jima *Town* Ethiopia 67 E9
Jinan *Town* China 85 E11
Jinzhou *Town* China 85 D11
João Pessoa *Town* Brazil 37 C12
Jodhpur *Town* India 77 D8
Johannesburg *Town* South Africa 69 J9
John o'Groats *Town* Scotland, UK 41 C9
Johor Baharu *Town* Malaysia 80 F2
Joliet *Town* Illinois, USA 20 G6
Jönköping *Town* Sweden 42 H7

Jordan *Country* 73
Jordan *River* Jordan 73 H9
Jorhat *Town* India 77 D12
Joseph Bonaparte Gulf 90 B7
Juazeiro *Town* Brazil 37 C11
Juazeiro do Norte *Town* Brazil 37 C11
Juba *Capital* South Sudan 67 F8
Judenburg *Town* Austria 40 G11
Juliaca *Town* Peru 36 D6
Juneau *State capital* Alaska, USA 25 C11
Jyväskylä *Town* Finland 43 F10

K2 *Mountain* China/Pakistan 77 B9
Kabul *Capital* Afghanistan 76 B7
Kabwe *Town* Zambia 69 F9
Kachchh, Rann of India 76 E7
Kaduna *Town* Nigeria 65 H10
Kagoshima *Town* Japan 82 I5
Kairouan *Town* Tunisia 62 D7
Kaiserslautern *Town* Germany 50 G7
Kalahari Desert Namibia 68 H7
Kalamata *Town* Peleponnese, Greece 49 I11
Kalamazoo *Town* Michigan, USA 20 G7
Kalemie *Town* DRC 69 E9
Kalgoorlie *Town* Australia 90 G5
Kaliningrad *Town* Russia 58 G5
Kalisz *Town* Poland 56 E7
Kamina *Town* DRC 69 E8
Kamloops *Town* British Columbia, Canada 28 H6
Kampala *Capital* Uganda 67 G8
Kampong Cham *Town* Cambodia 78 H5
Kananga *Town* DRC 69 E8
Kanazawa *Town* Japan 83 F8
Kandy *Town* Sri Lanka 77 J9
Kankan *Town* Guinea 64 H5
Kano *Town* Nigeria 65 G10
Kanpur *Town* India 77 D9
Kansas *River* Kansas, USA 27 D13
Kansas *State* USA 27
Kansas City *Town* Missouri, USA 22 B4
Kansk *Town* Russia 86 G6
Kaposvár *Town* Hungary 54 D5
Karabük *Town* Turkey 73 B8
Karachi *Town* Pakistan 76 D6
Kara Sea 17 G14, 59 B10, 86 D4
Karbala *Town* Iraq 74 C7
Kardhitsa *Town* Greece 49 G11
Karlovac *Town* Croatia 49 C8
Karlovy Vary *Town* Czech Republic 56 G4
Karlskrona *Town* Sweden 42 I7
Karlsruhe *Town* Germany 50 H7

Karlstad *Town* Sweden 42 G7
Kars *Town* Turkey 73 C13
Kasai (Cassai) *River* Angola/DRC 68 D7
Kashi *Town* China 84 E4
Kassala *Town* Sudan 67 C9
Kassel *Town* Germany 51 E9
Katherine *Town* Australia 91 B8
Kathmandu *Capital* Nepal 77 D10
Katowice *Town* Poland 57 G8
Katsina *Town* Nigeria 65 G10
Kattegat *Sea* 42 H6
Kaunas *Town* Lithuania 58 G5
Kaválla *Town* Greece 49 F12
Kawasaki *Town* Japan 83 G10
Kayseri *Town* Turkey 73 D9
Kazakhstan *Country* 86
Kazan *Town* Russia 59 F9
Kecskemét *Town* Hungary 54 D6
Kelang *Town* Malaysia 80 E2
Kemerovo *Town* Russia 86 G5
Kemi *Town* Finland 43 D9
Kénitra *Town* Morocco 62 D3
Kentucky *State* USA 23
Kenya *Country* 67
Kerman *Town* Iran 75 D10
Kesennuma *Town* Japan 83 E10
Kettering *Town* Ohio, USA 21 H8
Key West *Town* Florida, USA 23 J11
Khabarovsk *Town* Russia 87 H9
Kharkiv *Town* Ukraine 58 H7
Khartoum *Capital* Sudan 67 C8
Khaskovo *Town* Bulgaria I11
Khon Kaen *Town* Thailand 78 G4
Khulna *Town* Bangladesh 77 F11
Kiel *Town* Germany 51 B10
Kiev *Capital* Ukraine 58 G6
Kigali *Capital* Rwanda 66 G7
Kigoma *Town* Tanzania 66 H7
Kikwit *Town* DRC 68 D7
Kilimanjaro, Mount Tanzania 67 H9
Kimberley *Town* South Africa 69 I8
Kimberley Plateau Australia 90 C6
Kingston *Capital* Jamaica 35 D8
Kingstown *Capital* St. Vincent 35 E12
Kinshasa *Capital* DRC 68 D6
Kiribati *Country* 93 I13
Kirikkale *Town* Turkey 73 C9
Kirkuk *Town* Iraq 74 B7
Kirov *Town* Russia 58 G6
Kiruna *Town* Sweden 43 C8
Kisangani *Town* DRC 69 C8
Kismaayo *Town* Somalia 67 G10
Kisumu *Town* Kenya 67 G8
Kitakyushu *Town* Japan 82 H5
Kitchener *Town* Ontario, Canada 29 J11

Kitwe *Town* Zambia 69 F9
Kivu, Lake DRC/Rwanda 66 H7, 69 D9
Klagenfurt *Town* Austria 40 H11
Klamath Falls *Town* Oregon, USA 24 G3
Knoxville *Town* Tennessee, USA 23 C9
Kobe *Town* Japan 82 H7
Koblenz *Town* Germany 50 F7
Kochi (Cochin) *Town* India 77 I8
Kochi *Town* Japan 82 H7
Kodiak *Town* Alaska, USA 25 C10
Kofu *Town* Japan 83 G9
Kokshetau *Town* Kazakhstan 86 H3
Kolhapur *Town* India 76 G7
Kolkata (Calcutta) *Town* India 77 F11
Kolwezi *Town* DRC 69 E8
Komatsu *Town* Japan 83 F8
Komsomol'sk-na-Amure *Town* Russian Fed. 87 H9
Konya *Town* Turkey 73 E8
Koper *Town* Slovenia 48 B7
Korçë *Town* Albania 49 F10
Korea, North *Country* 85
Korea, South *Country* 85
Korea Strait Japan/South Korea 82 H4, 85 E13
Koriyama *Town* Japan 83 F10
Korla *Town* China 84 E6
Kortrijk *Town* Belgium 50 E4
Kosice *Town* Slovakia 57 I10
Kosovo *Country* 49
Kosovska Mitrovica *Town* Kosovo 49 D10
Koszalin *Town* Poland 56 B6
Kotka *Town* Finland 43 G10
Kotte *Capital* Sri Lanka 77 J9
Kotto *River* CAR 68 B7
Kozáni *Town* Greece 49 F11
Kozhikode (Calicut) *Town* India 77 H8
Kragujevac *Town* Serbia 49 D10
Kraków *Town* Poland 57 G9
Krasnodar *Town* Russia 58 I7
Krasnoyarsk *Town* Russia 86 G5
Krefeld *Town* Germany 50 E7
Kristiansand *Town* Norway 42 H5
Krusevac *Town* Serbia 49 D11
Kryvyy Rih *Town* Ukraine 58 H6
Kuala Lumpur *Capital* Malaysia 80 E2
Kuala Terengganu *Town* Malaysia 80 E2
Kuching *Town* Malaysia 80 F4
Kugluktuk *Town* Nunavut, Canada 28 E7
Kumamoto *Town* Japan 82 I5
Kumanovo *Town* Macedonia 49 E11

Kumasi *Town* Ghana 64 I7
Kunlun Shan *Mountain range* China 84 F6
Kunming *Town* China 85 I9
Kuopio *Town* Finland 43 E10
Kupang *Town* Indonesia 80 H7
Kure *Town* Japan 82 H6
Kushiro *Town* Japan 83 B11
Kütahya *Town* Turkey 72 D7
Kuwait *Country* 75
Kuwait City *Capital* Kuwait 75 E8
Kwangju *Town* South Korea 85 E13
Kwango *River* DRC 68 E6
Kwilu *River* DRC 68 D7
Kyoto *Town* Japan 83 G8
Kyrgyzstan *Country* 86
Kyushu *Island* Japan 82 I5
Kyustendil *Town* Bulgaria 55 I9

Labrador Sea 29 F12
La Ceiba *Town* Honduras 34 D5
La Coruña *Town* Spain 44 B5
La Crosse *Town* Wisconsin, USA 20 F4
Ladoga, Lake Russia 58 E6
Lafayette *Town* Louisiana, USA 22 H5
Lagos *Town* Nigeria 65 I8
Lagos *Town* Portugal 44 H5
Lahore *Town* Pakistan 77 C8
Lahti *Town* Finland 43 F10
Lake Charles *Town* Louisiana, USA 22 H5
Lakewood *Town* Colorado, USA 27 D10
Lalitpur *Town* India 77 E9
Lamía *Town* Greece 49 G11
Lansing *State capital* Michigan, USA 20 F7
Lanzhou *Town* China 85 F9
Laoag *Town* Philippines 79 D10
Laos *Country* 78
La Paz *Capital* Bolivia 36 D7
La Paz *Town* Mexico 30 F5
La Plata *Town* Argentina 37 G8
Laptev Sea 17 D13, 87 D8
Laredo *Town* Texas, USA 27 I12
Larissa *Town* Greece 49 G11
Larkana *Town* Pakistan 76 C7
La Rochelle *Town* France 46 E6
La Romana *Town* Dominican Republic 35 D10
Las Cruces *Town* New Mexico, USA 27 G9
La Serena *Town* Chile 36 F6
La Spezia *Town* Italy 48 C5
Las Vegas *Town* Nevada, USA 26 E6
Latina *Town* Italy 48 E6

Latvia *Country* 58
Launceston *Town* Australia 91 J11
Lausanne *Town* Switzerland 52 G1
Laval *Town* France 46 C7
Lawton *Town* Oklahoma, USA 27 F12
Lebanon *Country* 73
Lecce *Town* Italy 49 F9
Leeds *Town* England, UK 41 F9
Leeuwarden *Town* Netherlands 50 C7
Legnica *Town* Poland 56 F6
Le Havre *Town* France 47 B8
Leicester *Town* England, UK 41 G9
Leiden *Town* Netherlands 50 D6
Leipzig *Town* Germany 51 F11
Le Mans *Town* France 47 C8
Lena *River* Russia 86 G7
León *Town* Mexico 31 G8
León *Town* Nicaragua 34 E5
León *Town* Spain 44 C7
Lerwick *Town* Scotland, UK 41 A9
Leskovac *Town* Serbia 49 D11
Lesotho *Country* 69
Lethbridge *Town* Alberta, Canada 28 I7
Leuven *Town* Belgium 50 E5
Lewis *Island* Scotland, UK 40 C7
Lewiston *Town* Idaho, USA 24 E5
Lewiston *Town* Maine, USA 21 D13
Lexington *Town* Kentucky, USA 23 B8
Lhasa *Town* China 84 H7
Lianyungang *Town* China 85 F12
Liberec *Town* Czech Republic 56 F5
Liberia *Country* 64
Libreville *Capital* Gabon 68 C5
Libya *Country* 63
Libyan Desert Egypt/Libya/Sudan 63 G11, 66 A6
Liechtenstein *Country* 52
Liège *Town* Belgium 50 F6
Liepaja *Town* Latvia 58 F5
Likasi *Town* DRC 69 F8
Lille *Town* France 47 A10
Lillehammer *Town* Norway 42 F6
Lilongwe *Capital* Malawi 69 F10
Lima *Capital* Peru 36 D5
Limassol *Town* Cyprus 73 G8
Limerick *Town* Republic of Ireland 40 G6
Limoges *Town* France 47 E8
Limpopo *River* South Africa 69 H9
Linares *Town* Spain 45 G9
Lincoln *State capital* Nebraska, USA 25 I14
Lincoln Sea 17 G11
Lindi *Town* Tanzania 67 J10
Linköping *Town* Sweden 42 H7

Linz *Town* Austria 40 E11
Lipetsk *Town* Russia 58 G7
Lisbon *Capital* Portugal 44 G4
Lithuania *Country* 58
Little Rock *State capital* Arkansas, USA 22 E5
Liuzhou *Town* China 85 I10
Liverpool *Town* England, UK 41 G8
Livingstone *Town* Zambia 69 G8
Livorno *Town* Italy 48 D5
Ljubljana *Capital* Slovenia 48 B7
Lleida *Town* Spain 45 C11
Lobamba *Capital* Eswatini 69 I9
Lobito *Town* Angola 68 F6
Lodz *Town* Poland 57 E8
Logroño *Town* Spain 45 C9
Loire *River* France 46 D7
Lomami *River* DRC 69 D8
Lomas de Zamora *Town* Argentina 37 G8
Lomé *Capital* Togo 65 I8
London *Capital* England, UK 41 H10
London *Town* Ontario, Canada 29 J11
Londonderry *Town* Northern Ireland, UK 40 E7
Long Beach *Town* California, USA 26 F5
Long Island New York, USA 21 F12
Longview *Town* Texas, USA 27 G14
Lorca *Town* Spain 45 H10
Lorient *Town* France 46 C6
Los Angeles *Town* California, USA 26 F5
Los Angeles *Town* Chile 36 H6
Los Mochis *Town* Mexico 30 E6
Louisiana *State* USA 22
Louisville *Town* Kentucky, USA 23 B8
Lowell *Town* Massachusetts, USA 21 E13
Lower Hutt *Town* New Zealand 93 F9
Luanda *Capital* Angola 68 E6
Lubango *Town* Angola 68 F6
Lubbock *Town* Texas, USA 27 F11
Lübeck *Town* Germany 51 B10
Lublin *Town* Poland 57 F11
Lubumbashi *Town* DRC 69 F9
Lucknow *Town* India 77 D9
Lüderitz *Town* Namibia 68 I6
Ludhiana *Town* India 77 C8
Ludwigshafen *Town* Germany 51 G7
Luena *Town* Angola 68 F7
Lugano *Town* Switzerland 52 H4
Lugo *Town* Spain 44 B6
Luleå *Town* Sweden 43 D9

Lund *Town* Sweden 42 I7
Lüneburg *Town* Germany 51 C10
Luoyang *Town* China 85 F10
Lusaka *Capital* Zambia 69 F9
Luxembourg *Capital* Luxembourg 50 G6
Luxembourg *Country* 50 G6
Luxor *Town* Egypt 63 G13
Luzon *Island* Philippines 79 E10
Lviv *Town* Ukraine 58 H5
Lynchburg *Town* Virgina, USA 23 B11
Lyon *Town* France 47 F10

Maas (Meuse) *River* Belgium/ France/Netherlands 50 E6
Maastricht *Town* Netherlands 50 E6
Macapá *Town* Brazil 37 B9
Macau *Town* China 85 I11
Macdonnell Ranges Australia 91 E8
Macedonia *Country* 49
Maceio *Town* Brazil 37 C11
Mackay *Town* Australia 91 D12
Macon *Town* Georgia, USA 23 E9
Ma'daba *Town* Jordan 73 I10
Madagascar *Country* 69
Madeira *River* Brazil 37 B8
Madison *State capital* Wisconsin, USA 20 F5
Madras *See Chennai*
Madrid *Capital* Spain 45 E8
Madurai *Town* India 77 I8
Magadan *Town* Russia 87 G11
Magdeburg *Town* Germany 51 D10
Magnitogorsk *Town* Russia 59 G10
Mahajanga *Town* Madagascar 69 G12
Maiduguri *Town* Nigeria 65 H11
Main *River* Germany 51 G10
Maine, Gulf of 21 D14
Maine *State* USA 21
Mainz *Town* Germany 51 G8
Maitri (India) *RS* Antarctica 16 C5
Malabo *Capital* Equatorial Guinea 68 C5
Málaga *Town* Spain 45 I8
Malakal *Town* South Sudan 67 D8
Malang *Town* Indonesia 80 H4
Malatya *Town* Turkey 73 D11
Malawi *Country* 69
Malaysia *Country* 80
Mali *Country* 64
Mallorca Balearic Islands, Spain 45 E13
Malmö *Town* Sweden 42 I7
Malta *Country* 48
Manado *Town* Indonesia 80 F7
Managua *Capital* Nicaragua 34 E5
Manama *Capital* Bahrain 75 F8
Manaus *Town* Brazil 37 B8

Manchester *Town* England, UK 41 G9

Manchester *Town* New Hampshire, USA 21 E13

Mandalay *Town* Burma (Myanmar) 78 E2

Mangalore *Town* India 76 H7

Manila *Capital* Philippines 79 F10

Manisa *Town* Turkey 72 D5

Manitoba *Province* Canada 29

Manizales *Town* Colombia 35 H8

Mankato *Town* Minnesota, USA 20 F3

Mannheim *Town* Germany 51 G8

Manta *Town* Ecuador 36 B5

Maputo *Capital* Mozambique 69 I9

Marabá *Town* Brazil 37 B9

Maracaibo *Town* Venezuela 35 F9

Maracay *Town* Venezuela 35 F10

Maradi *Town* Niger 65 G10

Marajo Island Brazil 37 B9

Marambio (Argentina) *RS* Antarctica 16 D1

Marbella *Town* Spain 45 I8

Mardan *Town* Pakistan 77 B8

Mar del Plata *Town* Argentina 37 G8

Maribor *Town* Slovenia 49 B8

Marie Byrd Land Antarctica 16 F3

Marka *Town* Somalia 67 G11

Marmara, Sea of 72 C6

Marquette *Town* Michigan, USA 20 D5

Marrakech *Town* Morocco 62 E2

Marseille *Town* France 47 H10

Marshall Islands *Country* 93 H12

Martin *Town* Slovakia 57 H8

Martinique *Dep. territory* France 35 E12

Maryland *State* USA 21

Masaka *Town* Uganda 67 G8

Maseru *Capital* Lesotho 69 I8

Mashhad *Town* Iran 75 B11

Massa *Town* Italy 48 C5

Massachusetts *State* USA 21

Massawa *Town* Eritrea 67 C9

Massif Central France 47 F9

Matadi *Town* DRC 68 D6

Matamoros *Town* Mexico 31 E10

Mataram *Town* Indonesia 80 H5

Mataró *Town* Spain 45 C13

Matsue *Town* Japan 82 G6

Matsumoto *Town* Japan 83 G9

Matsuyama *Town* Japan 82 H6

Matterhorn, Mount Switzerland 52 H2

Maun *Town* Botswana 69 G8

Mauritania *Country* 64

Mauritius *Country* 69

Mawson (Australia) *RS* Antarctica 16 E6

Mayotte *Dep. territory* France 69 F12

Mazar-e Sharif *Town* Afghanistan 76 A7

Mazatlán *Town* Mexico 30 F7

Mbabane *Capital* Eswatini 69 I9

Mbandaka *Town* DRC 68 C7

Mbeya *Town* Tanzania 67 I9

Mbuji-Mayi *Town* DRC 69 E8

McMurdo (US) *RS* Antarctica 16 H5

Mecca *Town* Saudi Arabia 74 G5

Mechelen *Town* Belgium 50 E5

Medan *Town* Indonesia 80 E1

Medellín *Town* Colombia 35 G8

Medicine Hat *Town* Alberta, Canada 28 I7

Medina *Town* Saudi Arabia 74 F5

Mediterranean Sea 45, 47, 62, 73

Meerut *Town* India 77 D9

Mekong *River* Asia 78 G5, 85 I9

Melbourne *Town* Australia 91 I11

Melilla *Town* Spain 45 J9, 62 D4

Melville Island Canada 17 E9

Memphis *Town* Tennessee, USA 22 D6

Mendoza *Town* Argentina 36 G7

Menorca Balearic Islands, Spain 45 E14

Mérida *Town* Mexico 31 G13, 44 F7

Mérida *Town* Spain 44 F7

Mesa *Town* Arizona, USA 26 F7

Messina *Town* Sicily, Italy 48 H7

Metairie *Town* Louisiana, USA 22 H6

Metz *Town* France 47 C11

Meuse (Maas) *River* Belgium/ France/Netherlands 50 F5

Mexicali *Town* Mexico 30 B4

Mexico, Gulf of 23 H8, 27 J14, 31 F11

Mexico *Country* 30

Mexico City *Capital* Mexico 31 H9

Miami *Town* Florida, USA 23 I12

Michigan, Lake USA 20 E6

Michigan *State* USA 20

Micronesia *Country* 93 H11

Middlesbrough *Town* England, UK 41 F9

Midland *Town* Texas, USA 27 G11

Milan *Town* Italy 48 B5

Miles City *Town* Montana, USA 25 F10

Milwaukee *Town* Wisconsin, USA 20 F6

Mindanao *Island* Philippines 79 G12

Mindoro Strait South China Sea 79 G10

Minneapolis *Town* Minnesota, USA 20 E3

Minnesota *State* USA 20

Minot *Town* N Dakota, USA 25 E12

Minsk *Capital* Belarus 58 G6

Mirny (Russian Federation) *RS* Antarctica 16 F7

Mirpur Khas *Town* Pakistan 76 D7

Miskolc *Town* Hungary 54 B7

Mississippi *River* USA 20 F4, 22 E6

Mississippi *State* USA 22

Missouri *River* Montana, USA 25 E10

Missouri *State* USA 22

Mito *Town* Japan 83 F10

Miyako *Town* Japan 83 D10

Miyakonojo *Town* Japan 82 I5

Miyazaki *Town* Japan 82 I6

Mobile *Town* Alabama, USA 22 G7

Modesto *Town* California, USA 26 C4

Mogadishu *Capital* Somalia 67 F11

Moldova *Country* 58

Molucca Sea 80 F7

Mombasa *Town* Kenya 67 H10

Monaco *Capital* Monaco 47 H11

Monaco *Country* 47

Monclova *Town* Mexico 31 E9

Mongolia *Country* 85

Monroe *Town* Louisiana, USA 22 F5

Monrovia *Capital* Liberia 64 I4

Mons *Town* Belgium 50 F5

Montana *State* USA 25

Montana *Town* Bulgaria 55 H9

Montauban *Town* France 46 G7

Mont Blanc *Mountain* France 47 F11

Mont-de-Marsan *Town* France 46 F7

Montego Bay *Town* Jamaica 35 C8

Montélimar *Town* France 47 G10

Montenegro *Country* 49

Monterey *Town* California, USA 26 D4

Montería *Town* Colombia 35 F8

Monterrey *Town* Mexico 31 E9

Montevideo *Capital* Uruguay 37 G8

Montgomery *State capital* Alabama, USA 23 F8

Montluçon *Town* France 47 E9

Montpelier *State capital* Vermont, USA 21 D12

Montpellier *Town* France 47 H9

Montreal *Town* Quebec, Canada 29 I12

Montserrat *Dep. territory* UK 35 D12

Monza *Town* Italy 48 B5

Moorhead *Town* Minnesota, USA 20 D2

Mopti *Town* Mali 64 G6

Morelia *Town* Mexico 31 H8

Morocco *Country* 62

Moroni *Capital* Comoros 69 F12

Moscow *Capital* Russia 58 F7

Mosselbaai *Town* South Africa 68 J7

Mossoró *Town* Brazil 37 B11

Mostar *Town* Bosnia and Herz. 49 D9

Mosul *Town* Iraq 74 B6

Moulmein *Town* Burma (Myanmar) 78 G3

Moundou *Town* Chad 65 I12

Mount Isa *Town* Australia 91 D10

Mozambique *Country* 69

Mufulira *Town* Zambia 69 F9

Mulhouse *Town* France 47 D12

Multan *Town* Pakistan 77 C8

Mumbai (Bombay) *Town* India 76 F7

Muncie *Town* Indiana, USA 20 H7

Munich *Town* Germany 51 I10

Münster *Town* Germany 50 D7

Murcia *Town* Spain 45 G10

Murmansk *Town* Russia 58 C7

Muroran *Town* Japan 83 C10

Murray *River* Australia 91 H11

Muscat *Capital* Oman 75 F11

Mwanza *Town* Tanzania 67 H8

Mweru, Lake DRC 69 E9

Myanmar *See Burma*

Myrtle Beach *Town* S Carolina, USA 23 D11

Mysore *Town* India 77 H8

Myvatn *Lake* Iceland 43 H13

Nacala *Town* Mozambique 69 F11

Nagano *Town* Japan 83 F9

Nagaoka *Town* Japan 83 F9

Nagasaki *Town* Japan 82 I5

Nagoya *Town* Japan 83 G8

Nagpur *Town* India 77 F9

Nain *Town* Newfoundland and Labrador, Canada 29 G12

Nairobi *Capital* Kenya 67 G9

Nakhon Ratchasima *Town* Thailand 78 G4

Nakhon Sawan *Town* Thailand 78 G4

Nakhon Si Thammarat *Town* Thailand 78 I4

Nakuru *Town* Kenya 67 G9

Namangan *Town* Uzbekistan 86 I4

Nam Dinh *Town* Vietnam 78 E5

Namib Desert Namibia 68 H6

Namibe *Town* Angola 68 F6

Namibia *Country* 68

Nampula *Town* Mozambique 69 F11

Namur *Town* Belgium 50 F5

Nanchang *Town* China 85 G11

Nanchong *Town* China 85 G9

Nancy *Town* France 47 C11

Nanjing *Town* China 85 F12

Nanning *Town* China 85 I10

Nantes *Town* France 46 D6
Napier *Town* New Zealand 93 D10
Naples *Town* Italy 48 F7
Narvik *Town* Norway 43 C8
Nashville *State capital* Tennessee, USA 23 C8
Nassau *Capital* Bahamas 35 A8
Nasser, Lake Egypt 63 H13
Natal *Town* Brazil 37 C12
Nauru *Country* 93 H12
Naypyidaw *Capital* Burma (Myanmar) 78 F2
Nazareth *Town* Israel 73 H9
Nazilli *Town* Turkey 72 D6
Nazret *Town* Ethiopia 67 E10
N'Djamena *Capital* Chad 65 H12
Ndola *Town* Zambia 69 F9
Neápolis *Town* Greece 49 I11
Near Islands Alaska, USA 25 B8
Nebraska *State* USA 25
Negev Desert Israel 73 I9
Negotin *Town* Serbia 49 C11
Negro *River* Brazil 36 B7
Nellore *Town* India 77 H9
Nelson *Town* New Zealand 93 F8
Nepal *Country* 77
Netanya *Town* Israel 73 H9
Netherlands *Country* 50
Neubrandenburg *Town* Germany 51 C11
Neuchâtel *Town* Switzerland 52 F2
Neumayer III (Germany) *RS* Antarctica 16 C4
Neuquén *Town* Argentina 36 H7
Nevada *State* USA 26
Newark *Town* New Jersey, USA 21 F12
New Brunswick *Province* Canada 29
New Caledonia *Dep. territory* France 93 J12
Newcastle *Town* Australia 91 G12
Newcastle upon Tyne *Town* England, UK 41 E9
New Delhi *Capital* India 77 D9
Newfoundland and Labrador *Province* Canada 29
New Guinea *Island* Indonesia 81 G10
New Hampshire *State* USA 21
New Haven *Town* Connecticut, USA 21 F12
New Jersey *State* USA 21
New Mexico *State* USA 27
New Orleans *Town* Louisiana, USA 22 H6
New Plymouth *Town* New Zealand 93 D9
Newport *Town* Vermont, USA 21 C12
Newport *Town* Wales, UK 41 H8

Newport News *Town* Virginia, USA 23 B12
New South Wales *State* Australia 91
New York *State* USA 21
New York City *Town* New York, USA 21 F12
New Zealand *Country* 92
Nha Trang *Town* Vietnam 78 H7
Niagara Falls USA 21 F9
Niamey *Capital* Niger 65 G8
Nicaragua *Country* 34
Nice *Town* France 47 H11
Nicobar Islands India 77 J12
Nicosia *Capital* Cyprus 73 F8
Niger *Country* 65
Niger *River* West Africa 65 I9
Nigeria *Country* 65
Niigata *Town* Japan 83 F9
Niksic *Town* Montenegro 49 D9
Nile *River* East Africa 63 F13, 66 B7
Nîmes *Town* France 47 G9
Ningbo *Town* China 85 G12
Nis *Town* Serbia 49 D11
Nitra *Town* Slovakia 57 I8
Niue *Dep. territory* New Zealand 93 I13
Nizhnevartovsk *Town* Russia 86 G4
Nizhniy Novgorod *Town* Russia 59 F8
Nobeoka *Town* Japan 82 I6
Norfolk *Town* Nebraska, USA 25 H13
Norfolk *Town* Virginia, USA 23 B12
Noril'sk *Town* Russia 86 E5
Norman *Town* Oklahoma, USA 27 F13
Norrköping *Town* Sweden 43 H8
Northampton *Town* England, UK 41 H9
North Cape New Zealand 93 A8
North Cape Norway 43 A9
North Carolina *State* USA 23
North Dakota *State* USA 25
Northern Ireland *Country* UK 40
Northern Mariana Islands *Dep. territory* USA 93 G11
Northern Territory *State* Australia 91
North Island New Zealand 93
North Korea *See* Korea, North
North Sea 41, 42, 50
Northwest Territories *Province* Canada 28
Norway *Country* 42
Norwegian Sea 17 I11, 43 J13
Norwich *Town* England, UK 41 G10
Nottingham *Town* England, UK 41 G9

Nouadhibou *Town* Mauritania 64 D3
Nouakchott *Capital* Mauritania 64 E3
Nova Iguaçu *Town* Brazil 37 E10
Novara *Town* Italy 48 B4
Nova Scotia *Province* Canada 29
Novaya Zemlya *Island* Russia 17 G13, 59 B10
Novgorod *Town* Russia 58 F6
Novi Sad *Town* Serbia 49 C10
Novokuznetsk *Town* Russia 86 H5
Novolazervskaya (Russia) *RS* Antarctica 16 C5
Novosibirsk *Town* Russia 86 H5
Nubian Desert Sudan 67 A8
Nueva Gerona *Town* Cuba 34 B6
Nuevo Laredo *Town* Mexico 31 D9
Nunavut *Province* Canada 29
Nuremberg *Town* Germany 51 H10
Nyala *Town* Sudan 66 D6
Nyíregyháza *Town* Hungary 55 C8

Oakland *Town* California, USA 26 C4
Oamaru *Town* New Zealand 92 I7
Oaxaca *Town* Mexico 31 I10
Ob *River* Russia 86 G4
Obihiro *Town* Japan 83 B11
Oceanside *Town* California, USA 26 F5
Odense *Town* Denmark 42 I6
Oder *River* Poland 56 F7
Odessa *Town* Texas, USA 27 G11
Odessa *Town* Ukraine 58 H6
Offenbach *Town* Germany 51 G8
Ogaden Plateau Ethiopia 67 E11
Ogbomosho *Town* Nigeria 65 I9
Ogden *Town* Utah, USA 27 C8
Ohio *State* USA 21
Ohrid, Lake Albania/Macedonia 49 F10
Oita *Town* Japan 82 H6
Okavango Delta Botswana 68 G7
Okayama *Town* Japan 82 H7
Okeechobee, Lake Florida, USA 23 I11
Okhotsk, Sea of 87 G10
Oklahoma *State* USA 27
Oklahoma City *State capital* Oklahoma, USA 27 F13
Öland *Island* Sweden 43 I8
Oldenburg *Town* Germany 51 C8
Olomouc *Town* Czech Republic 56 H7
Olsztyn *Town* Poland 57 C9
Olympia *State capital* Washington, USA 24 D3
Olympus, Mount Greece 49 F11
Omaha *Town* Nebraska, USA 25 I14
Oman, Gulf of 75 F11

Oman *Country* 75
Omdurman *Town* Sudan 67 C8
Omsk *Town* Russia 86 H4
Onega, Lake Russia 58 E7
Onega *Town* Russia 58 D7
Onitsha *Town* Nigeria 65 I9
Ontario, Lake USA 21 E10
Ontario *Province* Canada 29
Opole *Town* Poland 56 F7
Oradea *Town* Romania 55 C8
Oran *Town* Algeria 62 D5
Orange *River* South Africa 69 I8
Orcadas (Argentina) *RS* Antarctica 16 C1
Ordu *Town* Turkey 73 C11
Örebro *Town* Sweden 42 G7
Oregon *State* USA 24
Orenburg *Town* Russia 59 G10, 86 H2
Orense *Town* Spain 44 C6
Orkney Islands Scotland, UK 41 B9
Orlando *Town* Florida, USA 23 H11
Orléans *Town* France 47 D8
Örnsköldsvik *Town* Sweden 43 E8
Orsk *Town* Russia 59 G10
Oruro *Town* Bolivia 36 D7
Osaka *Town* Japan 83 H8
Oshawa *Town* Ontario, Canada 29 J11
Oshkosh *Town* Wisconsin, USA 20 F5
Osijek *Town* Croatia 49 B9
Oslo *Capital* Norway 42 G6
Osmaniye *Town* Turkey 73 E10
Osnabrück *Town* Germany 51 D8
Osorno *Town* Chile 36 H6
Ostend *Town* Belgium 50 E4
Östersund *Town* Sweden 42 E7
Ostrava *Town* Czech Republic 57 H8
Otago Peninsula New Zealand 92 I7
Otaru *Town* Japan 83 B10
Ottawa *Capital* Canada 29 I12
Ouagadougou *Capital* Burkina Faso 64 G7
Oujda *Town* Morocco 62 D4
Oulu *Town* Finland 43 D10
Outer Hebrides *Island group* Scotland, UK 40 C7
Oviedo *Town* Spain 44 B7
Owensboro *Town* Kentucky, USA 22 B7
Oxford *Town* England, UK 41 H9
Oxnard *Town* California, USA 26 E5

Pachuca *Town* Mexico 31 G9
Pacific Ocean 24, 25, 26, 28, 30, 36, 79, 83, 85, 87, 91, 93
Padang *Town* Indonesia 80 F2
Paderborn *Town* Germany 51 E8
Paducah *Town* Kentucky, USA 22 C7

Pakistan *Country* 76
Pakxe *Town* Laos 78 G5
Palau *Country* 93 H10
Palawan Passage *South China Sea* 79 H9
Palembang *Town* Indonesia 80 G3
Palencia *Town* Spain 45 C8
Palermo *Town* Sicily, Italy 48 H6
Palma *Town* Mallorca, Spain 45 E13
Palmer (US) *RS* Antarctica 16 D1
Palmerston North *Town* New Zealand 93 E9
Palo Alto *Town* California, USA 26 D4
Palu *Town* Indonesia 80 F6
Pamplona *Town* Spain 45 B10
Panama, Gulf of 34 G7
Panama *Country* 34
Panama Canal *Panama* 34 F6
Panama City *Capital* Panama 34 F7
Pancevo *Town* Serbia 49 C10
Papua New Guinea *Country* 93
Paraguay *Country* 37
Paramaribo *Capital* Suriname 35 G13
Pardubice *Town* Czech Republic 56 G6
Paris *Capital* France 47 C9
Parma *Town* Italy 48 C5
Parnaíba *Town* Brazil 37 B11
Pasadena *Town* California, USA 26 F5
Pasadena *Town* Texas, USA 27 H14
Pasco *Town* Washington, USA 24 E5
Passau *Town* Germany 51 I11
Pasto *Town* Colombia 34 I7
Patagonia *Argentina* 36 I7
Paterson *Town* New Jersey, USA 21 F12
Patna *Town* India 77 E10
Pátrai *Town* Greece 49 H11
Pau *Town* France 46 G6
Pavlodar *Town* Kazakhstan 86 H4
Pearl *River* Mississippi, USA 22 G6
Pejë *Town* Kosovo 49 E10
Pechora *River* Russia 59 D9
Pécs *Town* Hungary 54 E5
Pedro Juan Caballero *Town* Paraguay 37 E8
Pegu *Town* Burma (Myanmar) 78 G2
Pekanbaru *Town* Indonesia 80 F2
Pennines *Hills* England, UK 41 F9
Pennsylvania *State* USA 21
Penza *Town* Russia 59 G8
Peoria *Town* Illinois, USA 20 H5
Pereira *Town* Colombia 35 H8
Perm *Town* Russia 59 F9
Pernik *Town* Bulgaria 55 I9
Persian Gulf 75 E8

Perth *Town* Australia 90 G4
Perth *Town* Scotland, UK 41 D8
Peru *Country* 36
Perugia *Town* Italy 48 D6
Pescara *Town* Italy 48 E7
Peshawar *Town* Pakistan 77 B8
Peterborough *Town* England, UK 41 G10
Petropavlovsk-Kamchatskiy *Town* Russia 87 H11
Petrozavodsk *Town* Russia 58 E7
Pforzheim *Town* Germany 51 H8
Philadelphia *Town* Pennsylvania, USA 21 G12
Philippines *Country* 79
Phnom Penh *Capital* Cambodia 78 H5
Phoenix *State capital* Arizona, USA 26 F7
Phuket *Town* Thailand 78 I3
Piacenza *Town* Italy 48 C5
Pierre *State capital* S Dakota, USA 25 G12
Pietermaritzburg *Town* South Africa 69 I9
Pietersburg *Town* South Africa 69 H9
Pinar del Río *Town* Cuba 34 B6
Pine Bluff *Town* Arkansas, USA 22 E5
Piraeus *Town* Greece 49 H12
Pisa *Town* Italy 48 D5
Pistoia *Town* Italy 48 C6
Pitesti *Town* Romania 55 F10
Pittsburgh *Town* Pennsylvania, USA 21 G9
Piura *Town* Peru 36 B5
Plano *Town* Texas, USA 27 G13
Platte *River* Nebraska, USA 25 I12
Plauen *Town* Germany 51 F10
Plenty, Bay of *New Zealand* 93 C10
Pleven *Town* Bulgaria 55 H10
Plock *Town* Poland 57 D9
Ploiesti *Town* Romania 55 F11
Plovdiv *Town* Bulgaria 55 I10
Plymouth *Town* England, UK 41 I8
Plzen *Town* Czech Republic 56 G4
Podgorica *Capital* Montenegro 49 E9
Pointe-Noire *Town* Republic of the Congo 68 D5
Poitiers *Town* France 46 D7
Pokhara *Town* Nepal 77 D10
Poland *Country* 56
Pontianak *Town* Indonesia 80 F4
Poona *See Pune*
Popayán *Town* Colombia 34 H7
Pori *Town* Finland 43 F9
Port Arthur *Town* Texas, USA 27 H14

Port Augusta *Town* Australia 91 G9
Port-au-Prince *Capital* Haiti 35 D9
Port Elizabeth *Town* South Africa 69 J8
Port-Gentil *Town* Gabon 68 C5
Port Harcourt *Town* Nigeria 65 J9
Portland *Town* Maine, USA 21 D13
Portland *Town* Oregon, USA 24 E3
Port Louis *Capital* Mauritius 69 H14
Port Macquarie *Town* Australia 91 G13
Porto *Town* Portugal 44 D5
Porto Alegre *Town* Brazil 37 F9
Port-of-Spain *Capital* Trinidad and Tobago 35 F12
Porto-Novo *Capital* Benin 65 I8
Porto Velho *Town* Brazil 36 C7
Portoviejo *Town* Ecuador 36 B5
Port Said *Town* Egypt 63 E13
Portsmouth *Town* England, UK 41 I9
Portsmouth *Town* New Hampshire, USA 21 D13
Portsmouth *Town* Virginia, USA 23 B12
Port Sudan *Town* Sudan 67 B9
Portugal *Country* 44
Potosí *Town* Bolivia 36 E7
Potsdam *Town* Germany 51 D11
Poznan *Town* Poland 56 E7
Prague *Capital* Czech Republic 56 G5
Praia *Capital* Cape Verde (Cabo Verde) 64 F1
Prato *Town* Italy 48 D6
Presidente Eduardo Frei (Chile) *RS* Antarctica 16 D1
Presov *Town* Slovakia 57 H10
Prespa, Lake *Macedonia* 49 F10
Presque Isle *Town* Maine, USA 21 B13
Pretoria *Capital* South Africa 69 H9
Préveza *Town* Greece 49 G10
Prichard *Town* Alabama, USA 22 G7
Prilep *Town* Macedonia 49 E11
Prince Edward Island *Province* Canada 29
Princess Elisabeth (Belgium) *RS* Antarctica 16 D5
Prince George *Town* British Columbia, Canada 28 H6
Pristina *Capital* Kosovo 49 D10
Prizren *Town* Kosovo 49 E10
Prome *Town* Burma (Myanmar) 78 F2
Providence *State capital* Rhode Island, USA 21 E13
Provo *Town* Utah, USA 27 C8
Pucallpa *Town* Peru 36 C6
Puducherry *Town* India 77 H9
Puebla *Town* Mexico 31 H10

Pueblo *Town* Colorado, USA 27 D10
Puerto Ayacucho *Town* Venezuela 35 G10
Puerto Montt *Town* Chile 36 H6
Puerto Princesa *Town* Philippines 79 G10
Puerto Rico *Dep. territory* USA 35 D11
Pula *Town* Croatia 48 C7
Pune (Poona) *Town* India 76 F7
Puno *Town* Peru 36 D6
Punta Alta *Town* Argentina 37 H8
Punta Arenas *Town* Chile 36 J7
Puntarenas *Town* Costa Rica 34 F5
Pusan *Town* South Korea 85 E13
Putrajaya *Capital* Malaysia 80 E2
Pyongyang *Capital* North Korea 85 D12
Pyrenees *Mountain range* France/ Spain 45 C11, 46 H7

Qamdo *Town* China 85 H8
Qatar *Country* 75
Qattara Depression *Egypt* 63 F12
Qena *Town* Egypt 63 G13
Qilian Shan *Mountain range* China 85 F8
Qingdao *Town* China 85 E12
Qom *Town* Iran 75 C8
Quebec *Province* Canada 29
Quebec *Province capital* Quebec, Canada 29 I12
Queen Elizabeth Islands *Canada* 17 F9
Queensland *State* Australia 91
Queenstown *Town* Australia 91 J11
Quelimane *Town* Mozambique 69 G10
Querétaro *Town* Mexico 31 G9
Quetta *Town* Pakistan 76 C7
Quezaltenango *Town* Guatemala 34 D4
Quibdó *Town* Colombia 34 G7
Quimper *Town* France 46 B5
Qui Nhon *Town* Vietnam 78 G7

Rabat *Capital* Morocco 62 D3
Radom *Town* Poland 57 F10
Ragusa *Town* Sicily, Italy 48 H7
Rainier, Mount *Washington, USA* 24 D4
Raipur *Town* India 77 F9
Rajshahi *Town* Bangladesh 77 E11
Raleigh *State capital* N Carolina, USA 23 C11
Rancagua *Town* Chile 36 G7
Randers *Town* Denmark 42 I6
Rapid City *Town* S Dakota, USA 25 G11

Rasht *Town* Iran 75 B8
Rat Islands Alaska, USA 25 C8
Ravenna *Town* Italy 48 C6
Rawalpindi *Town* Pakistan 77 B8
Reading *Town* England, UK
    41 H9
Reading *Town* Pennsylvania, USA
    21 G11
Recife *Town* Brazil 37 C12
Red *River* USA 22 G5
Red Deer *Town* Alberta, Canada
    28 H7
Redding *Town* California, USA 26 B4
Red Sea 63 G14, 67 B9, 74 G5
Regensburg *Town* Germany 51 H10
Reggio di Calabria *Town* Italy 49 H8
Reggio nell' Emilia *Town* Italy 48 C5
Regina *Province capital*
    Saskatchewan, Canada 29 I8
Reims *Town* France 47 C10
Rennes *Town* France 46 C7
Reno *Town* Nevada, USA 26 C5
Republic of Ireland *See Ireland,*
    Republic of
Republic of the Congo *See Congo,*
    Republic of
Resistencia *Town* Argentina 37 F8
Resita *Town* Romania 55 E8
Réunion *Dep. territory* France
    69 H14
Reus *Town* Spain 45 D12
Reutlingen *Town* Germany 51 I8
Reykjavik *Capital* Iceland 43 I11
Reynosa *Town* Mexico 31 E10
Rhine *River* Europe 50 F7, 52 E4
Rhode Island *State* USA 21
Rhódes *Town* Rhodes, Greece 49 I14
Rhodope Mountains Bulgaria 55 J10
Rhône *River* France 47 F10
Richmond *State capital* Virginia, USA
    23 B12
Richmond *Town* Kentucky, USA
    23 B9
Riga, Gulf of 58 F5
Ríga *Capital* Latvia 58 F5
Rijeka *Town* Croatia 48 C7
Rimini *Town* Italy 48 C6
Riobamba *Town* Ecuador 36 B5
Río Cuarto *Town* Argentina 37 G7
Rio de Janeiro *Town* Brazil 37 E10
Rio Gallegos *Town* Argentina 36 J7
Rio Grande *Town* Brazil 37 G9
Rivera *Town* Uruguay 37 F8
Riverside *Town* California, USA
    26 F5
Rivne *Town* Ukraine 58 G6
Riyadh *Capital* Saudi Arabia 74 F7
Roanoke *Town* Virginia, USA 23 B11
Rochester *Town* Minnesota, USA
    20 F4

Rochester *Town* New York, USA
    21 E10
Rockford *Town* Illinois, USA 20 G5
Rockhampton *Town* Australia
    91 E12
Rocky Mountains Canada/USA
    24 F7, 27 D9, 28 G6
Roeselare *Town* Belgium 50 E4
Romania *Country* 55
Rome *Capital* Italy 48 E6
Ronne Ice Shelf Antarctica 16 E3
Rosario *Town* Argentina 37 G8
Roseau *Capital* Dominica 35 D12
Ross Ice Shelf Antarctica 16 G4
Ross Sea 16 H4
Rostock *Town* Germany 51 B11
Rostov-na-Donu *Town* Russia 58 H7
Roswell *Town* New Mexico, USA
    27 G10
Rothera (UK) *RS* Antarctica 16 E1
Rotorua *Town* New Zealand
    93 C10
Rotterdam *Town* Netherlands 50 D5
Roubaix *Town* France 47 A10
Rouen *Town* France 47 B8
Rukwa, Lake Tanzania 67 I8
Ruse *Town* Bulgaria 55 G11
Rushmore, Mount S Dakota, USA
    25 H11
Russian Federation *Country* 59,86
Rwanda *Country* 66
Ryazan *Town* Russia 58 G7
Rybinsk *Town* Russia 58 F7
Rzeszow *Town* Poland 57 G11

Saarbrücken *Town* Germany 50 G7
Saba *Dep. territory* Netherlands
    35 D12
Sabac *Town* Serbia 49 C10
Sabah *Region* Malaysia 80 E5
Sabha *Town* Libya 63 F8
Sacramento *State capital* California,
    USA 26 C4
Safi *Town* Morocco 62 E2
Saginaw *Town* Michigan, USA 20 F7
Sagunto *Town* Spain 45 F11
Sahara Desert North Africa 62 H5,
    64 E7
Saiki *Town* Japan 82 I6
St. Augustine *Town* Florida, USA
    23 G11
St. Barthelémy *Dep. territory* France
    35 D12
St. Eustatius *Dep. territory*
    Netherlands 35 D12
St. Étienne *Town* France 47 F9
St. George's *Capital* Grenada 35 E12
St. George's Channel 40 G7
St. John *Town* New Brunswick,
    Canada 29 I13

St. John's *Capital* Antigua and
    Barbuda 35 D12
St. John's *Province capital*
    Newfoundland and Labrador,
    Canada 29 H14
St. Joseph *Town* Missouri, USA
    22 B4
St. Kitts and Nevis *Country* 35
St. Lawrence Island Alaska, USA
    25 B10
St. Louis *Town* Missouri, USA 22 B6
St. Louis *Town* Senegal 64 F3
St. Lucia *Country* 35
St. Malo *Town* France 46 B7
St. Martin/Sint Maarten
    Dep. territory France, Netherlands
    35 D12
St. Moritz *Town* Switzerland 52 G5
St. Nazaire *Town* France 46 C6
St. Paul *State capital* Minnesota,
    USA 20 E3
St. Petersburg *Town* Florida, USA
    23 H10
St. Petersburg *Town* Russia 58 E6
St. Pierre and Miquelon *Dep.*
    territory France 29 H14
St. Quentin *Town* France 47 B10
St. Vincent and the Grenadines
    Country 35
Sakai *Town* Japan 83 H8
Sakata *Town* Japan 83 E10
Salamanca *Town* Spain 44 D7
Salem *State capital* Oregon, USA
    24 F3
Salerno *Town* Italy 48 F7
Salina *Town* Kansas, USA 27 D13
Salinas *Town* California, USA 26 D4
Salta *Town* Argentina 36 E7
Saltillo *Town* Mexico 31 E8
Salt Lake City *State capital* Utah,
    USA 27 C8
Salto *Town* Uruguay 37 F8
Salvador *Town* Brazil 37 D11
Salzburg *Town* Austria 40 F9
Samara *Town* Russia 59 G9
Samarkand *Town* Uzbekistan
    86 J3
Samoa *Country* 93 I13
Samsun *Town* Turkey 73 C10
Sanaa *Capital* Yemen 74 I7
Sanae IV (South Africa) *RS*
    Antarctica 16 C4
San Angelo *Town* Texas, USA
    27 H11
San Antonio *Town* Texas, USA
    27 I12
San Bernardino *Town* California,
    USA 26 F5
San Cristóbal *Town* Venezuela
    35 G9

Sancti Spíritus *Town* Cuba 34 B7
Sandakan *Town* Malaysia 80 E6
Sand Hills Nebraska, USA 25 H12
San Diego *Town* California, USA
    26 F5
San Francisco *Town* California, USA
    26 C4
San Francisco de Macorís *Town*
    Dominican Republic 35 C10
San José *Capital* Costa Rica 34 F5
San Jose *Town* California, USA
    26 D4
San Juan *Town* Argentina 36 F7
Sankt Pölten *Town* Austria 40 E12
San Luis Potosí *Town* Mexico 31 F9
San Marino *Capital* San Marino
    48 D6
San Marino *Country* 48
San Miguel de Tucumán *Town*
    Argentina 36 F7
San Miguelito *Town* Panama 34 F7
San Pedro Sula *Town* Honduras
    34 D5
San Remo *Town* Italy 48 C4
San Salvador *Capital* El Salvador
    34 D4
San Salvador de Jujuy *Town*
    Argentina 36 E7
Santa Barbara *Town* California, USA
    26 E5
Santa Clara *Town* Cuba 34 B7
Santa Cruz *Town* Bolivia 36 D7
Santa Fe *State capital* New Mexico,
    USA 27 E10
Santa Fe *Town* Argentina 37 G8
Santa Marta *Town* Colombia 35 F8
Santander *Town* Spain 45 B8
Santarém *Town* Brazil 37 B9
Santa Rosa *Town* California, USA
    26 C4
Santiago *Capital* Chile 36 G7
Santiago *Town* Dominican Republic
    35 C10
Santiago de Cuba *Town* Cuba 35 C8
Santo Domingo *Capital* Dominican
    Republic 35 D10
Santos *Town* Brazil 37 E10
São Luis *Town* Brazil 37 B10
São Paulo *Town* Brazil 37 E10
São Tomé *Capital* São Tomé and
    Príncipe 68 C4
São Tomé and Príncipe *Country* 68
Sapporo *Town* Japan 83 B10
Sarajevo *Capital* Bosnia and Herz.
    49 D9
Saratov *Town* Russia 59 G8
Sarawak Malaysia 80 F4
Sardinia *Island* Italy 48 F4
Sarh *Town* Chad 65 H13
Sariwon *Town* North Korea 85 D12

Sasebo *Town* Japan 82 H5

Saskatchewan *Province* Canada 29

Saskatoon *Town* Saskatchewan, Canada 29 H8

Sassari *Town* Sardinia, Italy 48 F4

Satu Mare *Town* Romania 55 C8

Saudi Arabia *Country* 74

Savannah *Town* Georgia, USA 23 F11

Savona *Town* Italy 48 C4

Saynshand *Town* Mongolia 85 D10

Scheldt *River* Belgium 50 E4

Schenectady *Town* New York, USA 21 E12

Schwaz *Town* Austria 40 F8

Schwerin *Town* Germany 51 C10

Scotland *Country* UK 41

Scott Base (New Zealand) *RS* Antarctica 16 G4

Scranton *Town* Pennsylvania, USA 21 F11

Seattle *Town* Washington, USA 24 D4

Ségou *Town* Mali 64 G6

Segovia *Town* Spain 45 D8

Seine *River* France 47 B9

Sejong *Town* South Korea 85 E13

Sekondi-Takoradi *Town* Ghana 64 I7

Semarang *Town* Indonesia 80 H4

Sendai *Town* Japan 83 E10

Senegal *Country* 64

Senegal *River* Senegal 64 F4

Seoul *Capital* South Korea 85 E13

Serbia *Country* 49

Serov *Town* Russia 86 G3

Sète *Town* France 47 H9

Setúbal *Town* Portugal 44 G5

Sevastopol *Town* Crimea, Ukraine 58 I7

Severn *River* England, UK 41 H9

Severnaya Zemlya Russia 17 F13, 86 C6

Seville *Town* Spain 44 H7

Seychelles *Country* 69

Sfax *Town* Tunisia 62 D7

Shanghai *Town* China 85 F12

Shannon *River* Republic of Ireland 40 G6

Sheberghan *Town* Afghanistan 76 A7

Sheffield *Town* England, UK 41 G9

Shenyang *Town* China 85 D12

Sherbrooke *Town* Quebec, Canada 29 I12

's-Hertogenbosch *Town* Netherlands 50 D6

Shetland Islands Scotland, UK 41 A9

Shimonoseki *Town* Japan 82 H5

Shinyanga *Town* Tanzania 67 H8

Shiraz *Town* Iran 75 D9

Shizuoka *Town* Japan 83 G9

Shkodër *Town* Albania 49 E10

Showa (Japan) *RS* Antarctica 16 D6

Shreveport *Town* Louisiana, USA 22 F4

Shumen *Town* Bulgaria 55 H12

Sibenik *Town* Croatia 49 D8

Siberia Russia 86 F7

Sibiu *Town* Romania 55 E10

Sicily *Island* Italy 48 H7

Sidi Bel Abbès *Town* Algeria 62 D5

Siegen *Town* Germany 51 F8

Siem Reap *Town* Cambodia 78 G5

Siena *Town* Italy 48 D6

Sierra de Gredos *Mountain range* Spain 44 E7

Sierra Leone *Country* 64

Sierra Nevada *Mountain range* California, USA 26 C5

Sierra Nevada *Mountain range* Spain 45 H9

Signy (UK) *RS* Antarctica 16 C1

Silver City *Town* New Mexico, USA 27 G9

Sincelejo *Town* Colombia 35 F8

Singapore *Capital* Singapore 80 F2

Singapore *Country* 80

Sinuiju *Town* North Korea 85 D12

Sioux City *Town* Iowa, USA 20 G2

Sioux Falls *Town* S Dakota, USA 25 H14

Siracusa *Town* Sicily, Italy 48 H7

Sittwe *Town* Burma (Myanmar) 78 E1

Sivas *Town* Turkey 73 D10

Skagerrak *Sea* Norway 42 H6

Skellefteå *Town* Sweden 43 D9

Skopje *Capital* Macedonia 49 E11

Slavonski Brod *Town* Croatia 49 C9

Sligo *Town* Republic of Ireland 40 F6

Sliven *Town* Bulgaria 55 H12

Slovakia *Country* 57

Slovenia *Country* 48

Smederevo *Town* Serbia 49 C10

Smolensk *Town* Russia 58 F6

Snake *River* Idaho/Oregon, USA 24 H6

Snowdon *Mountain* Wales, UK 41 G8

Socotra *Island* Yemen 75 J10

Söderhamn *Town* Sweden 43 F8

Södertälje *Town* Sweden 43 G8

Sofia *Capital* Bulgaria 55 I9

Soledad *Town* Colombia 35 F8

Solingen *Town* Germany 50 E7

Solomon Islands *Country* 93 I12

Solomon Sea 81 G13

Somalia *Country* 67

Songea *Town* Tanzania 67 J9

Songkhla *Town* Thailand 78 J4

Soria *Town* Spain 45 C9

Sorong *Town* Indonesia 81 F9

Sousse *Town* Tunisia 62 D7

South Africa *Country* 68

Southampton *Town* England, UK 41 I9

Southampton Island Nunavut, Canada 29 F10

South Australia *State* Australia 91

South Bend *Town* Indiana, USA 20 G6

South Carolina *State* USA 23

South China Sea 79 G8, 85 J12

South Dakota *State* USA 25

Southern Ocean 16, 90

South Georgia *Dep. territory* UK 37 J10

South Island New Zealand 92

South Korea *See* Korea, South

South Orkney Islands Antarctica 16 C1

South Ossetia *State* Georgia 59 I8

South Sudan *Country* 66

Soweto *Town* South Africa 69 I8

Spain *Country* 44

Spanish Town *Town* Jamaica 35 D8

Spartanburg *Town* S Carolina, USA 23 D10

Split *Town* Croatia 49 D8

Spokane *Town* Washington, USA 24 D5

Springfield *State capital* Illinois, USA 20 I5

Springfield *Town* Massachusetts, USA 21 E12

Springfield *Town* Missouri, USA 22 C4

Srebrenica *Town* Bosnia and Herz. 49 C9

Sri Lanka *Country* 77

Stamford *Town* Connecticut, USA 21 F12

Stara Zagora *Town* Bulgaria 55 I11

Stavanger *Town* Norway 42 G5

Stavropol *Town* Russia 59 I8

Stewart Island New Zealand 92 J6

Stockholm *Capital* Sweden 43 G8

Stockton *Town* California, USA 26 C4

Stockton Plateau Texas, USA 27 H10

Stoke-on-Trent *Town* England, UK 41 G9

Strasbourg *Town* France 47 D12

Stuttgart *Town* Germany 51 H8

Subotica *Town* Serbia 49 B10

Suceava *Town* Romania 55 C11

Sucre *Capital* Bolivia 36 E7

Sudan *Country* 66

Sudbury *Town* Ontario, Canada 29 I11

Suez, Gulf of 63 F13

Suez *Town* Egypt 63 F13

Sühbaatar *Town* Mongolia 85 C9

Sukkur *Town* Pakistan 76 C7

Sulu Archipelago Philippines 79 I10

Sulu Sea 79 H10

Sumatra *Island* Indonesia 80 F2

Sunderland *Town* England, UK 41 F9

Sundsvall *Town* Sweden 43 F8

Sunnyvale *Town* California, USA 26 D4

Superior, Lake USA 20 C5

Sur *Town* Oman 75 F11

Surabaya *Town* Indonesia 80 H4

Surakarta *Town* Indonesia 80 H4

Surat *Town* India 76 E7

Surgut *Town* Russia 86 G4

Suriname *Country* 35

Surt *Town* Libya 63 E9

Suwalki *Town* Poland 57 B11

Svalbard *Dep. territory* Norway 17 H12

Swansea *Town* Wales, UK 41 H8

Sweden *Country* 43

Swindon *Town* England, UK 41 H9

Switzerland *Country* 52

Sydney *Town* Australia 91 H12

Syktyvkar *Town* Russia 59 E9

Sylhet *Town* Bangladesh 77 E12

Syracuse *Town* New York, USA 21 E11

Syria *Country* 73

Syrian Desert Syria 73 G11, 74 C6

Szczecin *Town* Poland 56 C5

Szeged *Town* Hungary 54 D6

Székesfehérvár *Town* Hungary 54 D5

Szombathely *Town* Hungary 54 D4

Tabora *Town* Tanzania 67 H8

Tabriz *Town* Iran 74 B7

Tacoma *Town* Washington, USA 24 D3

Taegu *Town* South Korea 85 E13

Taejon *Town* South Korea 85 E13

Taguatinga *Town* Brazil 37 D9

Taipei *Capital* Taiwan 85 H13

Taiwan *Country* 85

Taiyuan *Town* China 85 E10

Ta'izz *Town* Yemen 74 I7

Tajikistan *Country* 86

Takasaki *Town* Japan 83 F9

Taklimakan Desert China 84 F5

Talcahuano *Town* Chile 36 G6

Taldyqorgan *Town* Kazakhstan 86 I4

Tallahassee *State capital* Florida, USA 23 G9

Tallinn *Capital* Estonia 58 E5

Tamale *Town* Ghana 64 H7

Tamanrasset *Town* Algeria 62 H6

Tampa *Town* Florida, USA 23 H10

Tampere *Town* Finland 43 F9

Tampico *Town* Mexico 31 G10

Tamworth *Town* Australia 91 G12

Tanami Desert Australia 91 D8

Tanga *Town* Tanzania 67 H9

Tanganyika, Lake DRC/Tanzania 66 I7, 69 E9

Tangier *Town* Morocco 62 D3

Tanzania *Country* 67

Taranto *Town* Italy 49 F8

Tarbes *Town* France 46 G7

Târgu Mures *Town* Romania 55 D10

Tarija *Town* Bolivia 36 E7

Tarim Basin China 84 E6

Tarnow *Town* Poland 57 G10

Tarragona *Town* Spain 45 D12

Tarsus *Town* Turkey 73 E9

Tartu *Town* Estonia 58 F6

Tartus *Town* Syria 73 G10

Tashkent *Capital* Uzbekistan 86 I3

Tasmania *State* Australia 91

Tasman Sea 91 I12, 92 F6

Tatra Mountains Slovakia 57 H9

Taupo, Lake New Zealand 93 D10

Tauranga *Town* New Zealand 93 C10

Taurus Mountains Turkey 73 E8

Tavoy *Town* Burma (Myanmar) 78 G3

Tbilisi *Capital* Georgia 59 I8

Tegucigalpa *Capital* Honduras 34 D5

Tehran *Capital* Iran 75 C9

Tehuantepec, Gulf of 31 I11

Tekirdag *Town* Turkey 72 B6

Tel Aviv *Town* Israel 73 H9

Temuco *Town* Chile 36 H6

Tennessee *River* Alabama/ Tennessee, USA 23 D8

Tennessee *State* USA 23

Tepic *Town* Mexico 30 G7

Teramo *Town* Italy 48 D7

Teresina *Town* Brazil 37 B10

Terni *Town* Italy 48 D6

Terrasa *Town* Spain 45 C12

Terre Haute *Town* Indiana, USA 20 H6

Teruel *Town* Spain 45 E10

Tete *Town* Mozambique 69 G10

Tétouan *Town* Morocco 62 D3

Texas *State* USA 27

Thailand, Gulf of 78 H4

Thailand *Country* 78

Thai Nguyen *Town* Vietnam 78 E5

Thames *River* England, UK 41 H10

Thanh Hoa *Town* Vietnam 78 E5

The Hague *Capital* Netherlands 50 D5

Thessaloníki *Town* Greece 49 F11

Thimphu *Capital* Bhutan 77 D11

Thiruvananthapuram (Trivandrum) *Town* India 77 I8

Thun *Town* Switzerland 52 G3

Thunder Bay *Town* Ontario, Canada 29 I10

Tianjin *Town* China 85 E11

Tibesti Mountains Chad 65 E13

Tibet China 84 G6

Tibet, Plateau of China 84 G7

Tigris *River* Iraq 74 C7

Tijuana *Town* Mexico 30 B3

Tilburg *Town* Netherlands 50 E6

Timaru *Town* New Zealand 92 H7

Timisoara *Town* Romania 54 E7

Tindouf *Town* Algeria 62 F2

Tiranë *Capital* Albania 49 F10

Tiraspol *Town* Moldova 58 H6

Tiruchchirappalli *Town* India 77 I8

Tisza *River* Central Europe 54 D7

Titicaca, Lake Peru 36 D6

Tocantins *River* Brazil 37 C10

Togo *Country* 65

Tokelau *Dep. territory* New Zealand 93 I13

Tokushima *Town* Japan 82 H7

Tokyo *Capital* Japan 83 G10

Toledo *Town* Ohio, USA 21 G8

Toledo *Town* Spain 45 E8

Toluca *Town* Mexico 31 H9

Tolyatti *Town* Russia 59 G9

Tomakomai *Town* Japan 83 C10

Tombouctou *Town* Mali 64 F7

Tomsk *Town* Russia 86 G5

Tonga *Country* 93 I13

Tonkin, Gulf of 78 E5, 85 J10

Tonopah *Town* Nevada, USA 26 D6

Toowoomba *Town* Australia 91 F13

Topeka *State capital* Kansas, USA 27 D13

Toronto *Province capital* Ontario, Canada 29 J11

Torun *Town* Poland 57 D8

Tottori *Town* Japan 82 G7

Touba *Town* Senegal 64 F3

Toubkal, Mount Morocco 63 E2

Toulon *Town* France 47 H10

Toulouse *Town* France 46 G7

Tournai *Town* Belgium 50 E4

Tours *Town* France 47 D8

Townsville *Town* Australia 91 D11

Toyama *Town* Japan 83 F8

Toyota *Town* Japan 83 G8

Trabzon *Town* Turkey 73 C12

Trans-Dniester *State* Moldova 58 H6

Transylvanian Alps Romania 55 E9

Trapani *Town* Sicily, Italy 48 H6

Trencin *Town* Slovakia 56 I7

Trent *River* England, UK 41 G10

Trento *Town* Italy 48 B6

Trenton *State capital* New Jersey, USA 21 G12

Treviso *Town* Italy 48 B6

Trier *Town* Germany 50 G6

Trieste *Town* Italy 48 B7

Trincomalee *Town* Sri Lanka 77 I9

Trinidad and Tobago *Country* 35

Tripoli *Capital* Libya 63 E8

Tripoli *Town* Lebanon 73 G10

Trivandrum *See* Thiruvananthapuram

Trnava *Town* Slovakia 56 I7

Trois-Rivières *Town* Quebec, Canada 29 I12

Troll (Norway) *RS* Antarctica 16 C4

Tromsø *Town* Norway 43 B8

Trondheim *Town* Norway 42 E6

Troy *Town* New York, USA 21 E12

Troyes *Town* France 47 C10

Trujillo *Town* Peru 36 C5

Tshikapa *Town* DRC 68 E7

Tubruq *Town* Libya 63 E11

Tucson *Town* Arizona, USA 27 G8

Tuguegarao *Town* Philippines 79 E10

Tula *Town* Russia 58 G7

Tulcea *Town* Romania 55 E13

Tulsa *Town* Oklahoma, USA 27 E13

Tunis *Capital* Tunisia 62 D7

Tunisia *Country* 62

Tunja *Town* Colombia 35 G8

Turin *Town* Italy 48 B4

Turkana, Lake Kenya 67 F9

Turkey *Country* 73

Turkmenabat *Town* Turkmenistan 86 J3

Turkmenistan *Country* 86

Turks and Caicos Islands *Dep. territory* UK 35 B9

Turku *Town* Finland 43 G9

Tuvalu *Country* 93 I12

Tuxtla Gutiérrez *Town* Mexico 31 I12

Tuz, Lake Turkey 73 D8

Tuzla *Town* Bosnia and Herz. 49 C9

Tver *Town* Russia 58 F7

Twin Falls *Town* Idaho, USA 24 H6

Tyler *Town* Texas, USA 27 G14

Tyrrhenian Sea 48 G6

Uberaba *Town* Brazil 37 E10

Uberlândia *Town* Brazil 37 D10

Ubon Ratchathani *Town* Thailand 78 G5

Uchiura Bay Japan 83 C10

Udaipur *Town* India 77 E8

Udine *Town* Italy 48 B7

Udon Thani *Town* Thailand 78 F4

Uele *River* DRC 69 C9

Ufa *Town* Russia 59 G10

Uganda *Country* 67

Ukhta *Town* Russia 59 D9

Ukraine *Country* 58

Ulaanbaatar *Capital* Mongolia 85 C9

Ulaangom *Town* Mongolia 84 C7

Ulan-Ude *Town* Russia 86 H7

Ulm *Town* Germany 51 I9

Umeå *Town* Sweden 43 E8

Umtata *Town* South Africa 69 J8

Ungava Peninsula Quebec, Canada 29 F11

United Arab Emirates (UAE) *Country* 75

Uppsala *Town* Sweden 43 G8

Ural Mountains Russia 59 F10, 86 G2

Uruguay *Country* 37

Urumqi *Town* China 84 D6

Usak *Town* Turkey 72 D6

Ushuaia *Town* Argentina 36 J7

Usol'ye-Sibirskoye *Town* Russia 86 H6

Ust'Ilimsk *Town* Russia 86 G6

Ústí nad Labem *Town* Czech Republic 56 G5

Ustyurt Plateau Uzbekistan 86 I2

Utah *State* USA 27

Utica *Town* New York, USA 21 E11

Utrecht *Town* Netherlands 50 D6

Utsunomiya *Town* Japan 83 F10

Uzbekistan *Country* 86

Vaal *River* South Africa 69 I9

Vaasa *Town* Finland 43 E9

Vadodara *Town* India 76 E7

Vadsø *Town* Norway 43 A10

Vaduz *Capital* Liechtenstein 52 F5

Valdivia *Town* Chile 36 H6

Valdosta *Town* Georgia, USA 23 F10

Valence *Town* France 47 G10

Valencia, Gulf of 45 F11

Valencia *Town* Spain 45 F11

Valencia *Town* Venezuela 35 F10

Valladolid *Town* Spain 45 D8

Valletta *Capital* Malta 48 I7

Valparaíso *Capital* Chile 36 G6

Van *Town* Turkey 73 D13

Vancouver *Town* British Columbia, Canada 28 I6

Vancouver Island British Columbia, Canada 28 H5

Vantaa *Town* Finland 43 G10

Vanuatu *Country* 93 I12

Varanasi *Town* India 77 E10

Varna *Town* Bulgaria 55 H13

Västerås *Town* Sweden 43 G8

Vatican City *Country* 48
Växjö *Town* Sweden 42 I7
Venezuela *Country* 35
Venice, Gulf of 48 C7
Venice *Town* Italy 48 C6
Veracruz *Town* Mexico 31 H10
Verkhoyanskiy Mountains Russia 87 F9
Vermont *State* USA 21
Verona *Town* Italy 48 B6
Versailles *Town* France 47 C9
Verviers *Town* Belgium 50 F6
Viareggio *Town* Italy 48 D5
Vicenza *Town* Italy 48 B6
Victoria, Lake Kenya/Tanzania/ Uganda 67 G8
Victoria *Province capital* British Columbia, Canada 28 I6
Victoria *State* Australia 91
Victoria *Capital* Seychelles 69 D14
Victoria Falls Zimbabwe 69 G8
Victoria Island Canada 17 E8, 29 E8
Vidin *Town* Bulgaria 55 G9
Vienna *Capital* Austria 40 E13
Vientiane *Capital* Laos 78 F4
Vietnam *Country* 78
Vigo *Town* Spain 44 C5
Vijayawada *Town* India 77 G9
Villach *Town* Austria 40 H10
Villahermosa *Town* Mexico 31 H12
Villavicencio *Town* Colombia 35 H8
Vilnius *Capital* Lithuania 58 G5
Vina del Mar *Town* Chile 36 G6
Vineland *Town* New Jersey, USA 21 G12
Vinh *Town* Vietnam 78 F5
Virginia *State* USA 23
Virginia Beach *Town* Virginia, USA 23 B12
Virgin Islands *Dep. territory* UK 35 D11
Virgin Islands *Dep. territory* USA 35 D11
Vishakhapatnam *Town* India 77 G10
Vitoria *Town* Brazil 37 E11
Vitória-Gasteiz *Town* Spain 45 B9
Vitsyebsk *Town* Belarus 58 F6
Vladikavkaz *Town* Russia 59 I8
Vladivostok *Town* Russia 87 I9
Vlissingen *Town* Netherlands 50 D5
Vlorë *Town* Albania 49 F10
Volga *River* Russia 59 F8
Volgograd *Town* Russia 59 H8
Vólos *Town* Greece 49 G11
Volta, Lake Ghana 64 I7
Vorkuta *Town* Russia 59 C11, 86 E3
Voronezh *Town* Russia 58 G7
Vosges Mountains France 47 D11
Voss *Town* Norway 42 F5

Vostok (Russian Federation) *RS* Antarctica 16 F5
Vratsa *Town* Bulgaria 55 H9
Vyborg *Town* Russia 58 E6

Waal *River* Netherlands 50 D6
Waco *Town* Texas, USA 27 H13
Waddenzee *Sea* Netherlands 50 B7
Wadi Halfa *Town* Sudan 66 A7
Wad Medani *Town* Sudan 67 C8
Wagga Wagga *Town* Australia 91 H11
Wakayama *Town* Japan 82 H7
Wakkanai *Town* Japan 83 A10
Walbrzych *Town* Poland 56 F6
Wales *Country* UK 41
Wallis and Futuna *Dep. territory* France 93 I13
Walvis Bay *Town* Namibia 68 H6
Wandel Sea 17 G11
Warren *Town* Michigan, USA 20 F8
Warsaw *Capital* Poland 57 E10
Washington, Mount USA 21 D12
Washington *State* USA 24
Washington D.C. *Capital* USA 21 H11
Waterford *Town* Republic of Ireland 40 H6
Waterloo *Town* Iowa, USA 20 G4
Watertown *Town* New York, USA 21 E10
Wau *Town* South Sudan 66 E7
Weddell Sea 16 D2
Weimar *Town* Germany 51 F10
Wellington *Capital* New Zealand 93 F9
Wels *Town* Austria 40 E10
Wenzhou *Town* China 85 G12
West Bank *Disputed region* Near East 73 H9
Western Australia *State* Australia 90
Western Ghats *Mountain range* India 76 F7
Western Sahara *Territory* 64
West Palm Beach *Town* Florida, USA 23 I12
West Virginia *State* USA 21
Whitehorse *Province capital* Yukon Territory, Canada 28 F5
White Nile *River* Sudan 67 D8
White Sea 58 D7
Whitney, Mount California, USA 26 D5
Wichita *Town* Kansas, USA 27 E13
Wichita Falls *Town* Texas, USA 27 F12
Wieliczka *Town* Poland 57 G9
Wiener Neustadt *Town* Austria 40 F13
Wiesbaden *Town* Germany 51 G8

Wilhelmshaven *Town* Germany 51 C8
Wilkes Land Antarctica 16 G6
Williston *Town* N Dakota, USA 25 E11
Wilmington *Town* Delaware, USA 21 G11
Wilmington *Town* N Carolina, USA 23 D12
Windhoek *Capital* Namibia 68 H7
Windsor *Town* Ontario, Canada 29 J11
Winnipeg *Province capital* Manitoba, Canada 29 I9
Winston-Salem *Town* N Carolina, USA 23 C10
Winterthur *Town* Switzerland 52 F4
Wisconsin *State* USA 20
Wloclawek *Town* Poland 57 D8
Wolfsberg *Town* Austria 40 H11
Wolfsburg *Town* Germany 51 D10
Wollongong *Town* Australia 91 H12
Wonsan *Town* North Korea 85 D13
Worcester *Town* Massachusetts, USA 21 E13
Worms *Town* Germany 51 G8
Wroclaw *Town* Poland 56 F7
Wuhan *Town* China 85 G11
Wuppertal *Town* Germany 50 E7
Würzburg *Town* Germany 51 G9
Wyoming *State* USA 25

Xiamen *Town* China 85 H12
Xi'an *Town* China 85 F10
Xining *Town* China 85 F8
Xuzhou *Town* China 85 F11

Yakima *Town* Washington, USA 24 E4
Yakutsk *Town* Russia 87 F9
Yambol *Town* Bulgaria 55 I12
Yamoussoukro *Capital* Côte d'Ivoire 64 I6
Yanbu *Town* Saudi Arabia 74 F5
Yangon (Rangoon) *Town* Burma (Myanmar) 78 G2
Yantai *Town* China 85 E12
Yaoundé *Capital* Cameroon 68 C5
Yaroslavl *Town* Russia 58 F7
Yazd *Town* Iran 75 D9
Yekaterinburg *Town* Russia 86 G3
Yellowknife *Province capital* Northwest Territories, Canada 28 F7
Yellow Sea 85 E12
Yemen *Country* 75
Yenisey *River* Russia 86 F5
Yerevan *Capital* Armenia 59 J8
Yinchuan *Town* China 85 E9

Yining *Town* China 84 D5
Yokohama *Town* Japan 83 G10
Yonago *Town* Japan 82 G7
York *Town* England, UK 41 F9
Youngstown *Town* Ohio, USA 21 G9
Yucatán Peninsula Mexico 31 G13
Yukon *River* Alaska, USA 25 B10
Yukon Territory *Province* Canada 28
Yuma *Town* Arizona, USA 26 G6
Yumen *Town* China 85 E8
Yuzhno-Sakhalinsk *Town* Russia 87 I10

Zadar *Town* Croatia 49 D8
Zagreb *Capital* Croatia 49 B8
Zagros Mountains Iran 75 C8
Zahedan *Town* Iran 75 D11
Zajecar *Town* Serbia 49 D11
Zambezi *River* Southern Africa 69 G8
Zambia *Country* 69
Zamboanga *Town* Philippines 79 H11
Zamora *Town* Spain 44 D7
Zanzibar *Town* Tanzania 67 I9
Zanzibar Island Tanzania 67 I10
Zaporizhzhya *Town* Ukraine 58 H7
Zaria *Town* Nigeria 65 H10
Zeebrugge *Town* Belgium 50 E4
Zenica *Town* Bosnia and Herz. 49 C9
Zhangjiakou *Town* China 85 E11
Zhanjiang *Town* China 85 I11
Zhengzhou *Town* China 85 F11
Zhezkazgan *Town* Kazakhstan 86 I3
Zhongshan (China) *RS* Antarctica 16 E7
Zibo *Town* China 85 E11
Zielona Gora *Town* Poland 56 E6
Zilina *Town* Slovakia 57 H8
Zimbabwe *Country* 69
Zinder *Town* Niger 65 G10
Zlin *Town* Czech Republic 56 H7
Zomba *Town* Malawi 69 F10
Zonguldak *Town* Turkey 73 B8
Zrenjanin *Town* Serbia 49 C10
Zug *Town* Switzerland 52 F4
Zürich *Town* Switzerland 52 F4
Zwettl Stadt *Town* Austria 40 D12
Zwickau *Town* Germany 51 F11
Zwolle *Town* Netherlands 50 C7

Index

Acknowledgements

Cover artwork by Collaborate

Map Artworker Julian Baker (J B Illustrations)

Mountain High Maps® Copyright © 1993 Digital Wisdom, Inc.

The publishers would like to thank Richard Burgess for his contribution to this book

All other artworks are from the Miles Kelly Artwork Bank

The publishers would like to thank the following source for the use of their photographs:

Cover © Globe Williams Noble/Dreamstime.com
Fotolia.com 10(b) Andrey Mirzoyants, Jean Luc Bohin, Giovanni Catalani, Kárpáti Gábor, Matt Ireland; 20 David Ruderman; 22 Daren Whitaker; 25 Sascha Burkard; 27 Tomasz Kawka; 28 Melissa Schalke; 29 Roman Krochuk; 30 Beatrice Preve; 31(t) Lein De Leon; 34 Françoise Bro; 35 pixphoto; 36(t) urbanhearts; 41(b) C J Photography; 43 Marco Regalia; 44 Hugues Argence; 48 Dubravko Grakalic; 50 Jarno Gonzalez/Fotolia.com; 51 Philip Lange; 52(t) Renato Francia; 54(b) Jozsef Szasz-fabian; 56(b) Bartlomiej Kwieciszewski; 57 Martin Džumela; 58(b) Salazkin Vladimir; 59 Jacek Malipan; 65(t) Natasha Owen; 74(t) Richard Connors, (b) MaxFX; 79(c) Dmitry Ersler; 80 Stuart Taylor; 81(b) TAOLMOR/; 83(t) Anna Cseresnjes; 87(b) NFive; 91 Flavia Bottazzini; 92(b) Rico Leffanta; 93 Adam Booth
Shutterstock.com 27 somchaij/Shutterstock; 29 Roman Krochuk/Shutterstock; 36(b) Mark Schwettmann; 41(t) ShaunWilkinson; 73(t) Nickolay Vinokurov; 74(b) Zurijeta; 75 S-S; 76(t) turtix; 83(b) SIHASAKPRACHUM; 84(b) ESB Professional; 90 totajla

All other photographs are from: Corel, digitalSTOCK, digitalvision, istock.com, John Foxx, PhotoAlto, PhotoDisc, PhotoEssentials, PhotoPro, Stockbyte

Every effort has been made to acknowledge the source and copyright holder of each picture.
Miles Kelly Publishing apologizes for any unintentional errors or omissions.